The Hardy Boys Mysteries,
1927–1979

ALSO BY MARK CONNELLY

The IRA on Film and Television: A History
(McFarland, 2012)

The Hardy Boys Mysteries, 1927–1979

A Cultural and Literary History

MARK CONNELLY

McFarland & Company, Inc., Publishers
Jefferson, North Carolina, and London

> *The present work is a reprint of the illustrated case bound edition of* The Hardy Boys Mysteries, 1927–1979: A Cultural and Literary History, *first published in 2008 by McFarland.*

LIBRARY OF CONGRESS CATALOGUING-IN-PUBLICATION DATA

Connelly, Mark, 1951–
    The Hardy Boys mysteries, 1927–1979 : a cultural and literary history / Mark Connelly.
        p.   cm.
    Includes bibliographical references and index.

ISBN 978-0-7864-7304-5
softcover : acid free paper ∞

    1. Stratemeyer, Edward, 1862–1930 — Characters — Hardy Boys. 2. Stratemeyer Syndicate. 3. Hardy Boys (fictitious characters) 4. Children's literature in series — History and criticism. 5. Children's stories, American — History and criticism. 6. Detective and mystery stories, American — History and criticism. 7. Children — Books and reading — United States — History — 20th century. 8. Literature and society — United States — History — 20th century. I. Title.
PS3537.T817Z595 2012
813'.50992826 — dc22

                                              2008028811

BRITISH LIBRARY CATALOGUING DATA ARE AVAILABLE

©2008 Mark Connelly. All rights reserved

No part of this book may be reproduced or transmitted in any form or by any means, electronic or mechanical, including photocopying or recording, or by any information storage and retrieval system, without permission in writing from the publisher.

Cover art © 2012 PicturesNow

Manufactured in the United States of America

McFarland & Company, Inc., Publishers
  Box 611, Jefferson, North Carolina 28640
    www.mcfarlandpub.com

To Matthew and Benjamin

Table of Contents

Preface   1

Introduction: The Hardy Boys at Eighty   5

1. Off the Assembly Line: The Fiction Factory of Edward Stratemeyer 23
2. The McFarlane Formula: "I Opted for Quality" 47
3. The Weird Period 66
4. The Hardy Boys in Peace and Cold War 72
5. Policing the Hardy Boys: The "Great Purge" 83
6. Into the Disco Age 91
7. Race 98
8. Class 130
9. Hardy Girls: Gender in the Hardy Boys 138
10. Hardy Family Values 150
11. Law and Order 166
12. Action, Not Violence 176
13. Bayport, USA 189

14. The Hardy Boys on Stage, on Screen, and in Parody 201
15. Book Wars: The Series Book Under Fire 215

Chronology   231

The Hardy Boys Canon   233

Twenty Opening Lines   239

Hardyisms   241

Chapter Notes   243

Bibliography   247

Index   251

Preface

Like most people of my generation, I learned about the Hardy Boys through *Mickey Mouse Club* serials. Day after day, my friends and I rushed home from school to catch the next installment. I recall the unease I felt whenever the irascible Mr. Applegate or hectoring Aunt Gertrude appeared onscreen. At school we debated the unfolding mystery, guessing where the missing treasure might be hidden or if, in fact, it existed at all. Playing in backyards, we acted out scenes, with older boys taking the parts of the dreaded Applegate and his sinister plumber Jackley. When Frank and Joe found the treasure in an abandoned railroad tower, we walked along the train tracks winding through the Jersey woods. We could not find a water tower, so we reenacted the finale by climbing a tree with a bag of play money.

One day my mother brought home some Hardy Boys books she found in a supermarket. Up to that point my reading had been limited to *Classics Illustrated* comics, thin Golden Books, and illustrated children's versions of *Robinson Crusoe* and *Sherlock Holmes*. The books she handed me were different. Some were freshly-printed blue hard covers while others were shopworn volumes with torn dust jackets.

The first thing that struck me was that these were *real* books. They had no pictures, only words. They were grownup books. They seemed amazingly thick and heavy. Soon, most of the boys and some of the girls in third grade were bringing Hardy Boys books to class. Golden Books vanished from our desks. These were big boy books connected to the Frank and Joe we had seen on TV.

Familiar with the general plot and characters, I began to read *The Tower Treasure*. It was slow going. The sentences were long and full of words not found in Dick and Jane stories. I had to ask my father what "justifiably" and "prosaic" meant. In addition, he had to explain to me what "touring cars" and "rain slickers" were. The Hardy Boys were a challenge to read, but I was determined to learn more about Frank and Joe. I often shared the book with a friend, and we helped each other with words and phrases. The books, written in the 1920s, were full of dated expressions and references, which we found intriguing. We quizzed each other on terminology and began talking Hardyspeak at school, using the word "latter" and the phrase "bet dollars to donuts" whenever we could.

We devoured Hardy Boys books. They were addictive. And it was a dependency our parents enabled. Seeing children reading books instead of watching cartoons comforted adults who feared a decline in reading skills in the age of TV. Hardy Boys books became standard presents on our block. I could count on finding three or four volumes under the Christmas tree wrapped in bright paper. Two or three others would appear among the plastic eggs full of candy in my Easter basket. My July birthday brought a fresh stack of summer reading.

As soon as I finished one Hardy Boys book, I wanted, needed to follow up with the next. I was puzzled by the fact that the books always ended with a preview of the next adventure. I wondered how anyone could predict what Frank and Joe would encounter next. How could they know the future?

Over the next few years Frank and Joe Hardy became constant companions. As my reading skills improved, I reread the first books I received and discovered what I previously missed. I could relate to Frank and Joe in a way I could never connect with anyone else I found in a book. They were American boys. They went to school and lived with their parents. They did chores and had homework. They had to study for exams. They were yelled at by adults.

They were not just characters in a book to me but living people. Curiously, I had no interest in Franklin W. Dixon. He was just a name on the cover, as forgettable as a credit scrolling at the end of a movie. Frank and Joe Hardy, on the other hand, were as real as distant cousins I only heard about through parents and saw in family snapshots.

An ongoing topic of debate among my friends was the location of Bayport, Frank and Joe's hometown. We poured over Esso maps taken from our parents' glove compartments and discovered the magic word "Bayport" next to a small circle on Long Island. There was no Barmet Bay or Willow River, but the town was located on the Atlantic Ocean and connected to New York City by rail. It had to be the right Bayport.

Every few months my parents took us to New York to spend a day visiting museums, going to Radio City Music Hall, riding to the top of the Empire State Building, or touring the newly completed Lincoln Center. On one trip I encouraged my father to drive to Bayport. We headed east, leaving Manhattan for Brooklyn, Queens, the suburbs, then the farmlands of Long Island. I sat in the back seat with my books and maps, tense with anticipation. I just knew what Bayport had to look like.

Bayport was on the Atlantic Ocean, but the sleepy village of eight thousand we pulled into bore little resemblance to the thriving city of fifty thousand where Frank and Joe lived. There were no seaside cliffs, seedy waterfront, busy commercial district, impressive Bayport High, steamship office, stately Tower Mansion, or wide-fendered touring cars. There was no intersection of High and Elm Streets, either. I knew on one level that Frank and Joe Hardy were fictional characters, but I fully expected there to be a large stone colonial house standing on High and Elm or at least a Hardy Boys museum. If nothing else, I thought the Disney movie set would be located there with Tim Considine and Tommy Kirk living inside. We drove around the prosaic town and stopped for lunch in a café. I remember eating a dish of yellow New York vanilla ice cream and studying a WPA era mural on the wall depicting a Long Island farm girl contemplating a shining art deco Manhattan skyline on the horizon. It looked like Oz.

I masked my utter disappointment and took comfort in reading *The Secret of the Old Mill* on the long ride home. I never told any of my friends about the trip, not wanting to shatter their illusions. I was especially concerned about my friends' younger brothers. To share the findings of my expedition would be like betraying Santa Claus.

I soon outgrew the Hardy Boys, but they remained on my bookshelves, along with model cars, old baseball cards, stacks of *Classics Illustrated*, and World's Fair memorabilia. I moved on in life, but I could not help thinking that those books had shaped my view of the world and maybe even of myself.

For eighty years young people have been discovering, reading, and living with the Hardy Boys. While other series books have faded into obscurity, the Hardy Boys remain in print, with new titles appearing every few months. In the United States alone the original fifty-eight novels sell a million copies a year. They have influenced the way generations of American children have viewed themselves, their society, and the adult world. Translated into twenty-five languages, the books have also shaped the way millions of children in other countries view American life and values.

Behind the Hardy Boys — and their literary siblings — is a fascinating story of a publishing empire and one of the most successful father and daughter enterprises in history.

Introduction:
The Hardy Boys at Eighty

> The Hardy Boys turn 75 next year, still living at home and enrolled in Bayport High. They are still well-scrubbed Boy Scout types from the 1920s, with personalities that barely extend beyond the color of their hair. And their books still sell more than a million copies a year.
> —David D. Kirkpatrick, *New York Times*, July 29, 2001

A week before Charles Lindbergh took off for Paris in May 1927, the Hardy Boys took to the road, roaring out of their first novel *The Tower Treasure* to become popular culture icons.

"After the help we gave dad on that forgery case I guess he'll begin to think we *could* be detectives when we grow up."

"Why shouldn't we? Isn't he one of the most famous detectives in the country? And aren't we his sons? If the profession was good enough for him to follow it should be good enough for us."

Two bright-eyed boys on motorcycles were speeding along a shore road in the sunshine of a morning in spring. It was Saturday and they were enjoying a holiday from the Bayport high school. The day was ideal for a motorcycle trip and the lads were combining business with pleasure by going on an errand to a near-by village for their father.

The older of the two boys was a tall, dark youth, about sixteen years of age. His name was Frank Hardy. The other boy, his companion on the motorcycle trip, was his brother Joe, a year younger [1–2].

How the "bright-eyed" brothers managed to hold this conversation over the noise of their engines was never explained. The author dismissed this as a necessary bit of suspension of disbelief. "Don't ask how they managed this with two motorcycles going full blast," he wrote. "They just did."[1]

Far greater suspension of disbelief is required to accept that the boys, aged sixteen and fifteen in 1927, are still attending Bayport High just over eighty years later. *The Great Airport Mystery*, released in 1930, includes a detailed description of the brothers' high school graduation ceremonies. This would leave the Hardys a single summer vacation to solve crimes with their chums before leaving for college. This gaffe in creative judgment was magically erased in *What Happened at Midnight*, published the following year. Inexplicably, the boys are back in high school, never to graduate again, not only frozen in adolescence, but ensured of never outgrowing their readers. The brothers do age, though only slightly. In the Fifties Frank and Joe are described as being eighteen and seventeen, evidently to allow them to have valid drivers' licenses. A short-lived series launched in 1997, aimed at younger readers, turned the clock back even more, regressing their ages to eight and nine. As elementary school boys, Frank and Joe solved the cases in *The Pumped-Up Pizza Problem* and *The Bike Race Ruckus*, leaving their teenage counterparts to tackle gangsters and terrorists.

Like their literary siblings Nancy Drew and Tom Swift, the Hardy Boys have endured long after other heroes of the juvenile series genre — the Rover Boys, the Dana Girls, Ted Scott, Bomba the Jungle Boy, Don Sturdy, and the Motion Picture Chums — evaporated from the American consciousness like silent movie cowboys and radio soap opera heroines.

Hardy Boys novels remain popular. *The Tower Treasure* alone sells more than 100,000 copies a year. The original fifty-eight-volume series published by Grosset & Dunlap (1927–1979) remains in print and had sold more than 50 million copies by 1975. The firm currently reports total annual sales of a million books. Though impressive, these figures grossly undercount the number of readers who have enjoyed the Hardy Boys. The number of children who read the Hardy Boys is many times the number of copies sold as hardcover series books are handed down through families, purchased second-hand, recycled through rummage sales, and checked out from libraries.

Simon & Schuster has continued the brothers' adventures with The Hardy Boys Mysteries (1979–2005, 132 volumes), The Hardy Boys Casefiles (1987–1998, 127 volumes) and The Hardy Boys: Undercover Brothers (2005–), and has stepped up production, releasing a new title every two months instead of annually. Hardy Boys novels still appear on lists of best-selling children's books throughout the English-speaking world. In 2006 the Brooklyn Public Library listed a Hardy Boys title on its summer "What Others Are Reading" list.

Hardy Boys books have become more than fiction; they have become cultural artifacts. When the Shelburne Museum in Vermont opened its 1950 House exhibit, Hardy Boys books were featured along with *Life* magazines, Sinatra recordings, and a Studebaker in the driveway.[2]

The original Frank and Joe Hardy resembled schoolboys. *The Tower Treasure*, 1927.

Frank and Joe: Ever Evolving Yet Unchanging

The Hardy Boys have stayed popular because they have been constantly reinvented to stay relevant — without changes to the basics that were established in their first adventure. Frank and Joe were created as positive role models in the era of Flaming Youth, flappers, speakeasies, Leopold and Loeb, petting parties, and reefer madness. They were clean-cut, honest, moral, and respectful of traditional values and institutions to win the approval of adults (who usually bought the books) and enjoyed enough freedom and adventure to appeal to children.

Dark-haired Frank and blond Joe Hardy are the sons of Fenton Hardy, a famous detective formerly with the New York City Police Department. Fenton Hardy retired to become a private investigator in Bayport, a thriving town of fifty thousand on Barmet Bay on the Atlantic seaboard. Mr. Hardy is an ideal father — strong, manly, athletic, and knowledgeable. He is constantly teaching his sons the subtleties of criminal investigation while sharpening their skills of perception. Though not wealthy, he is generous, supplying expense money without question. He can be counted on to pay for train tickets and hotel bills, and once he paid for a new car. In many of the boys' adventures he is more of a senior partner or an older brother than an authority figure. In several stories Frank and Joe come to their dad's rescue, earning his respect for their resourceful bravery. Laura (sometimes named Mildred) Hardy is a loving, doting mother, forever making sandwiches and reminding her sons to be careful. For all her maternal concern, she trusts her sons implicitly, never suspecting them of lying or misbehaving. She never questions their plans or forbids them from taking a cross-country trip. She only urges caution.

The Hardy Boys share adventures with their "chums" — portly Chet Morton, a teenage Falstaff, always eating and playing pranks; athletic Biff Hooper; Italian-American Tony Prito, captain of the *Napoli*; and brainy and benignly Jewish Phil Cohen. In many books the chums appear in the first chapters to set the stage for an adventure. They vanish when Frank and Joe tear off to solve a crime, then reappear in the final scene to cheer the Hardy victory, often over a celebratory feast.

The Hardy Boys mysteries, neatly packaged in the early years into twenty-five chapters of two hundred and sixteen pages, follow a standard formula set forth in the first volume.

The Tower Treasure is the Ur-Novel that introduces the basic themes and characters which change little except in costume and dialogue. The plot of the first book would become the basis for a television drama, a stage play, and a board game.

As the brothers roar down Shore Road, a red-haired "speed demon" nearly forces them over the bluff, spraying them with gravel. The brothers recover from their brush with death and dutifully complete their errand. On their way home they visit Chet Morton who informs them that his beloved yellow roadster has just been stolen. When the boys reach the police station to report the theft, they learn that Chet's "gay-looking speed wagon" has been used in a hold-up by a man described as having long red hair by one witness and short brown hair by another. Later, while on an outing, the boys discover Chet's car hidden in a grove. As they drive back to Bayport, their victory is muted by news that the Tower Mansion has been robbed of forty thousand dollars in securities and jewels. The Hardy Boys accompany their father to the mansion to investigate the crime and take a personal interest when the mansion's caretaker, the father of a Hardy chum, is implicated in the crime. A distraught Perry Robinson proclaims his father to be innocent and pleads with Frank and Joe to clear him.

Determined to help Perry, Frank and Joe start their own investigation. The brothers discover a valuable clue in a piece of a red wig, which their father traces to Red Jackley, a career criminal with a fondness for red hairpieces. Jackley is mortally injured in an escape attempt, and he confesses on his deathbed to Fenton Hardy that he committed the crime and hid the loot in the "old tower." The Hardy brothers search the mansion towers without success, confirming the doubts of Hurd Applegate, the cantankerous owner of the mansion, who dismisses Frank and Joe as meddling children.

The boys are stumped, their investigation stalled. On a motorcycle trip, the Hardys pause for a picnic lunch beside a rail line and notice a new water tower rising beside an old, weather-beaten tower.

> In the eyes of both was the light of a great discovery. They knew that they were both thinking of the same thing.
> "Two water towers," said Frank slowly.
> "An old one and a new one."
> "And Jackley said —"
> "He hid the stuff in the old tower."
> "He was a railway man."
> "Why not?" shouted Joe, springing to his feet. "Why couldn't it have been the old water tower? He used to work around here."
> "He didn't say the old tower of Tower Mansion, after all. He just said 'the old tower!'"
> "Frank, I believe we've stumbled on the clue!" [191].

The boys recover the stolen treasure and enjoy a triple triumph: they receive a thousand-dollar reward from the now-grateful Hurd Applegate, they exonerate their friend's father (who gets his job back with a raise and back pay), and win approval from adults they respect and defeat adults who ridiculed them.

In the next few volumes the brothers rid Bayport of smugglers, car thieves, and counterfeiters; rescue kidnapped chums from Blacksnake Island; and travel to Montana to recover hidden gold. Each book repeats a basic formula Arthur Prager has broken down into five stages.

First, the boys are handed a mystery by their father, receive a strange message, or are nearly run down by a car, boat, or plane. Second, the boys discover a clue by coincidence that puts them on the trail of suspects. Third, the boys get into "trouble" when they confront the villains. Fourth, the brothers close in on the hideout (often a cave or remote dwelling) where they are typically captured and tied up. In the last stage, the brothers turn the tables and triumph over the evil-doers: "And so the final phase of each book began with escape and retribution, punctuated by whines and muttered invective from sniveling felons, and ended with a reward—five hundred dollars, two hundred dollars, a gold watch and chain, a movie camera, the usufruct of a vacation island in the bay, a new vehicle of some kind. No adventure ever ended for Frank and Joe without cash profit and a pat on the back."[3]

The plots remain as standard as episodes of *Law and Order*. Each book, however, takes the brothers to a different part of the country, equips them with a new technology, or introduces them to a new criminal enterprise. Along the way, readers learn something about subjects ranging from coin collecting to taxidermy.

Eighty years later, the formula remains much the same, though a few details have been altered. Manners of speech and dress have been updated. The latest novels are written in first person, with Frank and Joe narrating alternating chapters. And the boys are no longer simply freelance detectives but undercover agents for ATAC—American Teens Against Crime. Despite these modifications, little has really changed since 1927. In 2006 the boys were still escaping and capturing villains and still on motorcycles.

> My brother Joe was pretty proud of himself.
> In a single day he had managed to cut through our ropes with a pocketknife, roll over a few times in a dune buggy, stop a pair of wanted criminals, and locate our hidden motorcycles.
> Okay, fine.
> But did he have to rub my nose in it?
> "Who's the man, Frank?" he asked, when we stopped our motorcycles at a red light.
> I rolled my eyes. "You're the man, Joe," I said. "Now will you cut it out? We're almost home."
> The light changed, and we rode our motorcycles through downtown Bayport. When we reached the end of Main Street, I noticed a bunch of police cars in front of the local bank [*Wanted* 16].

That the scenarios have remained basically unchanged has ensured the books' popularity with young readers. Teenagers love cars, and the Hardys always have access to the latest teen vehicles—roadsters, jalopies, hot rods, and dune buggies. They travel widely on their own, their early train trip to Chicago supplanted by jet flights to London and Marrakech in the later novels. Their adventures bring them in touch with the latest technology—long-distance telephone calls in the 1920s, short-wave radios in the 1940s, computers in the 1980s, and cell phones in the 1990s.

The enduring popularity of the Hardy Boys lies in their ability to grow and change with the times, always keeping up with the latest trends, fashions, and technologies while remaining the same age as their readers. Previous juvenile series had allowed characters to age over the years. The Rover Boys started as schoolboys being packed off to a military academy in 1899. The books followed them over the next two decades, through college and into adulthood. After graduation, they bought three adjacent houses in New York City, married, and by World War I had sons. As they aged, they became distanced from their readers, so their sons were sent to a military school to go on adventures juveniles could relate to. The elder Rovers, like aging femme fatales in a daytime drama, became supporting characters in their own series. Tom Swift, who began tinkering with motorcycles in 1910, got older and had to relinquish the title of young inventor to his son, Tom Swift, Jr., who could pilot a jet lab in the Fifties and contend with cosmic astronauts in the Sixties. But through the miracle of fiction, Frank Hardy, who would have been born the same year as Ronald Reagan, is perpetually enrolled at Bayport High, trapped in time as the world around him changes. He and Joe bring their adolescent energy and enthusiasm to fight an ever-changing list of evil-doers, from Oriental opium smugglers to international terrorists. As Carol Billman notes, "Frank and Joe bring to mind the dark side of Peter Pan's charmed existence as an eternal boy."[4] They remain in a "perpetual moratorium," never aging and "reenacting the same patterns," solving one mystery after another.[5]

The Hardys' adventures build upon teenage interests of speed, independence, freedom and travel, and often capitalize on current events. In the 1920s they track down automobile thieves stealing Franklins, Pierce Arrows, and $2800 Cadillacs. In 1930 they go airborne in *The Great Airport Mystery*. During the era of Roosevelt's Good Neighbor Policy, the Hardys travel to Mexico. In 1957 they foil attempts to foment a revolution in Cuba. In 1959, the year Alaska became a state, the boys pack off to Juneau. In 1967, when teenagers were watching television shows like *The Man From U.N.C.L.E., Mission Impossible,* and *Danger Man,* the Hardys get on the espionage bandwagon in *The Secret Agent on Flight 101.* More recently, they have investigated corruption in the oil industry and false hurricane warnings.

The early books were revised to update slang and delete unfamiliar references to keep the original novels popular with younger readers. The boys stopped wearing caps and slickers, touring cars became sedans, Bayport High dropped its Latin requirement, automats stopped selling slices of pie for a nickel, and the Hardy household got along without servants. Shortened and trimmed to emphasize action, the newer versions are faster-paced with clipped dialogue and simpler vocabulary.

The look of the Hardys changed as well. The first dust jackets of the Twenties depict the brothers as "boys" wearing caps, neckties, and sweaters. By the late thirties and early forties, they appear older, wearing suits or open neck shirts. On the 1931 cover of *What Happened at Midnight* the Hardy brothers are strikingly Kennedyesque. In the Fifties they wear casual sports clothes. In the seventies, with feathered hair and bell bottoms, they look like extras from *Saturday Night Fever*.

But the ongoing appeal of the Hardy Boys rests on more than just keeping them fashion current. The brothers act out many of the teenage conflicts and confusions experienced by their adolescent readers.

Wish Fulfillment and Anxiety

Northrop Frye stated that literature presents readers with two dreams: "a wish-fulfillment dream and an anxiety dream, that are focused together, like a pair of glasses, and become a fully conscious vision."[6] Although the work of imagination, literature provides "a perspective and dimension on reality that we don't get from any other approach to reality."[7] Frye was thinking of Plato and Shakespeare, but his observations apply to the Hardy Boys as well. Their books skillfully play on both the adolescent drive for independence and lingering desire for the security of the family.

The appeal of the Hardy Boys also lies, in part, in their uniquely believable brand of wish fulfillment. On one hand, the brothers have adventures their readers can only dream about. They have motorcycles, cars, and speedboats. They travel unaccompanied by parents, taking trains and flying planes to distant cities and foreign countries. They overcome adult adversaries and win approval from authority figures. They make money on their own terms by earning rewards or running their own businesses. On the other hand, they are linked to their readers in a way that Sherlock Holmes and James Bond are not. The Hardy Boys live with their parents, attend high school, study for exams, and count the days till summer vacation. They have chores and homework. Many of their adventures happen "after school" or when they secure parental permission to go out at night. They live in the same middle-class suburban world as many of their readers. A boy riding his bicycle home from school or delivering newspapers can grip his handlebars and imagine himself roaring down the Shore Road on his way to adventure and excitement. Carol Billman observes that Frank and Joe "are, paradoxically, average guys, 'fellows like yourself' as the publicity went, even as they perform wondrous feats of detection."[8]

No book illustrates the movement from realism to wish-fulfillment fantasy more than *The Great Airport Mystery*. In the opening chapters, the Hardys and their chums are studying for final examinations, discussing graduation, and contemplating their future careers with a mix of anxiety, excitement, and resignation. There is also a sense of loss.

> "I was so worried when I wrote those first papers that I'm sure I didn't get by."
>
> "Forget it," advised Frank. "The exams are over and we can't change the papers now. We'll just have to be patient and wait for the results."
>
> "I wish I knew them now," said Chet Morton. "If I don't pass this year, my dad will flay me alive. I might as well pack up and head for Alaska if I don't get through. What are you fellows going to do, now that school is over?"
>
> "Wait for the results," returned Frank. "If we pass, I think Dad wants us to go to college and we'll have to start making our plans."
>
> Jerry Gilroy, another chum of the Hardy Boys, sauntered up.
>
> "How about you, Jerry?" asked Frank. "What are you going to do now?"
>
> "I have a job," announced Jerry calmly.
>
> "Already?" the others exclaimed enviously.
>
> "I start work Monday as a reporter for *The Banner*." Jerry stuck out his chest and pulled his hat brim down over one eye.
>
> "That's a good job," said Tony Prito, who joined the group at that moment. "You'll be able to get into all the shows in town for nothing and get through the police lines at all the fires."
>
> "Well," said Jerry doubtfully, "just at first they're putting me at work writing up obituaries and real estate deals. But I'll soon work my way up," he added hastily.
>
> Tony Prito announced that his parents had decided on a college course for him and that Phil Cohen was bound in the same direction.
>
> "Looks as if the old gang will be broken up by next fall," said Joe glumly [36–37].

The Hardys are later falsely accused of a crime and arrested, invoking the teenage fear of suspicion and harassment by authority figures. Out on bail, the Hardys capture the real criminals and return to Bayport in triumph by airplane. Their arrival mirrors Lindbergh's landing in Paris, carrying readers from the familiar world of homework, exams, and entry-level jobs to the fantasy world of stardom, achievement, and public adulation.

> There was a big crowd at the airport. People were running down the field toward the plane. By the time the pilot cut off his engine, by the time the propeller stopped turning and the plane came to a stop, a mob had surrounded the machine.
>
> Frank and Joe looked wonderingly at one another.
>
> "Looks like a reception committee!" said the pilot. "The sheriff must have telephoned to Bayport about his prisoners."
>
> The Hardy boys stood up. They heard shouts:
>
> "There they are!"

"That's them!"

"Turn around a little—let's get a picture!"

The Hardy boys and the pilot had a confused impression of half a dozen cameras leveled at them. Flashlight powder began to explode until the whole scene was as bright as day. An enterprising reporter scrambled up over the side of the plane.

"Interview!" he clamored. "Give me the story, boys! What happened?" [202–203].

This scene of group approval is replicated decades later in the 1953 novel *The Crisscross Shadow*, but in more believable circumstances. Frank and Joe are football heroes. Frank, captain and quarterback, has led Bayport High to a 7–0 victory over Hopkinsville. The decisive play is Joe Hardy's "one-hundred-yard dash for a touchdown" (40). The crowd goes wild with exaltation.

"Yeah, Hardy boys!" the Bayport fans shouted as they poured out on the field. "Up with 'em!"

With cheers and singing, they were borne off the field on the shoulders of their teammates. When at last they were set down, more fans crowded around to pommel the boys and shake their hands [40–41].

The books also explore adolescent fears and concerns. The Hardy Boys, for all their heroic qualities and independence, experience separation anxiety. The childhood panic of losing one's mother in a store or a crowded street is repeatedly dramatized. In *What Happened at Midnight* (1931), the boys are robbed while in New York City. Unable to pay for a hotel room, they are forced to sleep in Central Park, ration their dimes and nickels for cheap meals, and hitchhike home. Frank and Joe are frequently victimized by adults. A man in Chicago who claims to work for their father puts them on the wrong train to delay their arrival in Montana. While shopping for their mother, the brothers naively fall for a simple ploy and change a five-dollar bill for a man passing counterfeit money. Time and again, the boys encounter situations where they are tricked, overpowered, swindled, reprimanded, or chased by adults. These scenes prey on adolescent insecurity, the fear of leaving home, loneliness, and the sense that the outside world is dangerous, threatening, and hostile. The boys' eventual triumph represents more than a solution to a crime but a victory over anxiety, a triumph over insecurity about living and succeeding in the adult world. Carol Billman sees the books as providing young people with stories of continuing assurance of their safety in a confusing and sometimes threatening world.

> The security of the Hardys' existence (though always in danger, they are never seriously harmed) offers comfort as well from the anxieties brought on by the biological and psychological pressures of growing up in a world that most likely resembles Bayport and its extended universe but little. Readers need to spend quiet hours in such a retreat—in a moratorium, if you will—during which they

In the Thirties and Forties the Hardy Boys became young men in suits. *What Happened at Midnight*, 1931.

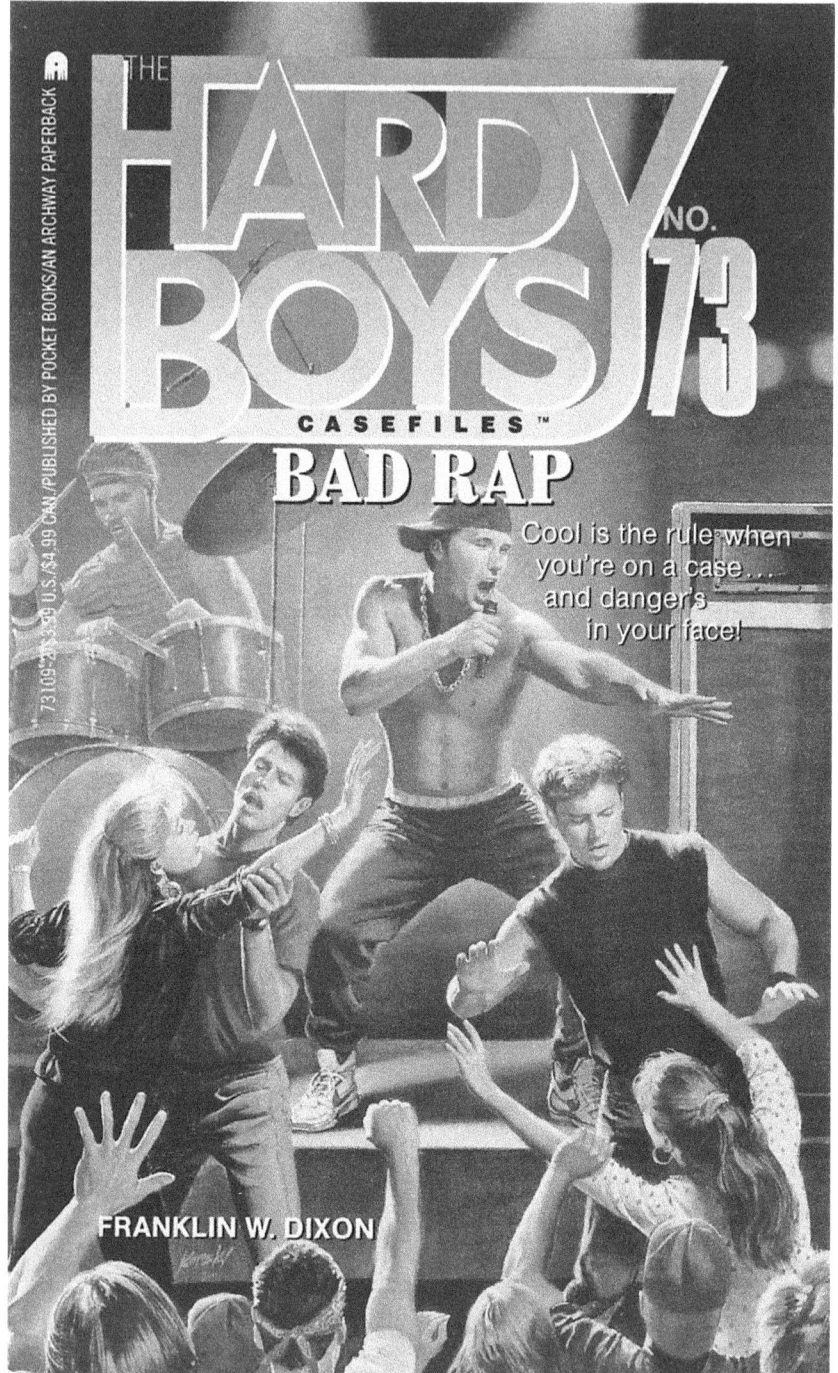

can amass latent energy for the last stage of growth into adulthood. The readily available, jam-packed, and familiar mystery adventures of Frank and Joe Hardy fill that time slot to a T.[9]

Unlike their readers, Frank and Joe never suffer "biological" anxieties or "psychological pressures." They never go through puberty. Their bodies are sanitized, youthful but not virile, male but not masculine. They are as sexless as Ken dolls. In addition, they have no doubts or confusions about their role in society, their futures, their personal security. They maintain an optimistic confidence no matter what the challenge.

Even minor scenes in the books present experiences adolescent readers will recognize and connect with. Though never reckless, the boys are often impulsive. On their first long train trip, Joe is captivated by the novelty of being served dinner while speeding across the country.

> "When I grow up, if I have money enough, I'll just live on the trains," he said solemnly.
> "You'd soon get tired of it."
> "Not me!" And not until the novelty of the long journey began to wear off did Joe admit to himself that possibly such an existence might be wearisome in the long run [*Hunting for Hidden Gold* 57].

These moments create emotional bonds with readers that transcend fascination with cliffhangers and car chases. Readers feel they are part of the stories, that they are becoming the Hardys themselves or at least one of their chums.

So in one way they are very much like their readers — living at home, going to school, having troubling encounters with the adult world — but at the same time they are very different.

> What made the Hardy Boys ... so cool, and keeps them popular today, is not only who they are and what they stand for, but what they aren't. The characters escape the bondage that keeps most teenagers toeing the line. They're never trapped by petty chores, curfews, or the short leash of meager allowances. Frank and Joe don't feel even a twinge of sibling rivalry.... They're not joiners; the 4-H, the Y, church groups, the Scouts have nothing to offer them. Because these teen detectives live so relentlessly in the present, they have no regrets about the past and no worries about their futures.[10]

Frank and Joe are fictional characters any boy can relate to. The athlete, the shy introvert, the troubled child in a dysfunctional family, the student bored with algebra, the teenager working a menial after-school job, and the awkward adolescent can savor a world in which confident boys enjoy individuality and

Opposite: Later series reinvented Frank and Joe to appeal to new generations of teenagers. *Bad Rap*, 1993.

freedom in the adult world while maintaining good relationships at home with family.

Multimedia Legends

While other series books of the Twenties were eclipsed by radio, comic books, motion pictures, and television, the Hardy Boys made an easy and profitable transition into other media, inspiring five television productions, stage plays, comic books, graphic novels, magazines, audio books, Viewmaster slides, VHS tapes, and DVDs.

Hardy Boys memorabilia include lunch boxes, coloring books, activity books, wall clocks, board games, posters, toys, action figures, and computer games. The Hardy Boys have generated an online nostalgia industry of book clubs, fan websites, e-Bay auctions, trivia quizzes, drinking games, and blogs. In 2003 Hardy Boys ornaments graced the White House Christmas tree.

Nostalgia also created a demand for authentic versions of the early novels. In the 1990s Applewood Books began printing facsimile editions of the original Hardy Boys books, restoring 1920s references to roadsters and reproducing expressions like "betting dollars to donuts" that were deleted from revised editions.

Icons of Satire

The Hardy Boys became such iconic figures of all-American youth they could not help but become objects of satire. In 1971 *National Lampoon* ran an adult parody called "Chums in the Dark." Fourteen years later, the magazine featured another parody, "The Undiscovered Notebooks of Franklin W. Dixon." In 2006 the "Hardly Boys" made an appearance in an episode of *South Park*.

"Queer Doin's"

The Hardy Boys' male-dominated cast, coolly platonic relationships with Callie Shaw and Iola Morton and general indifference to girls, the book jackets depicting Frank and Joe in bondage (the brothers were frequently bound and gagged by burly gangsters), and the continual use of the word "queer" to refer to anything unusual or suspicious made the books a perfect target for gay satire.

"Queer" was a favorite word in the series, especially in the novels of the

Twenties and Thirties. In 1927's *The Secret of the Old Mill*, Fenton Hardy confronts a counterfeiting suspect with the accusation, "They tell me you were 'shoving the queer' down in Barmet village this morning" (100). In *The Mystery of Cabin Island* (1929), the detective describes Elroy Jefferson to his sons, noting that "something happened" to make "'the old fellow very queer'" (25). In 1931's *What Happened at Midnight*, a farmer warns Frank Hardy to stay away from a roadhouse because "'they're a queer outfit'" (37).

The Secret of the Caves (1929) is filled with references to "queer doin's" as Frank, Joe, and the chums take a camping trip to Honeycomb Cliffs. They encounter an old storekeeper who warns the boys against "camping" in the area, advising them to "'stay away from the caves'" (63). When the chums announce they plan to explore the caves, the storekeeper tells them they are crazy. Going near the caves, he declares, is "'agin common sense.'" When the chums ask why, the old man gives them dire warnings.

> "There's some queer things been goin' on down there lately. Folks tell me the fishermen down that way are scared nigh to death."
> "What are they afraid of?" asked Biff.
> The old man shrugged eloquently.
> "That's just it. Nobody knows. But there's been queer lights seen down around them caves. And shootin'."
> "Shooting!"
> "Guns goin' off," explained the storekeeper, as if they had failed to understand the word. "Mighty queer doin's, they say" [64].

Undeterred, the boys press on and encounter an old fisherman, who also warns them against entering the caves.

> Chet Morton laughed.
> "We heard there were some queer things happening around here, but that does not frighten us."
> "There's nothing to laugh at, young man," returned the fisherman tartly. "I've lived here for twenty years and I'm no fool. The caves ain't healthy just now."
> …"There's been no queer doin's on the road at all. All the queer doin's are right in the caves"[69].

When the chums insist on entering the caves full of "queer doin's," the fisherman shrugs, saying, "'I'm thinkin' you'll come away from there a lot faster than you go in'" (71).

The chums explore the caves and discover that one has been lived in. They notice blankets, boxes, a crude table, and a mattress.

> "Well, I'll be switched!" declared Joe. "We have a neighbor."
> "We certainly have. And if I'm not mistaken, here he comes now."
> Frank was looking down the beach. The others turned.
> "What a queer duck he is!" exclaimed Biff.

"I'll say he is!" ejaculated Chet Morton. "Where do they get 'em like that?" Coming around a jutting promontory of rock was a queer old man [114–115].

Queer doin's continue in subsequent novels. In *The Disappearing Floor* (1940) Aunt Gertrude points out a strange-looking man on a train platform, warning her nephews that the man is a criminal. Joe "dryly" dismisses her concerns but does admit he is a "queer-looking individual" (3). Later, a state trooper tells Frank and Joe that the Ozonites, a group of sun worshippers, are a "queer bunch" (66). Mabel Maney's satiric parody novel *A Ghost in the Closet: A Hardly Boys Mystery* (1995) plays on a gay theme and makes extensive use of "queer doin's."

Theatrical Parodies

In recent years playwrights and comedy writers have used the Hardy Boys as characters in a variety of satiric skits, plays, and musicals. Recent stage productions include Christopher Durang's one-act drama *The Hardy Boys and the Mystery of Where Babies Come From*, in which the sexually clueless brothers try to figure out how Nancy Drew got pregnant. Like Maney's novel, *Nancy Drew & the Hardy Boys: The Wax Museum Mystery* by Richard Read and Flynn DeMarco plays on a gay theme between the brothers. Timothy Cope and Paul Boesing's gay musical *The Secret of the Old Queen* includes not only another naïve Frank and Joe mystified by sexual double entendre but the full Bayport cast of characters: Fenton Hardy, Callie Shaw, Iola Morton, Chet Morton, and Chief Collig.

Global Impact

The British firm William Collins Sons purchased the rights to publish Hardy Boys titles. The books were reset and edited. Spelling was Anglicized and Americanisms dropped or "translated" to appeal to English readers. The books were renumbered and provided with new illustrations and cover art. In later years, other British publishers would print paperback and multi-volume editions of Hardy Boys titles.

The Hardy Boys have been translated into more than twenty-five languages, including Spanish, Italian, Norwegian, Icelandic, Malay, Russian, German, French, Hebrew, and Japanese. The international drive to learn English has generated new legions of Hardy Boys readers, especially in Asia. In the late 1990s Japan's Kyoto Sangyo University listed twenty-one Hardy Boys books among its 700 titles in its reading program for freshmen English majors.[11]

Viet Dinh, a law analyst who came to the United States with his family after the fall of South Vietnam, explained to Mike Barnicle how he managed to learn English in two years. "One of the things that was a huge help," he said, "was that I read every single one of the Nancy Drew and Hardy Boys books. That's how I did it. English is a tough language to pick up, especially where I'm from."[12]

The influence of the Hardy Boys in India, for example, has been noted by a number of writers, critics, journalists, and bloggers. In "The Bibliophile in Me," Praveen from Banglaore says that books "have been an inseparable part of my life," noting that the novel he remembers reading first "was a Hardy Boys mystery which my aunt actually forced on me."[13] Amar Dev Dhindsa commented on the continuing imperialism in post-colonial Indian schools in an article called "Brown Man's Burden": "none of the books I remember reading from the library were written by Indian authors. The names of books in the library I remember are the Secret Seven, Hardy Boys, The Three Investigators, Coral Island, Treasure Island, Robinson Crusoe and piles of National Geographics."[14] Fifty years later, in the wake of the Harry Potter phenomenon, Kakoli Thakur noted in *Day After India*, "Talk to any school child, and it is certain that he has heard more of the likes of Harry Potter, the Hardy Boys, the Famous Five, Charlie and The Chocolate Factory, etc. than the *Panchatantra* or any other book by an Indian author."[15] This sense that the Hardy Boys were the spear tip of Western imperialism was also expressed in a two-part series in *Hinduism Today* in 1995 by Gowri Ramnarayan, who despaired of the state of children's literature in India where the bookstores "are embarrassingly choked with" Hardy Boys novels and adults confront "the ludicrous picture of India's brightest lads reading the Hardy Boys."[16] Neil Padayatty, a twenty-two-year-old law student, noted in his blog that he is an admitted "bookaholic" who devoured books in childhood, moving from folk tales to the "18-till-they-die Nancy Drew and Hardy Boys (that was a race for who among friends would complete the whole list first)."[17] He strongly suspected that the boy who "defeated" him in reading all the Hardy Boys titles had cheated by skimming only the last chapters. The Hardy Boys dominated the airwaves in India as well. In 2002 newspaper ads in *The Hindu* urged readers to "watch the adventures of the Hardy Boys in your living room, every alternate weekday at 4:30."

Hardy Boys books, like Hollywood films and music videos, have shaped the way millions of young people around the world perceive American life and values. The books themselves have taken a global reach. Once confined to solving crimes in Bayport, the Hardy Boys have gone international, traveling overseas in later novels to Australia, Iceland, Ireland, Britain, Hong Kong, Jamaica, Brazil, and Morocco. Along the way, they shed their Twenties nativism (when diversity meant boating with an Italian-American) to adopt Asian and African chums and dabble in foreign languages. Always all-American, the brothers exhibit traditional values of hard work, honesty, humility, clean-living, and respect for parents while defeating an endless stream of criminals.

The first Hardy Boys novel, *The Tower Treasure*, sold over two million copies and launched a worldwide merchandising empire.
For his efforts, the author received $125.

Chapter 1

Off the Assembly Line: The Fiction Factory of Edward Stratemeyer

> As oil had its Rockefeller, literature had its Stratemeyer.
> —*Fortune*

    The Hardy Boys novels were products of the Stratemeyer Syndicate. This "syndicate" was not a publisher. It did not own printing plants or warehouses. It was essentially a corporate author or "book packager" operating with a small staff out of modest offices in East Orange, New Jersey.

    The syndicate, founded by Edward Stratemeyer in 1905, dominated the juvenile serial fiction market for decades. By 1926 the firm had thirty-one series in production. That year the American Library Association released a survey showing that 98 percent of children polled listed a Stratemeyer book as their favorite.[1] The syndicate would ultimately turn out 125 series consisting of 1,600 separate titles that sold more than 200 million copies in more than two dozen languages.[2] Many Stratemeyer characters—the Hardy Boys, Nancy Drew, Tom Swift, the Bobbsey Twins, and the Rover Boys—became household names around the world, inspiring generations of media spin-offs.

    Stratemeyer did not write all these books himself. Instead, much like the creator of a television show, he typically developed concepts for series, established their basic premise, main characters, location, and dominant themes, then drafted plot outlines for individual novels. The books themselves were written by contract authors working in anonymity for a flat fee. Completed manuscripts were edited for content and format then submitted to publishers for printing and distribution. The literary assembly line was highly efficient. It took just forty days to move a book from original concept to production.[3] The names that appeared on the dust jackets — Franklin W. Dixon, Victor Appleton, and Carolyn Keene — were, like the books' protagonists, copyrighted syndicate creations. Up to half a dozen unnamed writers might work on a long-running series. At any one time Stratemeyer had as many as twenty writers under contract.[4] A total of a hundred contract writers worked for the syndicate over the years, their work appearing under seventy-five brand names. Howard R. Garis, a former *Newark Evening News* reporter, worked for the syndicate for thirty years, producing over three hundred books, among them many of the early Tom Swift novels. His wife also labored on the assembly line, hammering out books for the Bobbsey Twins and Outdoor Girls series. Later, their son and daughter would work for the syndicate.[5]

Although Stratemeyer would wield an influence in popular culture greater than that of any Hollywood mogul or newspaper baron, few people in publishing and fewer of his millions of readers knew of his existence. He shunned publicity and gave few interviews during his lifetime. Like the Wizard of Oz, he operated behind a curtain of secrecy, camouflaged by a hundred pseudonyms, so that eighty years after his death aging Baby Boomers are surprised when they learn that Franklin W. Dixon and Carolyn Keene were just as imaginary as the characters they supposedly wrote about. Because the various series had different authors and publishers, few consumers knew all these novels originated from a single source: the mind of Edward Stratemeyer, whose name rarely appeared in the books he created.

The Henry Ford of Fiction

For Stratemeyer, literature was a consumer product to be created, manufactured, and marketed. Success depended on not only a prolific imagination but also on understanding his consumer, streamlining production, and reducing overhead. During the first year of operation, his syndicate tripled his earnings. The next year he earned, after deductions for advertising and manuscript production, $6,490.18 ($140,000 in 2006 dollars).[6] By the early Twenties the syndicate would achieve gross sales of $9.1 million ($100 million in 2006 dollars).[7] Stratemeyer lived the life of a successful small manufacturer. He maintained a comfortable three-story home with a staff of servants and took his wife and daughters on family vacations to Atlantic City and Yellowstone. He had enough money to pursue his interest in automobiles and purchased several touring cars.[8] *Fortune* would later estimate his income at "a steady $50,000 a year" (twenty-five times the salary of a public school teacher at the time) and note that in 1930 his estate was worth one million dollars.[9]

Edward Stratemeyer, 1903. Stratemeyer Syndicate Records, Manuscripts and Archives Division, The New York Public Library, Astor, Lenox and Tilden Foundations.

Stratemeyer's reclusive nature led to speculative accounts of his production methods. Bruce Watson's 1991 *Smithsonian* article portrays Stratemeyer as a blend of Hans Christian Andersen and Walter Mitty:

> On the loveliest of spring mornings in 1910, a middle-aged juvenile awoke in his peaceful New Jersey home and his dreams began. Showering, he outlined the lively scenario for another title in the "Dorothy Dale, A Girl of Today" series.

Dressing in a tight starched collar, suspenders and tweeds, he sent Jack Ranger and his chums in search of danger. Shaving, he chuckled over the haps and mishaps of two adorable pairs of twins at the seashore. And if he seemed distracted at breakfast, blame it on the lion he was stalking with his electric rifle....[10]

In contrast, Meghan O'Rourke's 2004 *New Yorker* profile depicts Stratemeyer as a detail-oriented executive and shrewd businessman:

> Stratemeyer was a micromanager. During the syndicate's golden years, Stratemeyer, who lived in Newark with his wife and two daughters, would arrive in his Manhattan office at nine every morning, dictate two chapters, and then fire off a series of letters to publishers. No detail was too minor to escape his attention; once, while preoccupied with an important business deal, he noticed that a publisher had sent him a cover on which a Japanese life preserver bore an English name printed in tiny type, and immediately sent off a letter requiring a correction.[11]

In 1934 *Fortune* described Stratemeyer's creative process in wholly industrial terms, likening the process from idea to published book to a conveyor belt.

> Upon leaving the Stratemeyer brain, a fifty-center is crammed into a three page, typewritten outline in which the time elements, names of characters, and their destinies are logically arranged. Then comes the writer who is given the outline and anywhere from a week to a month to fill it out into a book.... [H]e is promptly given from $50 to $250, releases all claims to ownership of the piece, and the manuscript is thrown once again into the Stratemeyer hopper where it receives a final polishing. At the end of the chute stands a representative of the publisher who, acting like a U.S. Government meat inspector in a packing plant, certifies the manuscript as factually fit for consumption. The finished product is a set of electrotypes for a fifty-center, ready to be turned by the printer into thousands of books for waiting adolescents.... The whole process takes perhaps forty days, although on occasion books have sped from Stratemeyer brain to the immortality of print in considerably less time.[12]

Meghan O'Rourke argues that it was the "manufacturing" process that improved both the quality and popularity of Stratemeyer's titles. The rapid assembly line method of producing books "allowed Stratemeyer to learn from his mistakes more swiftly, making his series more sophisticated than many of the series penned by individual authors."[13] The success of syndicate books exploited the consumer's desire for quantity: "Stratemeyer realized that the way to move books was to keep them constant. The 'manufactured' nature of the series was curiously reassuring to kids, who felt that there was an endless supply of goods they knew and liked coming their way."[14]

Leslie McFarlane, who wrote for the syndicate for more than twenty years, considered Stratemeyer a sales genius, who developed "one of the great merchandising ideas in the history of American publishing."[15] McFarlane's

1976 autobiography provides an insider's somewhat sarcastic insight into Stratemeyer's business methods:

> His great idea was first, to insist on total ownership of the merchandise. Abolish all that royalty nonsense. Writers are always broke — pay them a flat rate, at the lowest possible figure. And never, under any circumstance, permit a writer to sign his own name to a book — that way lies disaster in the shape of future demands for more money. Give the author a pseudonym, make sure to have it copyrighted, and insist on a release of all rights to the manuscript.
>
> Second, show no mercy to any publisher. Make them sweat for every nickel they earn. Cut in on their racket by electroplating the books yourself. Then *lease*—do not sell—the plates.
>
> Third, avoid Alger's deplorable mistake of regarding each book as an entity. Alger conjured up a new hero every time he sat down to write a book. As a surcease from boredom this was understandable, but it was downright wasteful. *Ragged Dick* sold prodigiously, but think of what Alger could have done with twenty *Ragged Dicks: Ragged Dick in the Rockies*! *Ragged Dick in the Desert*! *Ragged Dick on the Midnight Express*! They'd have established sales records that would have staggered even Horatio Alger. Moral — always think in terms of a series. Squeeze the last dime out of a winner.[16]

Stratemeyer, like Ford and Rockefeller, rose from humble origins to revolutionize an industry through innovation, mass production, and lowered prices. Although largely unknown to the public, he would make an indelible mark on American society, shaping its values more than William Randolph Hearst or Louis B. Mayer. Two hundred million copies of his books would be read worldwide. In 1929 a survey showed that Tom Swift books were "second only to the Bible as the books most frequently read" by boys.[17] For girls, Stratemeyer's Outdoor Girls series topped the list.[18]

The Making of a Titan

The son of German immigrants, Edward Stratemeyer was born in Elizabeth, New Jersey, in 1862. Like other boys growing up in the 1870s and 1880s, he enjoyed reading popular literature, especially dime novels and the works of Horatio Alger. Fascinated with publishing at an early age, he amused childhood friends by printing stories on a small press. At fourteen he published his first story and, with the help of a friend, put out *Our Friend*, a one-issue newspaper. Months later Stratemeyer printed another single-issue paper called *The Young American*.[19] After graduating high school, Stratemeyer received additional tutoring in composition and rhetoric then took a job in one of his family's tobacco shops. Henry Stratemeyer did not consider writing a practical career for his son, whom he frequently accused of wasting his time reading trash literature. But the young tobacconist continued writing.

In 1883 he put out an eight-page publication for children called *Our American Boys* containing jokes, fillers, and short stories, some of which he is believed to have written.[20] He published stories in various magazines for small sums, but did not achieve a significant sale until 1889.[21]

Later, Stratemeyer would claim to have written "Victor Horton's Idea" on brown wrapping paper in the tobacco shop. The story was accepted by *Golden Days for Boys and Girls*, a popular children's magazine, and Stratemeyer earned his father's respect when he displayed his check for seventy-five dollars, more than many Americans earned in a month.[22] Like many of his future juvenile heroes, Stratemeyer overcame parental objections by accomplishing an unexpected triumph and making money. Now convinced of his son's talent and business acumen, the tobacconist endorsed his choice of career, reportedly telling him, "Well, you'd better write a lot more of them!"[23]

Stratemeyer, like other journeymen writers of the era, published stories under a number of pen names. He wrote "Poor but Plucky" under the pseudonym of Fred Frisky. As Roy Rockwood, he produced "Joe Johnson, the Bicycle Wonder" and published "Dashing Dave, the Ever Ready Detective" with not only a name, but a title: Captain Ravell Pinkerton of the Secret Service. Though frequently making sales, Stratemeyer could not support himself on writing alone and took a job in a stationery shop.[24]

He was hired by Street & Smith, a major publisher of dime novels. Dime novels were more like comic books without pictures. Usually consisting of sixteen to thirty-two pages of newsprint text with a vivid cover, they were issued monthly or even weekly. The repetitive and sometimes garish tales followed the exploits of a leading character, typically a cowboy, detective, or adventurer.

In mastering his craft, Stratemeyer followed the established conventions of the industry. Productivity rather than originality was the key to success for writers paid flat fees. In the early 1890s he wrote over forty dime novels. At Street & Smith he turned out stories about already established characters, completing 22 Nick Carter mystery stories before cranking out Westerns and producing more stories for a rival publisher under yet another pen name.[25] Many of Stratemeyer's Street & Smith titles explored the seedy side of urban life. As Jim Bowie, he published a number of Dead Shot Dave stories chronicling the exploits of a gentleman gambler. Dead Shot Dave and other Stratemeyer heroes engaged in adult — though non-sexual — activities of cigar smoking, drinking, and card playing. Dead Shot Dave patronized saloons, race tracks, dance halls, dog fights, and back alley dice games.[26] Stratemeyer's dime novels lacked the moral restraint found in the later syndicate novels. As Deidre Johnson notes, with the dime novel Stratemeyer was not concerned about winning adult approval because "the dime novels would not be purchased by adults for children but rather consumed as forbidden fruit by the children themselves."[27]

Edward Stratemeyer's first published story, "Victor Horton's Idea," 1889.

Throughout the 1890s Stratemeyer published magazine articles and newspaper serials in leading publications, including *Argosy*, *Chicago Ledger*, *New York Weekly*, *Holiday*, *Banner Weekly*, *New York Observer*, *Golden Hours*, and *Good News*. At the same time he continued producing a range of dime novels for various publishers. Stratemeyer also worked as a reporter for the *Newark*

Daily Advertiser under Noah Brooks, a juvenile author himself, who encouraged him to write novels full time.[28]

In 1898 life imitated art. In many of Horatio Alger's stories, the young hero achieves success not only by hard work but also through the intervention of an older patron. That year Stratemeyer was contacted by his boyhood idol Horatio Alger, who asked the industrious author to finish a manuscript he was unable to write because of failing health. Stratemeyer took on the assignment and went on to complete eleven other unfinished Alger volumes under the name Arthur M. Winfield.[29] These books appeared after Alger's death in 1899. During the next few years, Stratemeyer purchased a number of unfinished Alger manuscripts from Alger's sister Augusta. Stratemeyer revised and completed the pieces and sold them to publishers. Use of the Alger name gave Stratemeyer the ability to demand advances on royalties.[30]

Death of the Dime Novel

By the turn of the century the market for dime novels was declining. Many dime novel companies were hit hard by the 1897 depression and went out of business or scaled back production.[31] Because of their lurid nature, dime novels had become the target of clergymen, teachers, parents' groups, librarians, and social reformers. In their place, hard cover juvenile books began to command a stronger segment of the market. Like dime novels, they were often serials featuring stock characters and formulaic plots. Unlike dime novels, the protagonists tended to be juveniles whose more wholesome adventures avoided adult locales and vices. The Hardy Boys, for example, battled crime but generally tracked down their adversaries in tunnels, caves, or remote hideouts far from the urban underworld. Blacksnake Island was filled with danger and provided readers with plenty of action, but it was a safe distance from a city slum that might require the chums to walk past a speakeasy or brothel.

Because these books often sold for a dollar or more, they had to appeal to the middle class, especially parents who often bought them as presents. The growth of the hard cover juvenile novel marked a change in popular culture:

> The shift to clothbound books and to younger protagonists freed series books from some of the negative connotations of dime novels. Other aspects of series books also offered a surface respectability. The cover designs (and later, dust jackets) highlighted all–American boys and girls engaged in athletics, sampling new technologies, or visiting striking settings. Ads and book blurbs continued this theme, employing phrases like "clean," "bright," and "up-to-date" and an occasional reference to the factual information in the stories. Any parent

inspecting a series book would find that the heroes do not indulge in vices or even read dime novels. All of this must have assuaged the worries of many adults, for inscriptions in books show that older relatives bought series titles for children and teachers gave them as prizes for good conduct or attendance.[32]

Hardcover products could easily distinguish themselves from the thin cheaply printed dime novels and stand on a child's bookshelf alongside *The Three Musketeers* and *Robinson Crusoe*. They had the respectability of being "books." However, they still cost a dollar, a significant sum when factory workers earned as little as fifteen cents an hour.

Stratemeyer studied the changes in the marketplace. Half the population was under twenty-one. An expanding economy had created a rising middle class, giving children greater disposable income. Compulsory education increased literacy and instilled childhood reading habits. With more children attending school rather than working fourteen hours a day in shops and factories, there was an increase in adolescent leisure time. While dime novels were targeted to working class youths, the series book was aimed at middle-class children still in school, still living at home, and dreaming of independence and adventure free of parental restrictions. The books had to balance children's hunger for action and independence while not challenging mainstream moral standards or disparaging family values. The series heroes would have to be hard working, moral, decent, non-smoking, respectful, and idealistic to win parental approval yet enjoy enough freedom and adventure to appeal to children.

In 1899 Stratemeyer created his own series, the Rover Boys, again using Arthur M. Winfield as a pseudonym. According to some accounts, Stratemeyer's mother helped him concoct the pen name with Arthur standing for "Author," Winfield for "Winner in the Field," and M. for "Million."[33] Originally intended to be a trilogy about three brothers in military school, the books proved so successful that Stratemeyer expanded it into a series, adding twenty-seven novels until discontinuing the series in 1926.

The Rover Boys are notable for two reasons. First, they became one of the most long-running and popular juvenile series of the early twentieth century, selling five million copies by the mid–1930s.[34] Second, they established marketing and literary patterns that would be used to great success in the syndicate. Stratemeyer had released the first three volumes at the same time, his first "breeder" set. As characters, the Rover brothers exhibited values and attributes that would be imbued in future heroes and heroines. Their adventures in solving mysteries, rescuing kidnap victims, traveling cross country, surviving shipwrecks, and discovering hidden treasure would be reprised over and over in different formats in other series. The Rovers stayed "up-to-date" by keeping pace with new technology, driving motor cars in the early books and buying an airplane in 1912.

In 1904 Stratemeyer began another popular series, one that would remain in production until 1992 and total 115 novels. It, too, would sell millions of copies and become a household name. The Bobbsey Twins followed the adventures of two sets of twins: eight year olds Nan and Bert and four year olds Freddie and Flossie. With two sets of twins Stratemeyer could appeal to children of different age groups and feature the interplay between older and younger siblings children could easily relate to. The four Bobbsey children live in a privileged world of loving parents and live-in servants. The twins do face adversity, though hardly on the Rover Boys level. Their antagonist, a bully named Danny Rugg, steals ice cream and frames Bert for smoking. The Bobbsey Twins formed a pattern for the "tot series" genre aimed at younger readers.

These books clearly demonstrated to Edward Stratemeyer that he could succeed with his own hard cover book series. He had created characters and stories children identified with. More importantly, he had written stories that children wanted more of.

The popularity of the series books was due to their message and the fact they were series. As Deidre Johnson notes, the Stratemeyer books appealed to children's desire for individuality, success, and empowerment: "Above all, Stratemeyer and the Stratemeyer Syndicate's books preached success, the same message found in numerous other series, past and present. Children could be powerful, competent, and victorious through such books. No matter what the situation, a Stratemeyer or Syndicate hero or heroine eventually triumphs. No obstacle is too great, no adult too powerful, no competitor too skilled or too devious to fell the protagonist permanently."[35] Series books also capitalized on children's desire for repetition and their attachment to familiar characters who could become imaginary friends or alter egos they could return to again and again:

> In a world of changes, uncertainties, and disempowerment, series books provided children with a means of security and control. These elements were further heightened through the use of continuing characters, for here was even greater security, the guarantee not just of a happy ending but of meeting old friends over and over again. And when the adventure is over and the triumphant hero or heroine is toting treasures home, there is the promise of another round of adventures in a forth-coming book, reassuringly advertised on the last page.[36]

Birth of the Syndicate and the Fifty-Center

Having created a successful product, Stratemeyer, like other entrepreneurs, had only to step up production to become rich and famous, or at least rich. It is widely accepted that the syndicate came about simply because Stratemeyer wanted to produce more books than he could write. But additional factors coalesced to make the Stratemeyer Syndicate a success. New copyright laws guaranteed rights to owners, not writers, of literary works, ensuring his control over books produced by others.[37] High speed printing techniques had lowered the cost of publishing. Following the success of the Rover Boys, he approached publishers in 1906 with a new series, the Motor Boys, basically the Rover Boys on wheels. Instead of charging a dollar, he persuaded publishers to lower the cover price to fifty cents. The "fifty-centers" would look like the standard series books but cost half as much, expanding their market to children with modest allowances and price-conscious parents.[38]

At first, publishers resisted Stratemeyer's proposal because slashing prices by fifty percent would reduce their profit to a few pennies a copy. Stratemeyer argued that profits lay in volume rather than price. His strategy worked. The Motor Boys became a highly popular and profitable series. When Stratemeyer repackaged the Rover Boys as fifty-centers, their sales increased.[39] The fifty-center did for series fiction what the Model T did for the Ford Motor Company. Reduced prices increased demand and production soared. In 1927 80 percent of the books read by American children were products of the Stratemeyer Syndicate.[40] By 1934 *Fortune* estimated that Grosset and Dunlap, one of Stratemeyer's major publishers, had produced enough fifty-centers to build a monument 700 miles high.[41]

Because the profit margin for fifty-centers was slim and depended on volume sales, Stratemeyer concentrated on attaining mass production while maintaining a low overhead. He set up his original operation in East Orange, New Jersey, rather than in Manhattan, kept his staff small, and paid his writers flat fees rather than advances and royalties. Eliminating royalties meant that once a book earned a hundred dollars in profits, Stratemeyer was essentially the author. The use of syndicate-owned pen names prevented any real writer from gaining a fan base he or she might use as leverage to demand more money. It also avoided the danger of losing a popular author to a rival publisher. Writers came and went as anonymously as welders on an assembly line. Ironically, few readers ever questioned the authorship of the books, many fully believing that Carolyn Keene and Victor Appleton were just as real as Charles Dickens or Mark Twain (few readers seemed to question how Franklin W. Dixon, whose name appeared on *The Tower Treasure* in 1927 was able to write the Hardy Boys Undercover Brothers Super Mystery novel *Wanted* in 2006). Stratemeyer also kept his publishers in line, sometimes shifting a series to a rival firm to secure a better arrangement.

The writers hammering out the novels were mostly reporters and former dime novelists. Some applied to the syndicate, some were recruited, and others hired in response to blind want ads placed in trade publications. They labored in total obscurity, many dealing with Stratemeyer only by mail.

Mildred Wirt wrote for the syndicate for twenty-four years, producing twenty-three Nancy Drew titles while living in Iowa.[42] Leslie McFarlane typed Hardy Boys books in a cabin in Ontario, never meeting Stratemeyer in person or even speaking with him on the telephone.[43] Few authors knew the identity of others working for the syndicate. Those who produced satisfactory novels on time only earned the privilege of writing more books. Their fees ranged from $75 to $125 a book — one or two months' pay for a reporter in the Twenties. Sworn to secrecy, contract writers often never disclosed to their own families that they were the authors of some of the most popular juvenile books in American history.

Like other manufacturers, Stratemeyer demanded conformity to company standards. He was as much concerned about length and format as he was content, repeatedly reminding writers to make sure the novels had exactly twenty-five chapters and came in at two hundred and sixteen pages.[44] A non-smoking church-goer, Stratemeyer eschewed the gore, extensive gunplay, smoking, and drinking that marked his own dime novels. He was now producing books that would be purchased by adults and sold to libraries. Like a candy manufacturer, he had to assure parents that his product was wholesome if not exactly nutritious.

Stratemeyer dealt with teenage sex by avoiding it, segregating boys and girls into separate and often parallel series. When Stratemeyer launched books to capitalize on the automobile craze at the turn of the century, his characters took to the road not only in separate vehicles but in separate series: the Motor Chums and the Motor Girls. There were other parallel series: The Outdoor Chums and the Outdoor Girls, The Boys of Columbia High and The Girls of Central High.

To make sure his young readers understood he was launching a series and not introducing a single novel, he began with what he called his "breeders"— usually the first three volumes of a new series were released at the same time. Eighty years later, Grosset & Dunlap used the same technique, selling a boxed "starter set" of six Hardy Boy books in 2006. To further whet reader's appetites, he generally required that a series book summarize the previous novel (usually at the opening of chapter two) and provide a "throw-ahead" or preview of the next volume on the last page:

> And that ended the affair of the Tower Mansion, but it did not end the career of the Hardy boys as amateur detectives. They were soon to be called on to help solve another mystery, and the story of their adventures in this case will be told in the next volume of this series, entitled "The Hardy Boys: The House on the Cliff" [*The Tower Treasure*, 213].

Like other manufacturers of the era, Stratemeyer realized the importance of advertising and promotion. He purchased mailing lists from boys' and girls' organizations and sent out colorful catalogs to children. The catalogs included a form that asked children for the names and addresses of their friends. The novelty of getting mail addressed to them had great appeal to children. Many submitted lists of friends, and the mailing list grew. Children sent in questions and requests about upcoming titles and wrote fan letters to the fictional authors.[45] The direct mail campaign worked like "an insidious narcotic with the habit-forming properties of opium."[46] Later syndicate efforts would include book clubs and sales of introductory copies for ten cents. To maintain customer loyalty, the syndicate provided fresh dust jackets to children who wrote in stating that the cover of their favorite book had become worn. To win over parents, in 1911 Stratemeyer circulated a leaflet entitled "Safe and Sane Books for Boys and Girls" by John Tupper Brownell. This booklist was "Issued by Permission of the Good Reading Club of America." This reading club and its list was a Stratemeyer creation. The only books on the list, all of which were reviewed favorably, were syndicate productions.[47]

Now that Stratemeyer had the machinery to mass produce series fiction, he had to create products his consumers wanted. Stratemeyer's key strength was his understanding of child psychology and his ability to tap into current events, changing technology, and cultural fads. He instinctively understood what children were looking for in books. Analyzing a century of series fiction for a 2003 study, Nodelman and Reimer noted five characteristics of successful books:

1. A simple, straightforward writing style.
2. Central characters, who exhibit traits with which readers can identify.
3. Clear distinctions between "good" and "bad" characters.
4. Plots that focus on action with minimal attention to setting or character.
5. Plots that fulfill readers' wishful thinking.[48]

The Product Line

Stratemeyer created scores of series. Some, like failed television shows, were short-lived and cancelled after a few volumes. Others, like Tom Swift, would last for decades, often undergoing revisions and recreations. There were the "tot series" like the Bobbsey Twins, Six Little Bunkers, and Honey Bunch aimed at younger readers. Other series were knock-offs of adult fiction. The boom in hard-boiled detective fiction in the 1920s was largely responsible for the creation of the Hardy Boys, the Dana Girls, and Nancy Drew. The popularity of Tarzan led to Stratemeyer's juvenile version, Bomba the Jungle Boy (20 volumes, 1926–1938). Sports-oriented boys could read Baseball Joe, Mel Martin Baseball Stories, and the Gary Grayson Football Series. There were Westerns, school series, travel series, and books that focused on a particular industry or technology like Ralph of the Railroad and the Radio

Boys. He created historical fiction series and series based on current events. World War I inspired the Air Service Boys about young American aviators serving in France. Stratemeyer did not ignore girls. Numerous series featured female protagonists: Betty Gordon, Blythe Girls, Corner House Girls, Doris Force, Linda Craig, Nan Sherwood, and Ruth Fielding. At one point a third of the books sold were girls' series.

The burgeoning movie industry inspired no less than four Stratemeyer series, covering all aspects of film production. The Moving Picture Boys (15 volumes, 1913–1922) and the Motion Picture Comrades (5 volumes, 1917) traveled the world making movies, often filming actual events for documentaries or stock footage to be woven into fictional dramas. The Moving Picture Girls (7 volumes, 1914–1916) acted in front of the cameras. The Motion Picture Chums (7 volumes, 1913–1916) ran a series of movie theaters, blending fascination with the new entertainment medium with the earlier popularity of "boys in business" stories. Stratemeyer would also introduce the motion picture industry into other series, so that in the long-running Ruth Fielding series (30 volumes, 1913–1930) Ruth, wounded while doing intelligence work in World War I, returns home to write and produce motion pictures.

The Motion Picture Chums (1913–1916), one of the four early Stratemeyer series about the movie industry.

Perhaps no series better illustrates Stratemeyer's success in exploiting current events than the Ted Scott Flying Stories (20 volumes, 1927–1943). Though largely forgotten today, this series, launched the same year as the Hardy Boys, was immensely successful, selling twice as many copies as the Hardy Boys in its early years.[49]

Stratemeyer had published a number of aviation stories, but their popularity ebbed as airplanes became more commonplace. However, with the national hysteria that followed Charles Lindbergh's solo flight to Paris, Stratemeyer rushed a new series into production. He had the first Ted

Scott novel completed within two weeks and on bookstore shelves within a month.⁵⁰

The first volume of the series, *Over the Ocean to Paris*, describes how Ted Scott, once a humble mechanic with less than two dollars to his name, makes a solo flight across the Atlantic in a small monoplane resembling the *Spirit of St. Louis*. Like Lindbergh, Ted Scott becomes an international idol who is feted by heads of state, given a hero's welcome in New York on his return, and decorated by the President of the United States. Like Lindbergh, Ted Scott uses the word "we" to describe himself and his plane. Like Lindbergh, he is modest, turning down millions of dollars in endorsements, preferring not to cheapen his name by becoming a pitchman for shaving cream or a vaudeville performer. He does, like Lindbergh, lend his name to ventures that will "advance the cause of aviation." Subsequent volumes paralleled Lindbergh's flights to Latin America and Asia in the late Twenties. As aviation become more commercialized, the series moved beyond stories about record-breaking flights to mysteries and adventures. The airplane then became simply a vehicle to help Ted Scott defeat diamond smugglers and rescue missing explorers. With the advent of World War II, the last two Ted Scott volumes took on a military edge with stories about "sky spies" and pursuit planes.

Stratemeyer's series reflected the rapid industrial and technological expansion of the early twentieth century. As soon as the first automobiles began lurching down the unpaved roads of America, the Stratemeyer Syndicate launched series about young people's overland travels dealing with the state-of-the-art internal combustion engine and its mysterious components of batteries, inflatable tires, carburetors, and radiators. The Tom Swift series would begin in 1910 with *Tom Swift and His Motorcycle, Tom Swift and His Motor Boat, Tom Swift and His Airship*, and *Tom Swift and His Electric Runabout*. Four years later Tom Swift would be inventing something called a "photo telephone," and in 1918 he would help the war effort in *Tom Swift and His War Tank: Doing His Bit for Uncle Sam*. By 1928 Tom Swift would be making "talking pictures." By 1932 he was experimenting with television.

The reason for the longevity of Tom Swift, the Hardy Boys, and Nancy Drew was their ability to change. As inventors, Tom Swift, his son, and grandson could keep pace with state-of-the-art technology and grow with the century. As detectives, the Hardys could move from recovering stolen roadsters to combating international terrorism. The Motion Picture Chums, Air Service Boys, and the Radio Boys, however, were wedded to a single industry or historical event, and like many a TV series with limited appeal, they quickly exhausted available plots and lost their audience within a few years.

Death of the Founder

In 1930, the year Nancy Drew was introduced, Edward Stratemeyer's health began to fail. He suffered circulatory problems and a heart attack that sidelined him for months. He returned to his office for a few weeks until suffering a second heart attack. Though seriously ill, he was planning a new sports series when he suffered a third heart attack and died on May 10. Stratemeyer was buried in Evergreen Cemetery in Hillside, New Jersey (which also contains the graves of Stephen Crane and *Hans Brinker* author Mary Mapes Dodge). The family monument is bordered with carvings of bookshelves. Edward Statemeyer's own headstone bears the epitaph, "The final chapter closes, leaving in young hearts the memory of fine ideals."[51]

With Stratemeyer's death, the fiction factory ground to a halt. Despite its success and influence, the entire enterprise was only an extension of one man's imagination. Edward Stratemeyer had created the series, plotted the novels, given the contract writers their assignments, edited manuscripts, and negotiated with publishers. Without new ideas for books, the contract writers had nothing to write, the publishers no new books to print.

It was 1930. The Stratemeyer Syndicate, like so many other one-man companies, could have easily gone under during the Depression. There were no vice-presidents or senior executives in the chain of command. Stratemeyer had been the captain of a ship with a skeleton crew. Without his direction, the crew was helpless.

Stratemeyer's widow, who inherited her husband's business, was in poor health. Like characters in a girls' series, Harriet and Edna Stratemeyer stepped in to rescue their father's rudderless enterprise. Harriet Stratemeyer Adams, married with four children, and her younger sister, Edna, took over the syndicate. As a mark of success, Edward Stratemeyer had moved his operation to New York City. The sisters returned the offices to New Jersey, closer to Harriet's home.

Harriet Adams would soon play the dominant role in the sisters' partnership and eventually assume sole command of the syndicate. Born in 1892, she attended Wellesley, where she studied creative writing and edited the college newspaper. As a college journalist she sold articles to *The Boston Globe* and *The Newark Evening News*. In 1914 she was awarded a medal for bravery for her heroic actions during a dormitory fire, in which she and other girls entered a burning building to rescue valuable school documents. After graduation, she edited manuscripts for her father. With his death, Adams, then thirty-eight, completed unfinished manuscripts and began plotting new titles. Harriet Adams, like her father, shunned publicity, declining to list her position in the syndicate in alumni biographical statements.[52]

Edward Stratemeyer presided over his syndicate for twenty-five years.

1. Off the Assembly Line: The Fiction Factory of Edward Stratemeyer 39

Harriet Stratemeyer as a Wellesley senior, 1913–1914. Stratemeyer Syndicate Records, Manuscripts and Archives Division, The New York Public Library, Astor, Lenox and Tilden Foundations.

Harriet Adams would operate her father's fiction factory for another fifty, carrying it through the lean years of the Thirties and keeping the syndicate's series alive and profitable into the age of television and video games. Under her reign, the Hardy Boys would become international emblems of American youth and capitalize on new entertainment media. Not only would her teenage detectives compete with television, comic books, and video games — they would become television stars, comic book characters, and video games themselves.

During the Depression the syndicate stayed afloat, its survival due largely to the continued popularity of Hardy Boys, Nancy Drew, and Tom Swift titles. As *Fortune* reported in 1934, the fifty-center was far from dead. "For a while the movies, then the depression, damaged them," the article noted, "but the fifty-centers have never really lost their place in the literary sun."[53] During the Christmas season of 1933 Macy's alone sold six thousand Nancy Drew books.[54] The number of series was pared back, dropping from twenty-seven in 1930 to only seven by 1942.[55] Fees paid to writers were cut to $75.

Edna married and moved to Florida in 1942, leaving her sister to manage the syndicate. In 1948 Harriet Adams hired Andrew Svenson (1910–1975), a writer and journalism instructor, who pumped new blood into the syndicate. He wrote or co-wrote seventy novels and created three new series. Under the name Jerry West, he wrote The Happy Hollisters (1953–1970), an updated and energized family series similar to the Bobbsey Twins, which became one of the most popular series launched after World War II. The series ran for thirty-three volumes. In 1960 Svenson started the Bret King Mysteries under the name Don Scott. Though well-written, the juvenile Western series was discontinued in 1964 after nine volumes. Svenson also created the short-lived The Tolliver Adventure Stories in 1967. This series, modeled after the Happy Hollisters, told the adventures of the Tollivers, a black family. The syndicate's attempt at a minority series did not extend beyond the three-volume breeder set.[56]

In 1959 the syndicate began a twenty-year project of revising its old standards. The thirty-year-old Hardy Boy titles were becoming quaint and a bit shopworn with their dated references and now laughable teenage slang. Ethnic stereotypes, racial slurs, and negative depictions of the police were eliminated. The books were streamlined, trimming the word count by as much as 20 percent. Long descriptions and lengthy dialogue were cut or condensed to give the books a faster pace and emphasize action. Sentences were shortened and vocabulary simplified. Dedicated fans of the original versions would later call this change the "Great Purge."

Although television would be blamed for reducing children's interest in books, it benefited the syndicate. The Hardy Boys and Nancy Drew were adapted into a variety of television shows beginning in the late 1950s, giving the decades-old books new life. When the popular *Mickey Mouse Club* show featured a Hardy Boys mini-series, the books appeared in supermarket displays. The syndicate hired new writers and launched new series, including Chris Cool. And despite competition, some of the earliest series remained in demand. The original Bobbsey Twins series, first launched in 1904, continued to find new readers.

In 1961 Andrew Svenson became a partner, the first non–family member to take a leadership role in the syndicate. After East Orange was hit by riots in the late 1960s, the offices were moved to Maplewood, New Jersey.[57]

The 1970s witnessed a major changing of the guard. Edna Stratemeyer died in 1974. The following year Andrew Svenson died. Harriet Adams asked four staff members to become partners. The syndicate suspended less popular series and focused on its long running classics — the Hardy Boys, the Bobbsey Twins, Tom Swift, and Nancy Drew.[58]

Although by the 1970s the juvenile series book was being eclipsed by television and comic books, the Hardy Boys enjoyed booming sales in an overall declining market. Harriet Adams worked with media representatives, making arrangements to bring the Hardy Boys and Nancy Drew to television. Smart merchandising efforts paid off. In January 1973 Grosset & Dunlap issued Harriet Adams her largest royalty check to date. The last six months of 1972 had been the most financially successful sales period in sixty years. Two years later this record was broken. The $190,442.62 check was accompanied by a letter from Grosset & Dunlap's president stating, "Harriet, breaking records with you, although it is old history, is still something I regard as one of my favorite activities."[59] This record was surpassed in 1977 when Harriet Adams received a royalty check for $244,737.73.[60]

The $300 Million Lawsuit

Despite these successes and her publisher's appreciation, Harriet Adams was not satisfied with Grosset & Dunlap. Although the syndicate had been doing business with the firm since 1908, the relationship was often strained. Over the years Adams pestered Grosset & Dunlap for more advertising, stronger promotions, and a higher royalty schedule. She was aware that the standard author royalty was ten percent and felt that being bound by her father's original agreement, made when the fifty-center was an experimental venture, was unfair. The low-priced series book had proven successful for decades, and she believed the syndicate deserved a higher share of the profits. In 1969 she asked her publisher to reconsider their long-standing agreement: "It occurred to me recently that when my father signed a contract with your company some forty years ago ... Nancy Drew and the Hardy Boys books

Harriet Stratemeyer, 1980. Stratemeyer Syndicate Records, Manuscripts and Archives Division, The New York Public Library, Astor, Lenox and Tilden Foundations.

sold for fifty cents and he received a royalty of two cents; in other words four per cent. Since that time the rate has never changed, which makes a unique situation in publishing. Don't you agree that it is high time we update our thinking in line with present day practices and increase the percentage of royalty to world renowned Carolyn Keene [and] Franklin W. Dixon?"[61] Harriet Adams' lobbying for her fictional authors met with little success. Franklin W.

Dixon and Carolyn Keene, along with Victor Appleton, would get no raise. Adams was deeply disappointed when Grosset & Dunlap failed to capitalize on or even acknowledge the seventy-fifth anniversary of the Bobbsey Twins in 1979. When asked what plans the firm had for celebrating Nancy Drew's upcoming fiftieth anniversary the following year, Grosset & Dunlap was unresponsive. Believing that her long-running and highly profitable series deserved more recognition and promotion, Adams decided to look for a new publisher.

In 1979 Adams, then eighty-six, decided to move production of the Hardy Boys and Nancy Drew from Grosset & Dunlap to Simon & Schuster, which offered better terms and promised greater advertising and stronger marketing. The firm began issuing new titles in paperback, stepping up production from one to as many as six new titles a year. Grosset & Dunlap, unwilling to lose its grip on the consistently lucrative Hardy Boys and Nancy Drew market, sued the Stratemeyer Syndicate and Simon & Schuster, demanding $300,000,000 in punitive damages for breach of contract and copyright infringement. Grosset & Dunlap argued that the syndicate was not the sole author of the books, claiming that it shared ownership of the books' characters and copyrights. It was not, it insisted, simply a printing plant and distributor. A trial in 1980 ended with a compromise. The court ruled that the syndicate had the right to choose its publisher, but it also allowed Grosset & Dunlap to continue printing and selling hardcover editions of previously published books. The syndicate decided to retain Simon & Schuster as its new publisher, which would issue new titles in paperback.[62] The Hardy Boys canon of fifty-eight novels produced from 1927 to 1979 would remain in print and continue to sell millions of copies and provide Grosset & Dunlap an unprecedented income stream for decades.

In 1982 Harriet Stratemeyer Adams died at the age of eighty-nine. A grandson worked briefly with the syndicate. The remaining partners managed the fiction factory for two years, then were obliged — some contend forced — to accept Simon & Schuster's purchase offer. The overall market for the series book had declined, but in the early Eighties the syndicate maintained its near monopoly status, selling an estimated six million copies a year or 90 percent of series books sold in the United States. Hardy Boys books sold 1–2 million copies annually. Nancy Drew's numbers were even better, selling up to two million books a year.[63] In 1984 the syndicate was sold to Simon & Schuster, which would own the product line and exercise full rights, controlling the literary destinies of Stratemeyer's greatest creations: Frank and Joe Hardy, Tom Swift, and Nancy Drew.[64] The syndicate was no more, but Simon & Schuster followed its production methods, hiring contract writers for flat fees to write Hardy Boys books under the immortal penname of Franklin W. Dixon.

Claims and Denials

The secrecy of the syndicate's operations and continued questions of authorship led to various claims and disputes as to who should be considered the "real" Carolyn Keene or the "real" Franklin W. Dixon.

Mildred Wirt Benson was a syndicate writer who came to public attention following her testimony during the publishers' trial. Her growing reputation as being the "real" Carolyn Keene would vex Stratemeyer's great-granddaughter years after the syndicate ceased operation.

Born in 1905, the year the syndicate was founded, Mildred Augustine graduated from the University of Iowa with a degree in journalism. Her second husband, George Benson, was the editor of the *Toledo Blade* in Ohio, a newspaper Mildred would work for for fifty-eight years. Like Harriet Adams, Mildred Benson was an independent, indefatigable woman. She took up flying in her late fifties and continued working as a journalist, despite failing eyesight, until her death at ninety-six.

Benson's career with the syndicate began in 1926 when Edward Stratemeyer hired her as a ghostwriter. She wrote twenty-three of the first twenty-five Nancy Drew books. Like all syndicate writers, Benson signed a contract stipulating she would receive a flat fee and waive any claim of authorship or ownership of the books she produced.

But in the minds of much of the public her appearance at the publishers' trial revealed Benson to be the "real Carolyn Keene"—the woman who wrote the Nancy Drew books. Benson gave interviews and was the subject of several newspaper articles, some of which included a photograph showing her seated behind a desk piled high with "her books." She answered fan mail from Nancy Drew readers and noted in a Salon.com article in 1999 that she was glad that she was being acknowledged as the author because once her daughter came home from school upset by classmates who refused to believe her mother had written the Nancy Drew books.

This acknowledgment, however, was not shared by Stratemeyer's descendants. In response to the About.com question, "Who was the real author of the Nancy Drew books?" Cynthia Adams Lum, granddaughter of Harriet Adams and great-granddaughter of Edward Stratemeyer, posted a legalistic six-page article designed to lay the matter to rest.

In Adams' mind there was one author of Nancy Drew—her grandmother: "The Stratemeyer Syndicate's head had the full, legal and moral right to claim ownership and authorship of Syndicate books, their characters and pennames. As senior partner of the Syndicate, Edward, and then Harriet, exercised final authority over their books' content, with the right to assert authorship of their stories."[65]

The fifty ghostwriters, in Adams' view, were employed to complete plot outlines, which she deemed as virtual "rough drafts," provided by the syndicate that would edit final copy. Rather than use the well-established metaphor of the fiction factory, Adams used a more artistic analogy to explain the workings of her family's enterprise:

> In order to fully understand the position taken by the Syndicate's head, an analogy can be drawn with historical grand master painters and their studios. Various apprentices and other painters, needing work, were hired to assist in the master painter's commissions. This was acceptable in order to increase his output. They studied the master's style, under his direction, in order to mimic his work. Their contributions to his paintings varied from a few brush strokes, detailing work, to complete copies. The paintings, in subject, concept and detail, any work undertaken on the master's behalf and the final products were the property of the studio master. There was no question that he had the right to sign his name to his finished paintings.[66]

The syndicate book had, in Adams' view, only one possible author — the syndicate itself. Ghostwriters like Mildred Wirt Benson who cultivated the image of being the "real authors" were deceiving the public. Adams objected to Benson's donation of her typewriter to the Smithsonian which she claimed to have used to "write her" books, along with her suggestion to interviewers that she had created the Nancy Drew character. Adams insisted that Benson had merely supplied "narrative 'flesh'" to "Stratemeyer's story 'skeletons'" by adding dialogue and "text."[67] She could no more claim to be the author of Nancy Drew than a Ford spot welder could claim to be the inventor of the Model T.

"There is no mystery to the authorship of the *Nancy Drew* books," Cynthia Adams Lum concluded. "She was a prolific writer, successful business woman, mother and beloved grandmother. For inspiration and principles embodied in *Nancy Drew*, you need look no further than the life of Carolyn Keene, who was Harriet Stratemeyer Adams."[68]

The Legacy

The fiction factory operated for eighty years. It produced some of the most widely read books in the world and created characters that became popular culture icons. It influenced the way tens of millions of American children viewed society and thought of themselves, and shaped the way millions of children in other countries viewed the United States. The syndicate's power and influence was unprecedented. But unlike the dream factory of MGM, it came and went with little notice, an invisible empire. Stratemeyer and his legion of ghostwriters gave all the credit to imaginary authors whose names still appear on reincarnations of books that rolled off the syndicate assembly line eighty years ago.

Stratemeyer's method of mass-producing fiction, like Henry Ford's assembly line, was replicated by others. Dennis Duffy notes that Stratemeyer's methods were copied by Frank and Anne Hummert, who in the 1930s created an assembly line to produce radio soap operas. They developed concepts for shows, outlined episodes, then had "dialoguers" flesh out scripts for broadcast. Their "total packaging (script plus performance) of the product sold to the network or sponsor resembled the Stratemeyer Syndicate's."[69]

The Stratemeyer-Hummert model remains in use today in the production of both daytime dramas and primetime television shows, where a series creator employs a head writer who supervises a number of sub-writers who complete scripts. Like Stratemeyer's ghosts, these sub-writers follow outlines and mimic tones and styles developed by their employers. The production of popular narratives, in print or broadcast, is an industrial process. "To put it another way," Duffy observes, "however the Hummerts and their TV successors acquired their practices, a model of it existed during the golden age of popular print narrative. Edward Stratemeyer, in some fashion, became the mother of us all."[70]

Chapter 2

The McFarlane Formula: "I Opted for Quality"

> One day my son had come into the workroom, which had never been exalted into a "study," and pointed to the bookcase with its shelf of Hardy Boys originals. "Why do you keep these books, Dad? Did you read them when you were a kid?"
> "Read them? I wrote them." And then, because it doesn't do to deceive any youngster, "At least, I wrote the words."
> — Leslie McFarlane, *Ghost of the Hardy Boys*

Twenty of the original all–American Hardy Boys books were written by a Canadian, Leslie McFarlane (1902–1977), who developed a formula that elevated the series from juvenile hack fiction to memorable works of children's literature.

McFarlane grew up in Haileybury, a boom town in the rowdy silver-mining region of northern Ontario. Built on sloping hills overlooking Lake Temiskaming, Haileybury, like the mining towns of the Wild West, was populated by rough men, saloon keepers, and prostitutes. Fights and back alley shootings among drunken miners were common. McFarlane's father, a devout Bible-reader, was a school principal and a symbol of civilized morality in a frontier town. Like his future employer Edward Stratemeyer, McFarlane showed an early interest in writing and publishing. At thirteen he won an essay contest. At seventeen he attained second place in an Ontario literary contest. That year he helped found and edit his high school newspaper.[1]

Having published freelance articles in his hometown newspaper, the *Haileyburian*, McFarlane traveled five miles to interview for a reporter's job with the *Cobalt Nugget*. Hired at nine dollars a week, the teenage journalist developed enough experience to secure a higher paying position at the much larger *Sudbury Star*. He put in long hours doing the yeoman work of cub reporters, covering school board meetings, town council hearings, church picnics, ball games, and car accidents. Sudbury provided McFarlane with experiences that he would later weave into his fiction. The town of fifty thousand was not a sleepy farm town, but the center of a brawling lumber and mining region populated with tough characters, bootleggers, prostitutes, and the occasional murderer.[2]

McFarlane's dream, however, was to be writer, not a reporter. In his free time he wrote short stories, submitting them to the prestigious literary magazines of the day. During this period he met Ernest Hemingway, then a reporter for the *Toronto Star*.[3] In late 1924 he sold two stories to *Adventure* magazine, earning $775, a sizeable sum for the young reporter making a hundred dollars a month.[4] He briefly quit newspaper work and managed to support himself as a freelance fiction author. In 1926 he sought steady employment again, taking a job with the *Springfield Republican* in Springfield, Massachusetts. The city had two newspapers, but as McFarlane recalled, journalistic competition was almost non-existent. The papers had distinctly different readerships. Scoops were not encouraged, and the newsroom atmosphere was easygoing. Nearly all the reporters moonlighted, hoping to make it as actors, novelists, or songwriters.[5]

Seeking other outlets for his own writing talent, McFarlane noticed an ad in the trade magazine *Editor and Publisher*: "**Experienced Fiction Writer Wanted to Work from Publisher's Outline.**" There was no address, only a box number. He sat down at his city room typewriter and hammered out a reply. A few weeks later he received a letter postmarked East Orange, New Jersey:

> The letter was signed, in crabbed handwriting, "Edward Stratemeyer."
> This name meant nothing to me at all.
> How was I to know that I was gazing at the signature of the most prolific author of the day, a Henry Ford of fiction for boys and girls?
> *Yours truly, Edward Stratemeyer.*
> It didn't mean a thing.[6]

The letter explained the basic workings of the syndicate, which described itself as an organization that prepared manuscripts for publishers. Stratemeyer promised to send McFarlane two series books: a Nat Ridley mystery and a Dave Fearless adventure book. McFarlane was instructed to read both novels, then select one. Stratemeyer would then supply him with an outline of the opening chapters of the current title in production. McFarlane was asked to submit a 2,000-word sample. This assignment was simply a test. There would be no payment. If McFarlane passed, he would be commissioned to

Leslie McFarlane, Haileybury, Ontario, 1919. Research Collection, Mills Library, McMaster University.

finish the novel for a hundred dollars and earn the privilege of being considered for future assignments.[7]

For McFarlane this letter "opened a window on a very strange corner of the publishing world."[8] He had no idea that books could be mass-produced. When the novels arrived, he received a further shock. The Dave Fearless book listed Roy Rockwood as the author. Roy Rockwood, author of the popular Bomba the Jungle Boy books, had been one of McFarlane's favorite boyhood authors: "I pictured him seated at his desk, pen in hand, white shirt open at the throat, a bulldog pipe in his teeth. The creator of Bomba the Jungle Boy had a steady gaze, a firm mouth, a determined jaw. The walls of his study bristled with heads of leopard, grizzly and saber-tooth tiger. True, I had never actually seen a picture of the great author but I didn't have to. I just knew that's how he would look."[9] Roy Rockwood, whom McFarlane assumed was as real a person as Edgar Rice Burroughs, turned out to as fictitious as his jungle boy, a Stratemeyer house name. McFarlane had stumbled onto a trade secret and a uniquely American opportunity: "I realized then that America is truly the land of opportunity. America, where every little boy knows he can grow up to be President if he isn't careful. Being Canadian, I couldn't qualify. But I could be Roy Rockwood, once my favorite author. In fact, I even had a choice. I could be Nat Ridley, Jr. if I felt like it. Where else in the world could that happen, but in America?"[10]

McFarlane read the novels with distaste. At twenty-three, he found the juvenile stories he enjoyed as a teen flat and unpalatable. Neither had "even a smidgeon of merit" with "less content than a football bladder and no more style than a drunken camel."[11] But then he was not being asked to read the books, just "hammer out the words."[12] Measuring his typing skills rather than his creativity, McFarlane calculated that if he kept up production, he could double his income. He wrote Stratemeyer stating he would be interested in taking a chance at writing a Dave Fearless book.

Days later McFarlane received a three-page outline, briefly summarizing twenty-five chapters of *Dave Fearless Under the Ocean or The Treasure of the Lost Submarine*. Confident he would be hired to write the book, he kept working while waiting for Stratemeyer's verdict on his test chapters. He stayed up late at night, fleshing out Stratemeyer's sparse chapter outlines with shipwrecks, fires, deadly seaweed, and man-eating sharks.

Finding the sample chapters satisfactory, Stratemeyer informed the young reporter he was hired. McFarlane completed the novel and was gratified when he received his check for a hundred dollars along with a three-page outline for the next book, *Dave Fearless in the Black Jungle or Lost Among the Cannibals*. With the promise of continued employment as a syndicate novelist, McFarlane quit his newspaper job and returned to Canada, settling into a small cabin on Lake Ramsey in northern Ontario: "Now I had come full circle, back to the cabin on the bay, back at the typewriter. There were changes now. I was more experienced. I had become Roy Rockwood, author. The world was before me."[13]

Stratemeyer then approached McFarlane with his concept for a new series. The Hardy Boys would star Frank and Joe Hardy, sons of detective Fenton Hardy. They would live in a town called Bayport on Barmet Bay somewhere on the Atlantic coast. The brothers would have a group of chums, including an athlete named Biff Hooper and a chubby fun-loving farm boy named Chet Morton. There would be two girls, Callie Shaw and Chet's sister Iola. Their relations with Frank and Joe would be discreet, distant, and entirely wholesome. Accompanying this background information was an outline for the first novel about a robbery in a mansion. The author was to be called Franklin W. Dixon.

McFarlane greeted the prospect of the new series with delight:

> What a change from Dave Fearless! No man-eating sharks. No octopi. No cannibals, polar bears or man-eating trees. Just the everyday doings of everyday lads in everyday surroundings. They didn't go wandering all over the seven seas, pursued by imbecile relatives. They stayed at home, checked in for dinner every night like other kids. They even went to school....
>
> I was so relieved to be free of Dave Fearless and his dreary helpers that I greeted Frank and Joe Hardy with positive rapture, and I wrote to Stratemeyer to accept the assignment. Then I rolled a sheet of paper into the typewriter and prepared to go to work.[14]

McFarlane then gave his new book some careful consideration. The Hardy Boys promised to be a refreshing change from sensationalist pulp. But as a syndicate writer, McFarlane would be paid a flat fee. "The sensible course," he reflected, "would have been to hammer out the thing at breakneck speed, regardless of style, spelling or grammar, and let the Stratemeyer editors tidy it up. Bang it out, stuff the typed sheets in an envelope and put it in the mail, the quicker the better, and get going on the next book."[15]

But McFarlane was not sensible. He felt the Hardys deserved more than the "slapdash treatment" he had given the Dave Fearless titles. Recalling his own adolescence, he decided to add details that would appeal to teenagers. There would be descriptions of favorite foods. There would be pranks and jokes, especially ones directed at the Bayport cops whom he decided to portray as mindless dunderheads.

McFarlane's biographer saw this as a defining moment that would elevate Hardy Boys books from the forgettable genre of series fiction:

> On his own initiative, Les subtly and stealthily transformed some standard stereotypical characters, including three respectful policemen and a kindly aunt, into subversives. The policemen were not pillars of society but instead bumbling Keystone Kops who could barely show up for work on time, let alone

solve a case. And the stereotypical "kindly" maiden aunt was transformed into a comic dictatorial Cassandra, who always predicted a violent and tragic ending to her nephews' adventures.

In short, Les respected his adolescent audience and refused to write down to them.[16]

He was going to put thought, imagination, humor, and realism into the Hardy Boys. Amid the action and cliffhangers, he would inject references to Dickens, Poe, and Shakespeare. He would teach his readers something about different parts of the world and new technologies. The books would have depth and rigor and contain mature vocabulary. McFarlane realized that as a contract author, all this extra effort would bring him no additional rewards:

> But why go to all this trouble? If *The Tower Treasure* was a little better written than the usual fifty-cent juvenile, who would get the credit? The nonexistent Franklin W. Dixon. If better writing and a little humor helped make the series a success, who would benefit financially? The Stratemeyer Syndicate and the publishers. The writer who brought the skeleton outline to life wouldn't get a penny even if the books sold a million—which, of course, seemed impossible at the time.
>
> So what? I decided against the course of common sense. I opted for Quality.[17]

The McFarlane Style

McFarlane's refusal to write down to his readers is evidenced in his vocabulary. *The Tower Treasure*, for example, is sprinkled with what McFarlane called his "jawbreakers," words not commonly found in juvenile fiction—*prosaic, abated, spasmodic, ostensibly, diminutive, perceptible,* and *audacity*. He did, however, write with children in mind. Catering to their taste for sensationalism, his melodramatic prose could become quite purple:

> Frank Hardy felt an overpowering sense of loneliness as he wandered about among the rocks and the deep drifts. He seemed to be alone in a world of swirling, shrieking winds and flailing snow that stormed down from a sky of leaden hue [*Hunting for Hidden Gold*, 165].

> The sight of so much gold sent a thrill through them, just as it has sent a thrill through gold-seekers since the world began. Here was wealth, wealth in the raw, wealth for which men had fought and struggled, wealth that had been drawn from the depths of the earth [*Hunting for Hidden Gold*, 194–195].

McFarlane was a serious writer. He read Mencken, Conrad, Cather, and Joyce and briefly corresponded with F. Scott Fitzgerald. But he was writing for a flat fee at a brisk pace, and twenty-six-year-old McFarlane was capable of lapsing into awkwardly tangled and amateurish sentences. He especially seemed to have trouble pasting in Stratemeyer's required references to past and upcoming titles and slipping in opening exposition:

While the Hardy boys are scrambling out of their roadster and hastening back to the scene of the airplane crash that had so nearly cost them their own lives, the opportunity will be taken to introduce them more definitely [*The Great Airport Mystery*, 10].

While the boys are trudging out on the Shore Road toward the outskirts of the city, let us introduce them more definitely to readers who have not already made their acquaintance in the other books of this series [*While the Clock Ticked*, 13].

While Frank is waiting for an answer to his summons, we may take advantage of the moment to introduce the Hardy boys more clearly to those readers who have not already made their acquaintance in previous volumes of this series [*Footprints Under the Window*, 19].

For most adolescent readers these flaws were forgivable lapses. If anything, McFarlane's prose may have reminded teens of their own attempts at creative writing.

Probably the most significant words that bonded the Hardy Boys to their readers were the most ordinary. Throughout *The Shore Road Mystery* (1928), for example, McFarlane introduces events with phrases that immediately bring the Hardys into the everyday world of their readers: *As the Hardy boys were on their way to school on Tuesday morning.... At recess they gathered in little groups.... After school the following afternoon, the Hardy boys repaired to the boathouse.*

For many adolescents, the most telling scenes in the book are not the ones detailing another kidnapping and escape from an underground gang hideout but in classroom antics familiar to any high school student. Cars have been

Leslie McFarlane as a young reporter and Stratemeyer author. Research Collection, Mills Library, McMaster University.

stolen along the Shore Road, and the Hardy Boys attempt to solve the mystery. One night they follow suspicious characters along the shore only to discover they are on the trail of some men intent on illegal spear fishing. When a game warden casually mentions the Hardy misadventure to Chet Morton, the portly chum sees a great opportunity for a prank. On his way to school he purchases a fish and places the smelly package in Frank's desk. Discovering the fish, Frank withdraws a textbook as if nothing had happened, noting the disappointment on Chet's face. Frank whispers to Joe to lead Chet from the classroom, giving him time to quickly switch the fish to Chet's desk.

When the humorless mathematics instructor Mr. Dowd starts his lesson, he notices that Morton is unprepared and asks Chet to get his book. As he reaches into his desk, the fish lands on the floor "with a sickening thud." What follows is the kind of classroom drama every high school student can recognize: an embarrassing discovery and confrontation over some contraband:

"What have you there, Morton?"
"N-n-nothing, sir."
"Don't leave it lying there on the floor. Pick it up."
Chet gingerly picked up the package.
"Your lunch?" suggested Mr. Dowd.
"N-no, sir. I mean, yes, sir."
"Just what *do* you mean? Why are you looking at it with that idiotic expression on your face?"
"I — I didn't expect to find it there, sir."
"Morton, is this another of your jokes? If so, I wish you'd let us all enjoy it. Do you mind telling us what is in that package?"
"I — I'd rather not, sir. It's just a — a little present."
"A little present!" Mr. Dowd was convinced, by Chet's guilty expression, that there was more behind this than appeared on the surface. "Open it this instant."
"Please, sir — "
"Morton!"
Miserably, Chet obeyed. Before the eyes of his grinning schoolmates, he untied the string, removed the paper, and produced the fish. There was a gasp of amazement from Mr. Dowd and a smothered chuckle from every one else [95–96].

Ordered to get rid of the fish, Chet carries it by the tail out of the room where he runs into the principal who orders him to write two hundred lines of Latin.

Frank's ability to turn tables on a prankster friend is as great a wish-fulfillment dream as his ability to capture the snarling car thieves. More classroom antics occur in a later chapter when Frank and Joe, exhausted after a late night of sleuthing, vainly try to stay awake in class. Joe yawns and fumbles awkwardly to answer the history teacher's questions. Frank's head droops, and he falls asleep. Asked to relate details about Lincoln's assassination, Frank replies that he was stabbed to death by senators led by Mark Anthony, creating a "wave of laughter in which even Miss Petty was forced to join" (127–128).

These passages connect the world school-age readers know and experience every day with the dream world where juveniles like themselves drive cars, man speedboats, tackle criminals, earn reward money, and become leaders of their peers. The Hardy Boys, unlike other literary characters teens might encounter, were high school students. Like their readers, Frank and Joe had homework. They had dour teachers. They lived for the recess bell. They counted the days until vacation.

It is these passages that make McFarlane's books memorable. The plots of the Hardy Boys are dully predictable, repetitious, and dependent on absurd chains of coincidence.

In *The Secret of the Caves* (1929), the Hardy Boys rescue a woman jumping from a burning ship in Barmet Bay. The woman thanks the boys and tells them she must get to Bayport as soon as possible because she must see Fenton Hardy. The boys take her home where she explains that she is seeking help from the famous detective to locate her missing brother, Todham Todd, a professor, who became deranged after suffering a head injury in a train wreck. The boys, along with Biff Hooper and Chet Morton, take a motorcycle trip down the shore to explore some caves. On the way, Chet mentions that Carl Schaum, one of the car thieves captured in *The Shore Road Mystery*, has escaped from jail. When the boys pause for a swim a few hours later, Frank's motorcycle is stolen by Carl Schaum. The boys pursue him, and he runs off after taking a spill. When the chums arrive at the caves, they discover a drunken Carl Schaum on the beach, whom they deftly recapture. They also encounter a crazy old man living in a cave who calls himself Captain Royal. The boys suspect he is actually the missing professor. When Captain Royal is knocked unconscious in a fall, the boys rescue the old man, who not only turns out to be the missing professor but also wakes up with his memory and sanity magically restored. They decline a cash reward from the grateful sister but do accept her gift of a motion picture camera.

If this is one of the weakest of the early novels, it is understandable. Short of funds, Leslie McFarlane hammered out *The Secret of the Caves* on a borrowed typewriter in five days. He could have completed the novel in less time, he claimed, but a friend kept bringing people around to watch him work.[18]

In many ways McFarlane's books reverse the usual workings of detective fiction. The mystery, the action, the villains are almost forgettable, serving merely as vehicles for lively comic relief and classroom antics. The Hardy Boys are the most believable and most appealing when they are off duty, going to school, clowning with their chums, coping with humorless teachers and cops, and contending with Aunt Gertrude.

The Canadian Angle

One reason why Leslie McFarlane may have opted for quality was because he was keenly aware of the impact juvenile literature had on children. Growing up in Canada heightened his sensitivity to the lasting impact that fiction had on shaping children's views of themselves and the world. Aside from silent films, books offered Canadian children in the Twenties their only escape from long winters, homework, after school jobs, and chores. And nearly all the books were imports.

As McFarlane recalled in his autobiography, "At Christmas every normal Canadian lad felt neglected if he failed to receive a five-pound volume of either *The Boys' Own Annual* or *Chums*. These were the collected numbers of two weekly magazines for boys, published in England and bound annually in hard covers for export to the colonies. With pen and ink illustrations, printed in 1,000 pages of eyestraining type, they were packed with fiction calculated to brighten the most monotonous juvenile existence."[19]

Some of the serials depicted public school life in Britain as full of fun and adventure and no homework so that Canadian readers "went around envying the normal British schoolboy as fortune's favored son."[20] Other stories told heroic tales of English lads battling African savages, defeating pirates on the high seas, chasing highwaymen in Olde England, and outwitting any enemy foolish enough to defy British imperialism.

In contrast, the American imports such as Horatio Alger and the Rover Boys depicted American youths as hard working, resourceful, energetic, independent, successful, and clean-living. Whereas the British characters "spoke a strange language full of obscure references to 'pater' and 'mater,'" the American heroes spoke a more familiar North American English.[21]

Whether British or American, the books, McFarlane believed, had a profound and lasting influence on Canadian children:

> Under these literary influences the Canadian boy grew up in a state of proper humility. His reading taught him that British boys were courageous, daring, ingenious and always in the right so that they always came out on top while, incidentally, having more fun than anyone. At the same time his reading taught him that American boys were likewise courageous, daring and ingenious and, moreover, so devoted to honest toil that they always wound up rich. Canadian boys, who apparently had no history worth writing about and no forebears who ever made it as heroes of books, were clearly made of inferior stuff. This probably explains why the adult, male Canadian today is a docile, modest fellow who knows his place and is never given to throwing his weight around.[22]

Authority Figures

Edward Stratemeyer's original outline for *The Tower Treasure* briefly listed Chief Ezra Collig and Detective Smuff of the Bayport police department as members of the series' supporting cast. There was little to go on besides their names and ranks. McFarlane decided to portray them as pompous, self-righteous, and thick-headed — just the kind of authority figures his readers would love to see outwitted by teens like themselves.

Although the Hardy Boys demonstrate their wholesomeness, honesty, and devotion to their parents, they are not devoid of boyish enthusiasm, a love of fun and pranks, and a young person's quickness to spot a phony. For young males the police, whether big city cops or farm town deputies, usually mean trouble. Police represent adulthood, authority, government, rules, and restrictions. It is the police officer who monitors their driving, breaks up loud parties, patrols the beaches and parks where they play, enforces curfews, and in general dampers their fun.

Repeatedly, the Hardys solve crimes to the chagrin of Chief Collig and, especially, Detective Smuff, who jealously mutters about being beaten by a "couple of kids." The authority figure who bears the brunt of the Hardys' tempered adolescent rebellion is Patrolman Con Riley. A stage Irishman, Con Riley is both dumb and self-important, always using "we" to refer to police activities as if he were responsible for the whole force:

> Now, as old readers know, Riley was the sworn enemy of the youth of Bayport. A stolid, thick-set individual with more dignity and self-importance than brains, he took the responsibilities of his position on the Bayport police force very seriously. He had the view, too common to the type of elderly people who have forgotten that they once were young, that all enjoyment is sinful and that all young people are continually up to mischief [*Hunting for Hidden Gold*, 42].

When Riley spots the Hardys and chums bobsledding on a snow day, he attempts to enforce "an ancient and obsolete city ordinance" banning sledding outside of parks: "Majestically he stood at the bottom of the hill and held up his hand. Sled after sled pulled to a stop and Officer Riley, the personification of the majesty of the law, ordered the fun to cease" (*Hunting for Hidden Gold*, 43). The chums readily agree to stop their sledding and opt for snowballing instead. Riley can find no regulation against throwing snowballs, but he keeps his eye on the teens, hoping a stray snowball might break a window so he can put a stop to this fun as well. What follows is pure adolescent humor, the deliberate act camouflaged to look like an accident:

> Chet seemed to aim at one of the forts. But his foot appeared to slip and the snowball smacked Con Riley's helmet with deadly accuracy, knocking it off into the snow.

> Riley emitted a roar of rage and astonishment. Snow was trickling down his neck. He stooped merely long enough to pick up his helmet and thrust it back on his head, where it rested at a ridiculous and rather precarious angle [*Hunting for Hidden Gold*, 44].

The enraged cop plunges through the deep snow after Chet, following him into an ambush where he suffers a "merciless bombardment" of snowballs from the chums who keep their faces hidden. The words "volley" and "missile" are reminiscent of combat, as is the phrase "no man's land." Pelted by snow grenades, Riley retreats to downtown Bayport "where citizens were more law-abiding and where snowballs were unknown" (46). In this scene McFarlane gives vent to an adolescent revenge fantasy — within the safe limits of cheerful, clean-living chums who confine their attacks against police officers to tossing snowballs.

These scenes make *Hunting for Hidden Gold* memorable. The plot, in which the brothers travel to Montana to help their injured father recover stolen gold, relies on a wildly unbelievable pattern of coincidence and repetition. During a blizzard in Bayport the brothers rescue an old man, who turns out to be one of the rightful owners of the stolen Montana gold. The boys travel west, twice falling for ruses to keep them from catching a train. Once in Montana, they are twice captured by the Black Pepper gang. They escape twice, and on two occasions manage to get a gun away from a villain and to take the villain into the sheriff's office. In a replay of *The Tower Treasure*, the boys recover the stolen loot, win approval from their father, restore the reputation of someone falsely accused of theft, and receive a reward. What elevates the book from hack detective fiction is the humor.

There was for McFarlane some deeper message besides fun in these passages:

> I had my own thoughts about teaching youngsters that obedience to authority is somehow sacred. Where did it say that kids shouldn't size up people for themselves? Was it written in the Bible, the Talmud, the Koran, the British North America Act and the Constitution of the United States that everyone in authority was inflexibly honest, pious and automatically admirable? ... Was it a favor to let them grow up dumbly assuming that all is for the best in the best of all possible worlds? Wouldn't every kid be the better for a little shot of healthy skepticism at an early age?[23]

Edward Stratemeyer, however, had reservations about mocking the representatives of law and order. He wrote to McFarlane, instructing him to tone down the sarcasm and rebellious pranks. McFarlane reluctantly obeyed his employer and in future volumes the Bayport cops became more professional and the boys more respectful.

Aunt Gertrude

Edward Stratemeyer's outline for the fourth volume, *The Missing Chums*, included a suggestion for a new character. As Fenton Hardy and his sons would be away from Bayport, he thought it might be a good idea to add a maiden aunt who would visit Mrs. Hardy and keep her company. This could have been a throwaway character relegated to serving tea and asking foil questions to fill in exposition, explain a detail, or advance the plot.

McFarlane, however, saw this addition to the Hardy cast as a rare opportunity. The maiden aunt character was "Gold! Pure, gleaming, high-grade gold! ... I looked on the visiting relative as a godsend," he recalled, "spat on my hands and joyfully went to work making Aunt Gertrude a Character."[24]

Aunt Gertrude became for many readers the most memorable character after the Hardy Boys themselves. Aside from perhaps Chet Morton, no other character in the series is more discussed in blogs and websites than Aunt Gertrude. A proposed radio show about the Hardy Boys in the 1930s had the working title "Aunt Gertrude and the Boys." When television productions of the series aired in the 1950s Aunt Gertrude was featured but not Laura Hardy, leading viewers to assume the Hardy Boys' mother had died.

Aunt Gertrude makes her initial appearance in *The Missing Chums*. Described as Fenton Hardy's maiden aunt with no home of her own, she spends her life "in a sort of grand circuit series of visits to all her relatives, far and near" (50). Aunt Gertrude is a clear figure of stiff authority: "Aunt Gertrude was formidable. Her word was law. And, because she was possessed of a small fortune and a sharp tongue, none dared offend her. Relatives had discovered that the best plan was to suffer her visits in silence and pray for her speedy departure" (51). Aunt Gertrude becomes the kind of figure children immediately love to hate. She reminds adolescent readers of any number of aunts, uncles, or grandparents who insist on treating them like small children and lecturing them.

McFarlane, who identified Frank and Joe simply by age and hair color, lavished readers with extensive descriptions of Aunt Gertrude:

> Aunt Gertrude was one of the pepperiest and most dictatorial old women who ever visited a quiet household. She was a rawboned female of sixty-five, tall and commanding, with a determined jaw, an acid tongue and an eye that could quell a traffic cop. She was as authoritative as a prison guard, bossed everything and everybody within reach, and had a lofty contempt for men in general and boys in particular [*What Happened at Midnight*, 57].

Aunt Gertrude is an exaggeration of every stepmother, grandmother, guardian, teacher, or neighborhood old lady children encounter. Her dialogue is the most lively and colorful of any character in the entire Hardy Boys series. Greeting Frank at the train station, she lashes out with classic attacks young readers will identify with:

"You look it!" she snapped. "Where did you get the car? What a dangerous looking contraption! It's a wonder to me you haven't broken your neck in it. Looks as if it wouldn't go less than eighty miles an hour. You're too young to have a car anyway." She turned her attentions from the car to her nephew. "You've grown. But you haven't grown any fatter. What's wrong? Don't you eat enough? Or are you smoking cigarettes? If I ever catch you smoking a cigarette, young man, I'll whale you within an inch of your life. Here, take my suitcase. Don't stand there gaping. Tell me all the news. I've had a dreadful journey. The coach was so dusty I could hardly breathe and there was a baby across the aisle. It yelled and howled all the way. A man ate peanuts and oranges. I'm going to write to the railway company about it. Babies shouldn't be allowed on trains. And people who eat peanuts and oranges in the day coach ought to be sent to the penitentiary. It's an outrage!" [*What Happened at Midnight*, 60].

Teenage readers can particularly relate to the depictions of Aunt Gertrude as a backseat driver:

"Look! Look! Be careful, Frank! Look where you're going! Don't you see that truck coming right at you? Good grief! It's going to hit us. Stop the car! Oh, what a narrow escape. He just saw you in time. Why didn't you do something? We might have been killed. Look OUT! There's a streetcar. Are you clean crazy? Don't drive on the tracks! Are you sure we're on the right street? This isn't the way we went the last time I was in Bayport. I really believe you don't know your way about your own town" [*What Happened at Midnight*, 62].

These scenes not only provide humor but keep Frank Hardy on the same level as the readers. He may be a detective, have a car, a motorcycle, and a motorboat, but he is still a teenager subject to the tirades of an aunt who humiliates him and treats him like a child.

Although he enjoyed developing the Aunt Gertrude character, McFarlane was beginning to tire of the Hardy Boys. After completing *What Happened at Midnight* (1931), his tenth book, McFarlane considered resigning. He was making money from other publications and wanted to concentrate on a serious literary career. The Depression, however, led him to continue work for the syndicate, even though his fee dropped from $125 to $85.

In 1930 McFarlane received a letter announcing the death of Edward Stratemeyer, a man he had never met or had even spoken to on the telephone. Harriet Adams continued to send him outlines for new Hardy Boys books and asked him to develop a breeder set for another detective series. The Dana Girls were a blend of the Hardy Boys and Nancy Drew. Sisters Jean and Louise Dana attended a girls' boarding school and solved mysteries between classes. The books were written under the same house name as Nancy Drew, Carolyn Keene. It was 1934, and McFarlane took on the assignment with an air of sarcastic resignation:

I felt almighty foolish about becoming Carolyn Keene, but my wife promised she wouldn't tell anyone. So I spent a couple of months banging away at the

Dana sisters. Perhaps the expression is indelicate. Nobody ever banged the Dana girls — at least not for the record. Occasionally, I was tempted to turn them loose in one of Bayport's numerous abandoned buildings with the Hardy boys, just to see what would happen. It might have done the whole four of them no end of good.[25]

McFarlane wrote four of the books then asked to be released from the assignment. The Dana Girls never became as popular as Nancy Drew, leading him to speculate that the "virgins who followed the adventures of Jean and Louise sensed a lack of empathy."[26]

McFarlane continued writing Hardy Boys novels. The Depression was continuing, and the syndicate offered a steady, if diminished, paycheck. Freelance writing rarely provides a reliable income to support a family in the best of times, and in the 1930s McFarlane's situation was often desperate. "We had no car," his son Brian later recalled. "We had no coal. My mother always had food on the table, but sometimes it was spaghetti with tomato sauce on it."[27] McFarlane's diary includes entries documenting his lack of funds. He had to borrow ten cents from Brian's piggybank to buy stamps to mail a manuscript. Taking his young son for a walk one day, McFarlane had to return after the boy's shoes fell apart. "It is humiliating to be so hard up," he confessed.[28] Although the syndicate assignments meant a much-needed check, McFarlane was growing restless. His autobiography reflects a lack of interest and a mounting sense of boredom. He was no longer excited by the prospect of getting an outline for a new book or having the chance to invent a new character. The Hardy Boys were becoming increasingly forgettable piecework:

The Sinister Signpost, 1936, had to do with the disappearance of a valuable racehorse and concluded when Aunt Gertrude bawled out the boys on the iniquities of the track, then received a lawyer's letter informing her that she had been bequeathed a stable of horses.

A Figure in Hiding, 1937, was a mishmash which began with the hold-up of a Bayport theater box office, the mysterious activities of a pretty girl named Virginia and a phony eye doctor who called himself Grafton. There was also a deaf-mute, a character named Zeb and an associate villain named Rip Snider. The boys broke up the "eye syndicate," recovered the stolen money and picked up a reward of $500. After all, this was the Depression and rewards were sadly deflated.

The Secret Warning, 1938, has passed completely out of my memory and my records, definitely a loss to posterity.[29]

McFarlane took a break in 1938. The syndicate hired John Button to ghostwrite the Hardy Boys until McFarlane returned in 1942. Looking back, McFarlane remembered less about the plots of these last novels, recalling *where* rather than *what* he wrote. "*The Flickering Torch Mystery*, 1943," he noted, "was written in a stifling room during a heat wave in wartime Ottawa. The very thought of it brings out perspiration."[30] By then, he was working in

Canadian radio, the Hardy Boys providing a modest supplement to his annual income. He completed *The Phantom Freighter* in 1946 "in motel rooms at night on a location in Nova Scotia when I was directing a film."[31] Some sources indicate this novel was actually written by his wife, Amy.

The Phantom Freighter was his last Hardy Boys book. For McFarlane, saying good-bye to Frank and Joe, characters he had brought to life, evoked no strong emotions. "I didn't need them anymore," he reflected, "and certainly they didn't need me."[32] He was forty-four and had been working for the Stratemeyer Syndicate for twenty years.

McFarlane simply attached a note to his final manuscript stating that he no longer had time to accept further assignments. The syndicate did not ask him to stay on. There was always a large supply of writers looking for work. "If the parting involved any emotion at all," McFarlane recalled, "it was one of relief, as if a couple of relatives who came for the weekend had finally moved on after sticking around for years."[33] He had no emotional attachment to the books he had created. He never read them. When the syndicate mailed him a Hardy Boys book, he skimmed it "then the volume would join its predecessors on a bookcase shelf. Under glass, like a row of embalmed owls, so the dust wouldn't get at them."[34]

Though now most remembered for his Hardy Boys books, McFarlane, himself, dismissed them. The whole syndicate experience was forgettable:

> It was as if some force within my mind insisted on thrusting the books into limbo the moment the final page of a final chapter came out of the typewriter. Not revulsion. Complete indifference. Perhaps this also accounted for the fact that, although I had been in New York many times, I was never tempted to cross the river and drop into the Stratemeyer Syndicate office in East Orange. I had nothing whatever against Edward Stratemeyer or his daughters or the Syndicate people, and I am sure I would have been welcome, but somehow it just never seemed to matter.[35]

The Hardy Boys had served their purpose. McFarlane was ready to move on. In 1945 he wrote, produced, and directed a film for children called *The Boy Who Stopped Niagara* starring his fourteen-year-old daughter, Norah, and Jeff Martin. The short film was previewed not only in Canada but also in Great Britain, Australia, and New Zealand. Audience reactions and favorable reviews led to further screenings in Denmark, Ceylon, Holland, and Egypt.[36]

The Boy Who Stopped Niagara marked the beginning of McFarlane's long and distinguished career in Canadian film and broadcasting. He wrote 75 television scripts. He wrote, produced, and directed over fifty films for Canada's National Film Board. He wrote the script for the documentary *Herring Hunt* that earned an Academy Award nomination in 1953. He also wrote the script for *Royal Journey,* which won a British Film Academy Award that same year. Shot in 1951 in color, the hour-long documentary followed Queen Elizabeth

Leslie McFarlane (kneeling lower left) directing the cast of *The Boy Who Stopped Niagara*, Ottawa, 1945. Research Collection, Mills Library, McMaster University.

and Prince Phillip on their five-week tour of Canada and the United States. *Royal Journey* was one of the most successful documentary movies in Canadian history. Playing in over 1200 theaters and breaking box office records, the film was seen by millions of Canadians.

In 1958 he was hired by the Canadian Broadcasting Company to edit stories for two television series, the hour-long *General Motors Presents* and the half-hour show *The Unforeseen*. The latter program was one of the most innovative and popular shows in Canada. Many episodes were set in the future or explored the supernatural, leading critics to compare it to Rod Serling's American hit program *The Twilight Zone*. In 1960 *Liberty* magazine honored *The Unforeseen* as the best dramatic show on Canadian television and named Leslie McFarlane the country's best television writer.[37]

Never large to begin with, the market for script writing in Canada grew slimmer by the 1960s. McFarlane earned the distinction of being one of the few screenwriters, if not the only one, who could make a living in Canada. Although he was a strong nationalist, he decided to join the many other Canadian writers seeking more opportunities and higher pay in the United States. In 1969 he went to Hollywood and wrote scripts for the popular television show *Bonanza* starring Lorne Greene, a fellow Canadian he had worked with at the National Film Board. He also wrote scripts for the *Jane Wyman Show* and the *U.S. Steel Hour*. Although fairly successful at finding work in the competitive arena of American television, McFarlane disliked much of what he found in Hollywood and returned to Canada a year later.

In addition to his film and television work, McFarlane published four novels and hundreds of short stories, many of which appeared in national magazines. His literary achievement and contributions to Canadian culture were celebrated with the naming of a Whitby, Ontario, school in his honor.

Years later when his son told him about the popularity of the Hardy Boys books, McFarlane went to a department store and discovered shelves of all the old titles he had hammered out twenty years before. The books he had forgotten as soon as they left his typewriter had taken on a life he never expected:

> I began to see the Hardy Boys books wherever I went, in small bookstores and large, even in railway depots and corner stores. There seemed to be an epidemic. Whenever I saw a small boy on a train or plane, he was almost invariably absorbed in a bright blue volume, lost in Bayport and environs. "They must have sold a lot of those things," I reflected. "Maybe a hundred thousand or so."
> I asked a clerk if the Hardy Boys books were popular.
> "Most popular boys' books we carry," he said. "Matter of fact, they're supposed to be the best-selling boys' books in the world."
> "Imagine that!" I said in downright wonderment.[38]

The twenty titles he had written over two decades had sold twelve million copies. McFarlane calculated that during the twenty years he spent writing the Hardy Boys he had earned a total of five thousand dollars.[39]

In his later years, McFarlane was often asked if he felt cheated. He resented questions about the Hardy Boys, sensing that interviewers either regarded him as a "victim of one of the great swindles of modern times" or "the dumbest sucker of the age."[40] These questions maddened him: "I was not swindled. I accepted the terms of Edward Stratemeyer and the importance of money was related to my needs. I was free to reject any of the assignments. Writing is not a profession on which one embarks under duress. No one forces anyone to become a writer. No one even asks him. He writes because he enjoys writing."[41] What also maddened Leslie McFarlane was the universal indifference to his own novels and extensive work in film and broadcasting. The newspaper feature writers and reporters who sought him out invariably only wanted to know about Frank and Joe Hardy.

One reporter, Bob Stall, brought with him copies of the new versions of the novels McFarlane had written nearly forty years before. Looking at the shortened, streamlined revisions, McFarlane noted some of his favorite scenes had been cut. His beloved Aunt Gertrude was stripped of her dictatorial tirades and reduced to a colorless stage extra:

> The world had changed for the Hardy Boys as it had changed for everyone else. It was a very strange world indeed, when a ghost could be dispossessed by another ghost. There were fifty-three titles now.... And I had nothing to do with them.
> I had a sense of disinheritance.
> "Doesn't it upset you?" asked Stall.
> "Damn it all," I said, "what do you think? Even a ghost has feelings like anyone else."[42]

In the 1970s Leslie McFarlane began to claim a kind of inheritance. In 1974 he appeared on *I've Got a Secret* with two imposters claiming to be the real Franklin W. Dixon. McFarlane's actions did not spark the reaction Mildred Wirt Benson did when she claimed authorship of Nancy Drew. He never professed to be more than an employee on the assembly line. He readily acknowledged the fact that he was following Stratemeyer's outlines and suggestions. Eager to stress his own original writing and career in Canadian broadcasting, he was indifferent to the Hardy Boys, irked by reporters' questions about "his" books. He saw himself as a ghostwriter, not a creator or author. The title of his 1976 autobiography clearly indicated he claimed at best a secondary role. He summed up his life in a book called *Ghost of the Hardy Boys*.

Chapter 3

The Weird Period

> "Joe! I — I feel queer!" Frank whispered.
> — *The Disappearing Floor*, 1940

After writing the first sixteen Hardy Boys books, Leslie McFarlane took a hiatus in 1938 to pursue more serious and more lucrative writing opportunities. In his absence, five novels were written by John Button.[1] Although the outlines were produced by the Stratemeyer Syndicate, the books took a strange and surreal turn under his pen. The year 1938 began what many Hardy Boys collectors and enthusiasts call the "weird period."

In the early McFarlane novels, Frank and Joe Hardy solve crimes close to home, taking on counterfeiters, smugglers, and car thieves in and around Bayport. In later novels they travel cross-country by train or plane. But the basic tenor of the books remains the same. The brothers and their chums defeat lone outlaws like Red Jackley or small criminal gangs. In these novels the brothers employ contemporary technology. For all their power, the motorcycles, boats, cars, and planes the boys use are realistic representations of vehicles available to affluent adolescents of the 1920s and 1930s. The boys' lives are marked by the everyday realities of doing homework, studying for exams, running errands, going on hikes, and tinkering with their boat engine. The train ride to Montana in *Hunting for Hidden Gold* (1928) was a rare out-of-town trip for Frank and Joe, only made possible when storm damage to Bayport High fortuitously suspended classes for two weeks.

In the Button novels, Frank and Joe appear to be on an eternal summer vacation. There is only a passing mention of Bayport High and few references to schoolwork, chores, or common adolescent pursuits. Except for Chet Morton, the chums play much smaller roles. The boys work more closely with their father, often operating side by side with him rather than being given an assignment of their own.

Using an outline developed by Edna Squier, McFarlane's successor introduced new and darker elements to the world of the Hardy Boys in *The Secret Warning* (1938). The plot takes Frank and Joe underwater to assist a deep-sea diver and a salvage company recover a sunken treasure. Elements of the story echo *Twenty Thousand Leagues Under the Sea*. Frank and Joe have an improbable battle with a monstrous octopus. In a graphic scene, a trapped diver running out of air prepares to amputate his own leg until rescued by Frank. The novel in-

"LOOK, THERE'S THAT ICE MACHINE POINTING RIGHT AT DAD."
The Disappearing Floor   *Frontispiece (Page 208)*

Frontispiece from *The Disappearing Floor* by Franklin W. Dixon is a registered trademark of Simon & Schuster Inc. All rights reserved. Used by permission of Simon & Schuster Adult Publishing Group.

cludes an element of science fiction, describing a Tom Swift kind of camera unavailable in reality even today. One of the divers operates an underwater motion picture camera with an X-ray lens that can "'take pictures through wood or steel or almost any obstruction'" (174). This represents the first time in the Hardy Boys novels that the suspension of disbelief entails futuristic technology.

The following volume, *The Twisted Claw* (1939), is a strange anachronistic tale of international piracy. Posing as sailors, Frank and Joe board a tramp schooner called the *Black Parrot* crewed by old salts who talk like eighteenth-century seamen. In earlier novels, the Hardy Boys tracked criminals to isolated hideouts, usually caves or deserted buildings. Invariably, the gangsters slept on cots or used packing cases as furniture, their Spartan surroundings befitting criminals maintaining a low profile while on the run. In this novel, Frank and Joe land on a tropical island kingdom "alive with gorgeously-plumaged birds and chattering monkeys" (166) that is no mere gang hideout but a nation unto itself, ruled by a pirate monarch and patrolled by uniformed soldiers. The island is surreal. Instead of grass shacks, the boys discover "one of the most attractive but unusual cities either of them had ever seen" (173). The island features shaded avenues, stately homes, and a castle worthy of Oz's Emerald City:

> The most awe-inspiring sight of all was what undoubtedly was the ruler's palace, a huge, turreted structure rising from a hill on the opposite end of the city. It sparkled in the tropical sun like jewels. For a moment the brothers were too overcome to speak, but they soon realized that the entire civilization of Barracuda had been built on a foundation of smuggling.
> "It all looks wonderful," Frank remarked, "but when you get right down to it it's nothing more nor less than a robber's paradise!"
> "You're right!" his brother agreed with emphasis. "And it's up to us to do something about it!" [173].

Like Gulliver exploring one of his islands, the Hardys stroll down a "spacious" avenue crowded with "joyous throngs of merry-makers" celebrating a three-day holiday honoring the King's Grand Meeting for the Fleet, a pirate assembly. A Mardi Gras–like parade proceeds through the city. "Gaudily-decorated floats" laden with stolen cargo, each bearing the name of a pirate ship, trundle through the streets, followed by "a group of dignified looking individuals in blue pantaloons and scarlet jackets, with numerous medals and decorations dangling from their breasts" (176). The boys seem almost to have traveled through time as well as space to enter an island kingdom apparently unknown to the outside world. One of the nation's rules is that unauthorized visitors must remain in the kingdom for the rest of their lives.

Frank and Joe manage to sneak into the Grand Assembly and watch the entrance of His Majesty, King of Barracuda, Potentate of the Order of the Twisted Claw. Adorned with an ermine cloak and bejeweled gold crown, the "huge, bearded" king resembles Henry VIII. One by one, the sea captains of the pirate schooners, each named for a parrot of a different color, come forward and report their annual haul and present a tribute to the king. As the brothers watch, a branding ceremony takes place as candidates are marked with the emblem of the twisted claw on their index fingers. The king then awards a prize of half a million dollars in gold coins to the captain and officers of the *Black Parrot*.

Back aboard the *Black Parrot*, Frank and Joe send an SOS message that summons a U.S. revenue cutter carrying their father. In this novel the Hardys don't merely break up a Bayport gang with the help of the police. Instead, they take down an entire criminal "civilization" with the help of the armed forces. Orders are "broadcast to all nations" to seize the *Parrot* schooners and arrest men imprinted with the twisted claw. Within days, "a fleet of American warships seized the mysterious island and put a quick end to the vast smuggling operations of the King of Barracuda" (216).

The Disappearing Floor (1940) transports Frank and Joe Hardy into the equally unreal world of a mad scientist, who seems more at home in a Superman or Batman comic book. Along the way, Frank and Joe battle escaped tigers and encounter the Ozonites, a strange cult of sun-worshippers.

The book opens with Frank, Joe, and Chet boarding a train for a camping trip. The boys notice a "queer-looking" old man with long whiskers on the platform. Aunt Gertrude recognizes the stranger as Eben Adar, a former classmate who was "always snooping about and saying strange things" (3). Dismissing her warnings that Adar is probably a criminal, the chums take the train to Great Notch and hike to a campsite.

That night they awaken to discover a shadowy figure in their camp. Chasing the intruder, the chums fall through the earth into a cave that somehow seals itself shut. Trapped in darkness, Joe wishes he had a flashlight. Instantly a light snaps on, and the chums turn around to meet Fenton Hardy who informs them he is on the trail of a bank robber named Duke Beeson. The brothers eagerly offer to help their father. Fenton Hardy patiently explains they can do nothing but wait. At that moment a rock Frank was leaning against gives way, revealing a "small sack" full of silver dollars from the Wayne County Bank. Fenton Hardy announces that he is not surprised by the find, noting that he suspected the cave was a Beeson hideout. Hearing voices in the cave, Fenton Hardy vanishes, abandoning his sons. The boys are chased from the cave by Weeping Sam, a "lean, wolfish-looking man with small, calculating eyes, a hatchetlike nose and a thin, cruel mouth" (15–16).

The following day, the chums recover the "small sack" of coins that is now so "heavy" and "unwieldy" they must fashion a stretcher so the three of them can carry it. Reaching a town, they hail a taxi, assuming a strange cabbie would have no idea what was in the sack. The driver, however, turns out to be "sinister-looking" and drives crazily down a side street. Frank lunges for the steering wheel, and the cab plunges over an open drawbridge into the water. Somehow Frank and Joe manage to bear the heavy sack to the surface and head to the bank, where they are nearly savaged by a mob mistaking them for robbers.

After returning the money to the bank, the boys return to their campsite and discover Fenton Hardy, bruised and beaten, lying near the cave. Frank and Joe rescue their wounded father and set off to find Duke Beeson. The bank robber now poses as Chief Shining Light, leader of a thousand-strong organization of sun-worshippers called the Ozonites, a "queer bunch" who blend Indian costumes and ancient Egyptian mythology. Hunting for tigers that escaped from a private zoo, the brothers encounter a man dressed like a native of India who speaks in a cultist dialect:

> "Greetings, and may the sun's rays fall upon you both," he saluted in a gentle voice. Without waiting for them to answer he continued, "I am out hunting two tigers, as it pleaseth heaven."
> "So are we," Frank smiled. "We just heard that—"
> "Yes, it is true, sadly enough. The beasts have demoralized my people. Our camp is practically empty."
> He swished his robe around and made some sort of a sign.
> "Is your camp near here?" Joe asked.
> "About half a mile, as the sunflower points" [67].

Recovering from his injuries, Fenton Hardy returns, only to be sidelined again by an attack by one of the tigers. The plot gets even "queerer" when Frank and Joe "hastily" don women's clothes to disguise themselves from the bank robbers.

Captured by the Beeson gang, the brothers are driven to a mysterious mansion that turns out to the home of Eden Adar. Noticing the approach of visitors, the strange old man rubs his gnarled hands in "fiendish glee" as he contemplates the fate of the intruders. He switches on one of his many inventions and freezes the bank robbers and the Hardys.

Thirty-six hours later, the defrosted Hardy Boys wake up adrift in a boat. They return to the mansion and are admitted by the mad scientist who shows the brothers some of his inventions. At the touch of a switch, the furniture begins to glow and tables rise from trapdoors. Oversized plants grow without soil, fed by electricity. Electrified chickens lay five times the number of eggs. Electrically charged window screens zap insects. A decade before the invention of the microwave oven, Adar cooks food instantly in his electronic kitchen. When a fire breaks out in the mansion, Adar flips a switch that electrically neutralizes the flames. Even Adar's water is highly charged. He pours Frank and Joe glasses of his special water, which has a drug-like effect on the Hardys:

> "Drink! Drink it all! You will be amply rewarded!" Adar screamed at them.
> Frank summoned his courage and downed the draught at a gulp. Joe did likewise.
> "Say, I—I feel—wonderful!" said Frank a few moments later.
> "I feel as if I were walking on air. Golly, what was in that stuff anyhow, Mr. Adar? Tasted like ordinary water, but Jumping Jonah, what a kick!" [121–122].

Adar's strangest inventions come into play when Duke Beeson and his thugs attempt an attack. Adar engages a "bipolar field of magnetism" which protects him and the Hardys from the bank robbers who cannot penetrate the invisible shield. Using a small flashlight-like device, Adar aims a beam of light at the ceiling and a "queer-looking machine" descends into the room. Drawn to the machine by an "irresistible force," Beeson struggles helplessly. The machine, Adar states, will force the gang leader to tell the truth. Watching Beeson's face writhe "grotesquely," Joe begs Adar to stop, arguing that he has no right to take the law into his own hands. This rebuke causes Adar to turn on the Hardys. Promising them the same fate as the criminals, Adar "melts" into a secret panel and vanishes.

As the Hardys watch, Beeson is drawn upright under the machine's strange light and confesses his sins, starting with the admission of his first crime, the theft of a teacher's pocketbook.

The novel ends not only with Frank and Joe recovering stolen bank funds but also with assisting the eccentric inventor in publishing a book about his discoveries to benefit the scientific community.

In *The Mystery of the* Flying Express (1941) Fenton Hardy gives his sons a preposterous assignment. Instead of asking Frank and Joe for help in solving a criminal case, he announces, "'Our goal is to track down certain sinister spies who at present are endeavoring to destroy our whole social order'" (11–12). Instead of nabbing a housebreaker or car thief that eludes the bumbling Chief Collig and clueless Detective Smuff, teenage Frank and Joe are doing the work of J. Edgar Hoover's FBI. Although the "Federal Government" is involved in the case, it takes the Hardys to locate an ammunition-laden spy camp housing a thousand enemy agents.

The introduction of espionage in 1941 may have been an attempt to capitalize on current interests. FBI arrests of Nazi agents and stories of enemy saboteurs, along with widespread concern about Hitler Youth camps in the United States, made headlines prior to Pearl Harbor. Interestingly though, the novel makes no illusion to the politics or the nationality of the foreign agents, who are only identified by their halting attempts at speaking American English.

With the last Button novel, *The Clue of the Broken Blade* (1942), the "weird period" came to an end. In this adventure, Frank and Joe return to conventional crime-solving, breaking up a gang of thieves who rob ships and warehouses using camouflaged trucks and forged documents. There are no voyages to island kingdoms, futuristic technology, or foreign intrigue. The only bizarre element is a reprise of a theme from the McFarlane period. As in *The Secret of the Caves,* the Hardys rescue an amnesia victim who is magically restored to mental health by a shock.

CHAPTER 4

The Hardy Boys in Peace and Cold War

> We feel here that all of us should be alert to the changes that the end of the war will bring. That it will bring sweeping changes in the Juvenile field goes without saying.... We want to be ready when peace comes. We'll probably make some mistakes, but we can't afford to sit still and wait.
> — Hugh Juergens, Grosset & Dunlap

Leslie McFarlane returned to the Hardy Boys with *The Flickering Torch Mystery* published in 1943. In this story, Frank and Joe solve a mystery involving stolen silkworms and government construction supplies. Resolution of the crimes leads not to a thousand dollar reward from a wealthy citizen of Bayport but telegrams of "hearty congratulations" from "high government authorities in Washington."

The Mystery of the Missing War

Stolen silk worms and the spy camp in *The Mystery of the* Flying Express (1941) are as close as the Hardy Boys novels get to World War II. In neither book is the Second World War mentioned. This marks an odd and distinctive feature of the Hardy Boys series. At a time when popular culture — radio dramas, motion pictures, comic books, adult fiction, and Broadway plays — took on patriotic or military themes, Frank and Joe remain remarkably distant from the most significant events that shaped the twentieth century. While the dream factories of Hollywood sought to remain relevant and capitalize on wartime consciousness by making war movies and weaving in patriotic plot lines into popular film series such as Sherlock Holmes and the Bowery Boys, the fiction factory kept the Hardys propaganda free. Comic book publishers, in contrast, exploited the war, the Nazis with their swastikas and black SS uniforms providing their artists with easily identifiable foes and a shorthand for evil. But throughout the war years, when Superman and Wonder Woman battled the Third Reich and radio detectives fought Japanese spies, the Hardy Boys mysteries were notably Nazi free. There are no scenes of

The Mystery of the Flying Express, 1941.

bond drives, mention of blackouts, or shore surveillance (commonplace in a seaport town like Bayport). No chum ever talks about enlisting in any branch of the armed services or doing any war work. No uniformed characters appear in the novels, even in passing. No older chum goes into the army or comes back from the Pacific. Though real Nazi saboteurs landed on Long Island (fifty miles from the actual Bayport) in June 1942, they never penetrated the pages of the Hardy Boys. No U boats surface in Barmet Bay. No guttural speaking agents poke around Bayport's factories. No sinister Asians appear on the waterfront.

In the First World War Tom Swift came to the aid of Uncle Sam with the invention of his "war tank." Other Stratemeyer series exploited adolescent fascination with American flyers serving in France. But the Second World War never came to Bayport. There is no mention that America is at war or that the Germans and Japanese are enemies. While books like *Footprints Under the Window* (1933) evoke racist stereotypes of sinister Chinamen, the wartime novels never engage in the anti–Japanese sentiments widely expressed in popular culture following the Pearl Harbor attack.

The Flickering Torch Mystery makes only oblique references to current events. In the opening chapter an entomologist from a nearby experimental farm explains to the boys that he has developed a species of silkworm that produces "a silk thread stronger than any yet known" (7). This leads Frank to whistle, noting the importance of silk thread "especially in these times" (7). The scientist agrees, mentioning how the thread could be used in making parachutes. Later in the novel, he experiments with a new kind of synthetic rubber, another critical wartime necessity — but the need for artificial rubber is never explained. The impact of rationing is only hinted at. The novel points out that Fenton Hardy "used trains for his longer trips nowadays instead of his car" and that the staff of the experimental farm now uses horses instead of cars to tour the fields, though no explanation is offered. The Hardy Boys travel by bicycle for the first time in the series, evidently garaging their motorcycles to save gas. Even the stolen government building materials have nothing to do with the war effort. They are taken from a civilian highway construction project. The high cost and scarcity of copper wire is mentioned, but again no reason is given. The secretive gang that wears black robes and uses flaming torches as signals is comprised of common American criminals, not enemy agents. They are little different than the auto thieves in *The Shore Road Mystery*. None of them speaks with a foreign accent. The motives for the thefts are purely economic. They steal valuable construction supplies in wartime for the same reason the Shore Road gang stole Isaac Fussy's Cadillac in 1928. The fact that at novel's end the congratulations for rounding up the gang comes from Washington officials rather than the Bayport Police Department implies that solving the disappearance of construction materials has national significance. But no one in the final scenes says anything about helping the nation at large, protecting America, or supporting the war effort. The novel misses ample opportunities to tie the plot to events dominating the headlines and newsreels.

The Flickering Torch Mystery lacks the element of foreign terrorism the syndicate outline and McFarlane created for *The Sinister Signpost* published in 1936. Woven into that drama about a kidnapped racehorse is an ominous villain named Ivan Vilnoff, a "swarthy, well-dressed stranger" who speaks with a guttural accent (7). Frank encounters the "foreigner" at a high school football game and again at the racetrack. The following day, Fenton Hardy takes his sons to meet Vilnoff to ascertain his recent whereabouts. Polite and courteous, Vilnoff affably explains he attended a football game and happened to sit next to the detective's son. Frank confirms Vilnoff's alibi. Afterwards, Frank asks his father why he was tracking Vilnoff's movements. Fenton

Hardy's answer provides more drama about spies and enemy agents than McFarlane's wartime novel:

> "Oh, the government is just checking up on all visiting aliens," he remarked casually. "It wasn't very important."
> "A result of the explosion in the munitions factory?" Joe suggested shrewdly.
> "I wouldn't go so far as to say that I connect Vilnoff with that," returned Mr. Hardy.
> Although their father would say no more, the boys felt they could read between the lines. They were firmly convinced that his investigations had some connection with the factory explosion [32–33].

Sensing there is something suspicious about the foreigner, Frank and Joe return to Vilnoff's home. Spotting a lighted basement window, they move closer to investigate and discover a man working in an underground machine shop. Like many a spy novel villain, the mysterious Vilnoff appears to have a double. He is spotted in both New York and on Barmet Bay at the same time. Subsequent events lead Frank and Joe back to Vilnoff's basement, where they discover blueprints labeled "SUPER AERIAL BOMB" and "SECRET— LIGHTWEIGHT TORPEDO FOR SUBMARINE USE" (136). Their search also reveals "supplies of nitroglycerin, T.N.T, dynamite, gunpowder, guncotton, caps, fuses — enough deadly explosives to lay Bayport in ruins for blocks around" (136). They also find the model of a new type of machine gun. The Hardy Boys alert the police about their discovery and pursue the vanished Vilnoff.

When Frank and Joe finally confront the elusive Vilnoff, he is no longer the well-mannered gentleman but a raving lunatic planning a reign of terror not just on Bayport but on the entire United States. When Frank accuses him of "'inventing machines of warfare, probably to be used against our country'" (184) Vilnoff explodes in rage:

> "I am not a bad man as you think," he said. "But I hate Bayport!"
> He snapped out the words viciously.
> "I hate your whole country!" he repeated with sinister emphasis.
> "Why do you live here, then?" asked Joe.
> "I stay here only for the purpose of revenge," declared Vilnoff. "My vife — the best and finest woman who ever lived — she vas an American. But an American killed her! Right here in Bayport! She gave her life for a man who is in Washington now trying to urge your government to harm my country."
> His voice rose to a shout.
> "So I hate your land, and I have intended to make war on it!" he yelled, his eyes blazing as he shook both fists at the boys [184].

Vilnoff explains that he plans to create caches of explosives across the country that will be detonated at his signal. Vilnoff escapes, but the Hardys locate him in an underground maze of chambers filled with high explosives.

Cornered, Vilnoff throws himself into an instrument panel and electrocutes himself in a "livid blue flash" (196). While Joe mounts the rescued thoroughbred and gallops off to get help, Frank anxiously tears apart the wiring to Vilnoff's explosive mechanisms, knowing that he might "accidentally set off a connection that would blow him up and lay waste the entire countryside" (199–200). Frank manages to save Bayport from destruction, the racehorse is returned to its owner, and the twin mysteries are solved. Fenton Hardy surmises that Vilnoff's double, his brother, has escaped and is "'safe in hiding on the other side of the water'" (213).

None of these plot lines, developed in 1936, appear in any of the wartime novels. There are no strange foreigners with guttural accents, no plots to blow anything up, or links to hostile countries overseas. McFarlane's second wartime novel, *The Melted Coins* (1944), contains not even a vague reference to wartime rationing. The storyline involving buried treasure, stolen coins, a Chinese merchant, and yet another amnesia victim could just as easily have been written in the 1920s.

The absence of the war was deliberate. Harriet Stratemeyer Adams, with an eye to keeping her books current long after the conflict ended, explained to Leslie McFarlane in 1943 that she wanted to prevent the books from becoming time-bound by locking them too closely to contemporary events: "We are trying to play along with the War effort by not using gasoline, etc., in the stories. This need not be mentioned in the books, as we trust these stories will be read long after the War is over. We merely are trying to avoid criticism for the duration, so we are having our heroes do more walking, or going by bicycle. Here and there where a car is used, it might be termed 'essential driving.'"[1] As Melanie Rehak observes, Harriet Adams was trying to "have things both ways" by not offending wartime sensibilities about wasting fuel while not dating the books and damaging their longevity. Frank and Joe, always responsible, could not be shown joyriding in their roadsters or taking motorcycle outings when their readers were being daily admonished in school, on the radio, and in the movies to save gas. Car owners with the dreaded A card on their windshields were entitled to only four gallons of gas a week. Train and bus stations bore huge signs asking travelers, "Is This Trip Necessary?" So as not to offend or confuse juvenile readers, Frank and Joe's usual freedom of movement is curtailed. Adams directed Nancy Drew's ghostwriter to follow similar instructions, telling Mildred Wirt to "note here and there that Nancy is taking an airplane lesson, and infer that this has something to do with the war effort, without mentioning the war."[2]

Adams, however, could not excise the war from her own life. Her son Sunny, a naval flight instructor, was killed in a training accident in Florida in 1942. The syndicate offices were closed for several days, and it fell upon her sister Edna to explain to publishers and contract writers the reason for the uncharacteristic deceleration of the fiction factory's assembly line.[3]

Frank and Joe: Big Brothers

The Short-Wave Mystery (1945) makes no reference to the Second World War but is notable for introducing an element of social consciousness in the series. When Aunt Gertrude tells the brothers to clean out some old clothes, they come across a toy train set, which Frank suggests they donate to "some poor kid" (22).

This gesture foreshadows the brothers coming to the aid of a trio of "ragged youngsters" they encounter chasing a thief. At first the "urchins" regard Frank and Joe with suspicion when the Hardys offer to treat them to a soda. The brothers observe that "there was nothing vicious about them; but clearly, they were neglected" (30). Jimmy Gordon, leader of the group, tells Frank and Joe their parents are away from home all day, leaving the boys to their own devices. "'They don't know if I go to school or not,'" he tells them, almost boasting that all three had flunked (30). Asked about what they do for food, the boys scornfully state they are forced to fend for themselves.

Frank and Joe offer them dinner, breaking class barriers by bringing home "three of the dirtiest and raggedest urchins who ever had set foot on High Street" (31). Aunt Gertrude is initially shocked at the idea of having the "filthy little imps" sitting in the dining room. Frank agrees, noting, "'Of course they're dirty. They're neglected'" (31). Aunt Gertrude is mollified, suggesting Frank and Joe take the boys upstairs to be cleaned up, warning them, however, not to "use the good guest towels" (32).

Once the boys are "scrubbed and shampooed until they glowed with cleanliness," Aunt Gertrude has a change of heart, beaming with pride as the hungry boys devour their dinners. Later she declares "the highest compliment ever paid her cooking was the eating performance she witnessed that evening" (32).

After getting them to promise to attend summer school, Frank and Joe take the boys to their homes, described as "ramshackle flats." Watching Jimmy scramble up the "dimly lighted stairs of a shabby tenement," the Hardy Boys vow to prevent him from becoming a criminal like his uncle, Elly Batter:

"Jimmy's background is pretty bad," said Frank. "Poor kid! What chance has he got?"
"That's up to us," declared his brother. "We'll see that he gets a chance. We can't let him follow in his uncle's footsteps" [34].

On the track of a thief, Frank and Joe run into Jimmy Gordon and ask him to help them locate the criminal. Jimmy agrees, his eyes "shining" with enthusiasm. He is "thrilled" to help the detectives, deciding that "it was a great deal more fun to be on the right side of the law" (45). In turn, Jimmy asks Frank and Joe to help Mickey, one of the trio, who has been arrested for robbing a bakery.

The Hardy Boys speak with the juvenile court judge, assuring him that the boy is a victim of neglect rather than a delinquent. The judge listens intently as Frank pleads Mickey's case then makes a proposal:

> "Now if Mickey had a big brother—someone responsible and willing to look after him—"
> "How would two big brothers do, sir?" asked Joe eagerly. "Frank and I will take him in hand."
> "I hoped you'd say that," smiled the judge. "Very well, then. If you'll take an interest in Mickey, I'll turn him over to you on suspended sentence. But remember—he's no angel. You'll have your troubles" [72].

Frank and Joe take Mickey home for more Aunt Gertrude–cooked meals, and Chet Morton gives him a job in his taxidermy shop.

Jimmy Gordon proves helpful in the Hardy Boys' investigation of factory robberies. At novel's end, they give their old electric train set to Jimmy, instructing him to let Mickey play with it. The Hardy Boys also receive a gift from the FBI, which is a throwback to the weird period. For their help in solving the case, Frank and Joe receive a "television walkie talkie" in 1945.

End of an Era

The Phantom Freighter (1947) brought the second McFarlane period to an end. Some sources credit McFarlane's first wife, Amy, as the author. Syndicate records contain a letter from Leslie McFarlane announcing that his wife was "taking over" some of his freelance work.[4] McFarlane's time and attention were consumed by his work with the Canadian National Film Board, but the idea that he handed over writing assignments to his wife strikes both researchers and his own family as highly unlikely. Amy McFarlane was not a gifted writer, as evidenced by the letters she wrote to her children.[5] Norah Perez suggests that the reason McFarlane asked the syndicate to regard Amy as the author was financial. Troubled by his tax situation, McFarlane may have wanted to avoid declaring his syndicate fee as income. This desire to distance himself from the book may explain his request to Harriet Adams, "Will you be good enough to regard this manuscript as written by her, with payment to be made to her on delivery and acceptance, addressing correspondence regarding it to her at the above address."[6] If Amy McFarlane wrote, edited, or assisted in the completion of the book, it made little difference to the final product. *The Phantom Freighter* is a classic Hardy Boys tale involving Aunt

Gertrude, stolen documents, and smuggled goods along Bayport's seedy waterfront. The science fiction elements and preposterous plots of the "weird period" are absent, and the boys are back in high school.

New Writers, New Issues

After Leslie McFarlane left the series again, the Hardy Boys were written by a number of syndicate personnel and contract authors. As in Edward Stratemeyer's day, plot outlines were generated by the syndicate for writers to flesh out. Harriet Adams wrote several Hardy Boys books herself, assigning others to a number of ghostwriters, including George Waller Jr., Richard Cohen, William Dougherty, and James Duncan Lawrence.[7]

Although written by a number of different authors, the books maintain a general uniformity in tone and style. A few alterations in slang and vague references to social issues indicate that the world of the Hardy Boys has changed since 1927.

The Secret of Skull Mountain (1948) alludes to postwar economic expansion and the baby boom with Aunt Gertrude describing "the increasing number of families" moving to Bayport and "the lack of rooms in the schools for the extra children" (7). The novel's nomenclature is clearly postwar, with Frank and Joe saying "guy" rather than "fellow." The following novel *The Sign of the Crooked Arrow* (1949) includes more terminology that is clearly non–McFarlane. As Frank and Joe prepare for a trip West, the Hardy household is described as being "as busy as rodeo day in a prairie town" (86). Flying west, their chartered aircraft is chased by a "kibitzing plane" (94).

Overall, the postwar novels of the late Forties and early Fifties are reminiscent of the earliest books — with a few changes. Frank and Joe are described as being eighteen and seventeen in *The Secret of Wildcat Swamp* (1952), aging two years since *The Tower Treasure* was published twenty-five years before. Fenton Hardy does not age quite as gracefully, described as being forty-five instead of forty in *The Hooded Hawk Mystery* (1954).

The villains of the early Fifties, like the villains of the Twenties, are by and large small gangs involved in crimes like smuggling and robbery. Some books feature a single villain. The adventures are less dramatic. In one novel, Frank and Joe unearth a lost deed. In another, they find a missing will. In both, the Hardys ensure justice and social order by securing the property rights of legal heirs. The boys remain obedient sons, always taking direction from Fenton Hardy and asking permission to stay out late or travel beyond Bayport. The chums, especially Chet Morton, help out, and Callie and Iola take more active roles in brief scenes.

The Hardy Boys novels of the early Fifties contain more accurate and sensitive portrayals of ethnic groups, especially Native Americans and Asians. *The Crisscross Shadow* (1953) includes scenes clearly designed to acquaint young readers with the lifestyles of real Native Americans as opposed to the stereotype of the wild Indian depicted on TV Westerns. The author repeatedly points out how normal or all-American the Native Americans are in dress and language. Only the oldest tribal member speaks with a noticeable dialect. *The Hooded Hawk Mystery* (1954) parallels *Footprints Under the Window* (1933) in its theme of smuggled Asian immigrants. But unlike the earlier novel, the Asians, this time Indians rather than Chinese, are depicted in a more wholesome light. Fenton Hardy tells his sons that an Indian friend of his "'naturally frowns on anything that will reflect on his country's good reputation, and has offered to assist in every way he can'" (22). The Indian characters speak without accents, and the boys are deferential to Indian adults who teach them about their culture. Much of the novel is devoted to the sport of falconry. The novel includes an acknowledgment page thanking Dr. John J. Craighead, a falconer and research scientist, for "assistance in the preparation of the falconry material used in this story."

In the novels of the Fifties Frank and Joe are models of the Quiet Generation. There are fewer pranks. In addition, Frank and Joe's relationship with Chief Collig and the Bayport Police improves. No longer dismissive rivals, the Bayport cops cooperate with the teenage detectives and often come to their assistance to provide needed protection or surveillance. Chief Collig appears almost as an agent of the Hardys, assigning officers or making official queries whenever the boys call for assistance.

The books continue to parallel technological developments and social change. In the Twenties Frank and Joe tear around Bayport on motorcycles. In 1956 they go scuba diving in *The Secret of Pirates' Hill* and a year later take flying lessons in *The Ghost at Skeleton Rock*. The current events of the Cold War, like the Second World War a decade before, are barely hinted at. In *The Ghost at Skeleton Rock* Frank and Joe fly to Puerto Rico where they help foil the attempt by rebels to "overthrow the legally elected government" of Cuba by constructing a nuclear weapon. The words "terrorist" or "Communist" never appear. A Cuban official simply defines the adversaries as "criminals, crazy for power" (83). At the end of the novel, a Cuban official decorates Fenton Hardy for his "distinguished efforts for the cause of peace and justice" (184). Peace and justice are odd terms to apply to the Batista regime, which was widely known at the time for its corruption, oppression, and open cooperation with American organized crime figures who had interests in Havana's famed casinos and brothels. In the following novel, *The Mystery at Devil's Paw* (1959), the brothers track down spies hoping to recover a missing American moon rocket that crashed in Alaska. This adventure ends with a cinematic climax worthy of an action adventure film. Unlike previous novels, in which gangs are rounded up by a half dozen Bayport cops or state troopers, U.S. and Canadian jet fighters streak across the sky dropping flares, followed by assault helicopters and paratroopers. Again, the word "Communist" does not appear, and the unfriendly nation behind the espionage is never named.

The Mystery at Devil's Paw does follow Stratemeyer's long-established marketing strategy of capitalizing on major events. Set in Alaska, the 1959 novel contains a topical dedication: "*The author proudly dedicates this book to the boys and girls of Alaska, which became our forty-ninth state during the writing of* THE MYSTERY AT DEVIL'S PAW."

The book is one of the most overtly educational in the series, presenting children with travelogue and geographical details which figured in television programs, newspaper articles, and elementary and middle school lesson plans about the first new state to be added to the Union since 1911. A telegram from Tony Prito asking Frank and Joe to help him solve a mystery in Alaska sets up a patter of stilted, pedagogical dialogue worthy of an educational film:

> "Oh, Auntie!" Joe exclaimed. "Alaska isn't all ice and snow. A few days ago it was eighty degrees in Juneau."
>
> "Seems incredible," Mr. Hardy agreed, "but it's true. The Alaskan Panhandle has weather much like Washington or Oregon, with plenty of rain."
>
> "Then you will both get wet and die of pneumonia!" Aunt Gertrude went on, not to be deterred.
>
> The brothers suppressed a smile as the conversation about the new state continued. Only the far north was frigid, Joe recalled from his geography lessons. He even remembered that Alaska was an Aleut Indian name meaning "The Great Land," and was referred to as the "Crossroads of the World" [3].

The didactic travelogue continues as the Hardy Boys, accompanied by Chet Morton, fly to Juneau. When Chet mentions his surprise that it is a "real city" with modern buildings, Joe remarks, "'What did you expect — log cabins? ... This *is* the capital of Alaska'" (21). Although Tony is involved in a "weird mystery" and their lives have been threatened just trying to get airline tickets, the chums manage to squeeze in highly educational side trips.

Visiting the Alaska Historical Museum, they view wildlife exhibits and displays of Indian and Eskimo artifacts. Frank and Joe pause at a glass case containing a copy of the $7,200,000 U.S. Treasury check used to purchase Alaska from Russia. Noting the gold fortunes produced in Alaska, Frank declares the deal "some bargain" (23). Once outside, the brothers comment on other features of the northernmost state, such as the fact that the sun won't set until eleven o'clock.

After the chums locate Tony Prito, who has taken a summer job as a "stream guard" for the Fish and Wildlife Service, they are treated to further details about Alaska.

Tony welcomes them to the new state, reminding the chums that it is "twice the size of Texas" (36). Tony shows them a salmon run, explaining the use of fish ladders and the importance of the fishing industry. On a river trip, a guide points out species of flowers by name, including masses of yellow monkey flowers that appear to have miniature faces.

Even the typical chapter-ending cliff hangers serve an educational purpose as the boys are attacked by a bear in one instance and trapped on a glacier in another. On the glacier they rescue a couple of explorers. Though suffering a broken leg, a retired engineer expounds to the boys his theory that Indians originated in Alaska and did not cross from Asia over the Bering Sea as commonly believed. Throughout the book, the plot and dialogue make tie-ins to features of Alaska that would have saturated the consciousness of American schoolchildren in 1959.

In the last year of the Fifties, the Hardy Boys were seeking to maintain their relevance and capture a new generation of readers among children born in the television age. The final novels of the Fifties are shorter and were the first books to include more pictures than the customary frontispiece. Now as many as half a dozen drawings, some of them crude sketches, illustrated dramatic scenes of the novels.

More changes were soon to come to the Hardy Boys canon.

Chapter 5

Policing the Hardy Boys: The "Great Purge"

"It's mighty good of you, fellows," said Slim gratefully. "I won't forget it in a hurry. You've been pretty white to me all through this—"
— *The Tower Treasure*, 1927

"It's mighty good of you fellows," Slim said gratefully. "I won't forget it in a hurry." He tried to smile, but it was evident that the boy was deeply worried.
— *The Tower Treasure*, 1959

    The Second World War transformed America. The burst of postwar affluence, the Baby Boom, television, nuclear weapons, and the growing civil rights movement changed popular culture. The dark days of the Depression were over. The America of the New Deal, breadlines, CCC Camps, the Dust Bowl, Fireside Chats, and *The Grapes of Wrath* was replaced by the America of GI loans, Levittowns, shopping malls, drive-ins, credit cards, two-car families, and *The Man in the Gray Flannel Suit*.
    For the writers and publishers of series books the postwar era was filled with promise and misgiving. The soaring birthrate meant that the Fifties would be the decade of the child. The annual number of births reached four million in 1954. The nation's general prosperity meant that parents had more discretionary income to spend on children's entertainment. Parents who had grown up during the lean years of the Depression or wartime rationing wanted to make sure their children had better lives. Young mothers read Dr. Spock and celebrated Dr. Salk's triumph over polio, the disease that had crippled

FDR. The majority of young mothers worked only in the home, dedicating their lives to their children. PTA meetings, choir practice, orthodontist appointments, and Little League games dominated the rhythms of middle-class life in the ever-expanding subdivisions. The low-priced series book was well within children's allowances and parental budgets. Adults who had grown up with Tom Swift, the Hardy Boys, and Nancy Drew could be counted on to buy these wholesome books for their children.

The Baby Boom seemed to guarantee a children's book boom.

There was, however, an electronic specter on the horizon. The rapid growth and influence of television meant changes in education, entertainment, and reading habits. In 1947 only 178,571 television sets were manufactured in the United States. Within six years output would increase to 7,261,109.[1] Radio mysteries, comedies, variety shows, and soap operas moved to the new medium or vanished from the airwaves. Hollywood scaled back motion picture production and ceased making comedy shorts, newsreels, and series films. School teachers, librarians, and parents became concerned that children were no longer reading books. Would children and adolescents continue reading mystery and adventure books when they could watch *Superman* and *Dragnet* on television? By the Fifties, the series book could have become as obsolete as a Henry Aldridge film or a Little Orphan Annie radio show.

Television, however, would revitalize the thirty-year-old Hardy Boys series. Walt Disney's popular *Mickey Mouse Club* featured two Hardy Boys dramatic series in the 1956–57 and 1957–58 seasons. The show, which reached fourteen million viewers, drew attention to Hardy Boys books, as did a stream of Hardy Boys coloring books, board games, and comic books. Grosset & Dunlap benefited from the link to the popular Disney series and created promotional book wrappers featuring the series actors on the cover. Point of purchase displays appeared in supermarkets and drugstores, leading many parents who were eager to get their children to read in the television age to buy Hardy Boys books. Though no longer priced at fifty cents, they were still substantially cheaper than other children's books. Grosset & Dunlap helped consumers buy into the series by offering two volumes for the price of one. In the late Fifties the Hardy Boys again became popular Christmas and birthday gifts.

The new popularity of the Hardy Boys, however, generated criticism. As early as 1948 Grosset & Dunlap began to receive complaints about dated ethnic stereotypes in the early Hardy Boys novels, which were still in print.[2] *The Hidden Harbor Mystery* (1935), with its black villain, heavy dialect, and racist descriptions of "shuffling" and "stupid" Negroes offended many parents. Harriet Adams resented criticism of syndicate books and defended them against what she considered unfair attacks. She wondered why a minority could not be cast as a villain. But under pressure from her publisher, she agreed that many of the early titles needed to be revised.

McFarlane's books, the syndicate had to acknowledge, now seemed outdated, confusing, and to some, offensive. Few children in 1959 had ever seen a "roadster" or heard of a "touring car." Men no longer wore caps, few middle-class families had servants, the novelty of air travel had worn off, and Americans no longer referred to motorcycles or airplanes as "machines." More troubling was the presence of racist dialogue. McFarlane may have not been an overt bigot, but he was a provincial Canadian whose dialogue reflected the ethnic stereotypes of the 1920s and 1930s. Watching Frank struggle against pounding waves to rescue Captain Royal in *The Secret of the Caves* (1929), Joe observes that his brother "'hasn't a Chinaman's chance'" (182). In *The Great Airport Mystery* (1930) Frank comments that it was "'mighty white of Mr. Jefferson and Mr. Applegate to go bail for us'" (128). Even worse were the depictions of Rocco, the "excitable" Italian fruit peddler shouting about "'Da Blacka Hand!'" the Amos & Andy Negroes in their decrepit "autymobile" in *Hunting for Hidden Gold* (1928), and sinister Chinaman Louie Fong in 1933's *Footprints Under the Window*.

In the aftermath of the Montgomery bus boycott and Little Rock, it seemed wrong and distasteful to introduce stereotypes of dialect-speaking Negroes to another generation of American children. In addition, the early novels included pranks against adults and ridiculed the police. These may have been amusing elements in the Roaring Twenties, but by the Cold War Fifties, these themes seemed suspicious and anti-social in a time of worried conformity.

Syndicate files show that Harriet Adams and Andrew Svenson reviewed the first twenty-four novels for use of dialect and racial stereotypes. Notes were prepared on each book and revised outlines were presented to new ghostwriters. Starting in 1959, *The Tower Treasure* and *The House on the Cliff* were reissued in new editions.

These books still appeared until the name Franklin W. Dixon, but bore a brief notation on the copyright page that few children probably noticed: "*In this new story, based on the original of the same title, Mr. Dixon has incorporated the most up-to-date methods used by police and private detectives.*" For critics of series fiction, this statement was evidence of a continuing fraud. The non-existent Franklin W. Dixon was credited for making changes to books he never wrote for non-existent reasons.

Some books like *The Tower Treasure* were simply revised. The basic plot of the novel remains the same. The Hardy Boys (now aged eighteen and seventeen) are introduced riding their motorcycles and are nearly run down by a "speed demon." They visit Chet Morton who reports that his car has been stolen. He no longer drives a yellow "roadster" but a yellow "jalopy."

Detective Smuff is still a thickheaded cop, but the degree of derision is modified. Applegate's mansion is robbed and the caretaker is arrested. The Hardy Boys decide to take the case not only for the reward but also to clear Slim Robinson's father.

As in the original novel, the Hardys conspire with their chums to devise a ruse to delay Detective Smuff's departure from Bayport to give Fenton Hardy time to interview the dying Red Jackley. In this version, the idea is to get Smuff to miss a plane rather than a train. The scheme still involves Rocco, who now owns a "fruit store" rather than "fruit stand." He is still an Italian immigrant with a "genial" personality but is no longer described as having "an excitable nature." Rocco has lost his Chico Marx accent, his speech gently hinting that English is his second language: "'*Buona sera*,' he says. 'Good evening. How you like my fix the place?'"(111). There is no bomb, no mention of "Da Blacka Hand," no excited Rocco dancing in the street yelling in fright, and no dumb Irish Con Riley dumping buckets of water on an alarm clock. Instead, Frank offers to mind the store so Rocco can go home for an hour's rest. Frank volunteers to burn some rubbish in the back yard as a favor. He starts a roaring blaze. Joe flags down Smuff, tells him the store is on fire and tricks Smuff into racing into the yard to put out the inferno. The strategy works, and the inept detective is prevented from catching his flight.

Other ethnic stereotypes were dropped. *Hunting for Hidden Gold* was revised to have the Hardys take a plane rather than a train to Montana. They are kidnapped but escape without the appearance of Amos and Andy Negroes in their clattering Ford. *The House on the Cliff* was edited to delete the offensive phrase "nigger in the woodpile." *The Hidden Harbor Mystery* underwent major revisions to eliminate the offensive character of Luke Jones and all references to his wild colored society. There remains the elderly black servant, a family retainer loyal to his master. Deferential to the Hardys, he calls them "sir" but speaks without dialect, using words like "folks" to suggest a Southern or humble origin:

> Grover sighed. "All right, sir, I'll tell you folks what I can. I don't like trouble. The faster everything's cleared up, the happier lots of folks will be."
> "Did Mr. Blackstone send you here to hide from us?" Joe queried.
> "Yes sir, he did," Grover admitted [83].

Footprints Under the Window was not simply revised but rewritten, with an entirely new plot, characters, and locales. The Hardys no longer break up Louie Fong's sinister coolie smuggling operation or protect the submissive Tom Wat through crossdressing. In the 1960 version there are no Chinese characters. In this novel, published under the same title, the Hardy Boys head to South America to foil a plot to steal a top-secret instrument needed in the space program. Ethnic stereotypes are reduced to the boys spotting a dark-skinned man running from a photographic plant, leading to Joe to remark, "'He may be foreign-born,'" (3) suggesting that real Americans are light complexioned. This bit of racial profiling leads a security officer to tell the brothers, "'We already suspect that aliens who entered the country illegally are operating in this area. Your description may be a great help to us'" (3). The trip to South America features a number of conventional stereotypes — swarthy thieves, shabbily dressed people, poor hotels, rickety buildings, thuggish *Policia*, a dictator, and scruffy guerrillas. The vicious anti–Asian stereotypes of the 1930s were replaced by the benign stereotypes of Latin Americans found on television dramas in the wake of Castro's rise to power in Cuba. The only element linking the two novels is the clue that gives the books a common title.

In addition to removing racist statements and softening ethnic dialects, the new ghostwriters cut depictions of smoking and drinking, even by felons. *The House on the Cliff* (1927) not only lost its rogue Chinaman Li Chang, described as a "wizened little fellow with a villainous countenance," but also its violent ending. In the original version, Frank and Joe, along with their father, escape from a gang hideout only to be recaptured. The scene is filled with gunplay:

> The darkness was pierced by a flash of crimson and a revolver barked three times.
> From the lane came sounds of running feet. A man was shouting:
> "What is it? What's the matter?"
> "They've got away! Hardy and them boys! They've escaped. Look! There they are now — running across the yard!"
> The revolver spoke again. But the shots were wild, for the detective and his sons were soon lost to view in the shadows of the house....
> There was a deafening roar and a streak of flame. The man of the house had been armed with a shotgun, and in the struggle it had exploded....
> Then, in a moment, a perfect fusillade of shots broke out.
> But Fenton Hardy and the boys had withdrawn past the turn in the staircase and were well protected. They could hear the uproar of gunfire as the smugglers riddled the staircase with bullets.
> "That should have finished 'em!" they could hear Snackley saying. "If they're on the stairs at all they're as dead as mutton by now" [183–186].

Realizing that the Hardys had moved from the staircase to the attic, Snackley fires through the ceiling above him:

> A shot sounded from below and a bullet ripped its way savagely through the flooring but a foot or so away from where the three sat. Another bullet tore through the wood of the trapdoor....
> A few more shots resounded. The bullets were unpleasantly close....
> "Let 'em have a few more!"
> An angry chorus of revolver shots followed [189–190].

The 1959 version repeats the basic premise. The three Hardys attempt to flee but are spotted and move to the attic where they are cornered and recaptured — without a single shot being fired. No bullets rip through the floor. No villain says "Let 'em have a few more." The villain, now called Snattman rather than Snackley, only threatens to use his gun in recapturing the detectives. There is gunplay at the end but it is muted. There are no vivid descriptions of bullets tearing through wood or revolvers barking or shooting out streaks of crimson flame: "Others guarded the sides of the house to prevent any escape from the windows. A few shots were fired, but soon the smuggling gang gave up without fighting further. The capture of their leader and sudden attack had unnerved them (173)."

The revision process not only updated references and eliminated ethnic slurs but also simplified style, streamlined plots, shortened exposition, and trimmed the books' overall length. The standard McFarlane Hardy Boys book consisted of twenty-five chapters totaling 208 to 216 pages. Beginning in 1959 the books were shortened to twenty chapters totaling 180 pages. Sentences and vocabulary were simplified. The original 1927 *The Secret of the Old Mill*, for example, was 212 pages long. The new version was 174 pages. The long passages about Frank and Joe sweating over Latin and geometry were excised, along with schoolroom jokes and pranks on the hapless Con Riley. Gone as well were many of scenes of local color and caricatures. The pipe-smoking and straw-chewing farmer, with his "ain't's" and "dunno's," who tells the boys that the old mill is now occupied by "onpleasant chaps" vanishes. Aunt Gertrude's exaggerated tirades predicting doom and destruction were toned down and trimmed. Many of McFarlane's "jawbreakers" were deleted. The new versions were slimmer, less didactic, less descriptive, with more emphasis on action and shorter dialogue. The slimmer books and quicker syntax were geared to appeal to the shortened attention spans of children accustomed to fast-paced television programs.

These revised editions pained Leslie McFarlane when he discovered how his work had been altered. Bob Stall, a writer for *Weekend Magazine*, interviewed McFarlane in the early 1970s and presented him with his own boyhood copies of the original Hardy Boys. Looking at a faded volume, McFarlane told Starr not to bother asking him about the plot, admitting, "'I can't remember what happened in any of them."[3] By chance the book fell open to the passage describing Aunt Gertrude's initial appearance in the series. Reading the lines detailing her arrival at the Hardy home, hectoring the cab driver, and ordering Frank and Joe to carry her baggage, McFarlane recalled the scenes he had pounded out on his typewriter nearly fifty years before for roughly sixty cents a page.

Then Stall handed him the revised edition. The arrival scene had been deleted. Aunt Gertrude was simply present in the novel, her colorful persona drastically muted. As McFarlane studied the book, Stall voiced his own dismay:

> I've compared all my original copies, the ones I read when I was a kid, with all the new ones. They haven't just been streamlined. They've been gutted from beginning to end. Those old books were well written. They had words you could roll around in your mouth and taste. They had funny scenes. They had scenes you could wallow in. These new ones move faster, all right, but too fast. There's never a place to stop and linger. That's why the old ones were so great for a kid. They had flavor. And now the flavor is all gone.[4]

A resigned McFarlane reminded the agitated reporter that the books, characters, and even name on the cover were all property of the syndicate. He had been, after all, not so much the author of the books as the typist. But Stall was adamant, arguing that parents were now buying these "crappy books" thinking they were the same books they had read as children. They were simply not "the Hardy Boys they remember."[5] As Stall argued that the watered-down books would weaken children's literacy, McFarlane examined the remade novel with dismay. "Gone was the leisurely style," he noted. "Gone were the roadsters in which the Hardy Boys drove up and down the Shore Road. Maybe Snackley and Jackley were gone too. Gone was the humor, such as it was. Even Aunt Gertrude didn't bawl out the kids any more. Aunt Gertrude — God save us all! — was playing it straight."[6]

Restoring the Flavor: Hardy Boys Uncut

The streamlined editions pained collectors and readers of the originals as well. The revised editions were starker, less colorful, and simplistic. Baby Boomers who grew up reading reprints of McFarlane's originals felt cheated and disappointed when they glanced through the modern versions they bought for children and grandchildren. Nostalgia for the genuine article led collectors to buy old copies and created a market for reproductions.

In the early 1990s Applewood Books began printing replica copies of the early Hardy Boys books featuring the original text, block type style, art work, red cloth covers, and dust jackets. The fifty-center was back — for $17.95. These reproductions included an explanatory, almost apologetic, notice with a cautionary admonition about the book's contents:

> Much has changed in America since the Hardy Boys series first began in 1927. The modern reader may be delighted with the warmth and exactness of the language, the wholesome innocence of the characters, their engagement with the natural world, or the nonstop action without the use of violence; but just as well, the modern reader may be extremely uncomfortable with the racial and social stereotyping, the roles women play in these books, or the use of phrases

or situations which may conjure up some response in the modern reader that was not felt by the reader of the times.

For good or bad, we Americans have changed quite a bit since these books were first issued. Many readers will remember these editions with great affection and will be delighted with their return; others will wonder why we just don't let them disappear. These books are part of our heritage. They are a window on our real past. For that reason, except for the addition of this note, we are presenting *The Mark on the Door* unedited and unchanged from its first edition.

Applewood Books

Now restored, Leslie McFarlane's novels are available in fresh copies. Like a mint condition Model T or a DVD of *The Jazz Singer*, they provide the public with an unedited artifact of the past that shaped the consciousness of generations of American children.

Chapter 6

Into the Disco Age

> By jettisoning their creakier aspects and reformulating the Nancy Drew and the Hardy Boys characters, the series got new leases on life and proved once again that, for the Stratemeyer Syndicate, books were business, and business came first.
> — Kismaric and Heiferman, *The Mysterious Case of Nancy Drew & the Hardy Boys*

The shorter, streamlined novels of the Sixties and Seventies present straight-forward mysteries, without McFarlane's lush detail and humorous asides. Frank and Joe investigate crimes or suspicious doings in Bayport, which often turn out to be linked to larger investigations being carried out by their father. Descriptions are paired to quick expository sketches to establish settings and introduce new characters. Dialogue is clipped to provide just enough explanation between action scenes. Frank and Joe are still presented as high school students, but there are no classroom scenes, no references to waiting for recess, doing homework, or worrying about passing exams. Aunt Gertrude appears in the books, but her scenes are cut, and her histrionic diatribes are muted into cautionary warnings. Overall, the high school chums, except for Chet (who retains his love of food), make fewer appearances.

Fenton Hardy is no longer portrayed as a lone private investigator but the head of a small, elite detective agency. He is assisted by an operative named Sam Radley and employs Jack Wayne to pilot his small plane. Frank and Joe are not the eager but naïve amateurs depicted in *The Tower Treasure* in 1927. In the McFarlane books, they are energetic but clearly amateur detectives. Frank and Joe spot clues but depend on Fenton Hardy or police officials to evaluate evidence. Now eighteen and seventeen, they are shown as being experienced and trusted investigators, able to conduct independent testing of evidence: "The Hardys had a criminology laboratory over their garage, where they did scientific analyses for their clients. They matched fingerprints under the microscope and carried out chemical tests of poisons, explosives, and other materials from the scene of a crime" (*The Jungle Pyramid*, 7). The nature of the mysteries change as well. In the early novels Frank and Joe battle lone villains like Red Jackley or small gangs like the car thieves in *The Shore Road Mystery* (1928) or *The Great Airport Mystery* (1930). Many of the novels in the 1960s and 1970s deal with international intrigue. In *The Secret Agent on Flight 101* (1967) Frank and Joe search through Fenton Hardy's files looking for information about a magician named Hexton they suspect of kidnapping their father. They try looking under M for "magician" but find nothing. Joe notices a file marked "school" and discovers it contains a sheet on Hexton:

> Written at the bottom of the page was: "Last two years agent UGLI."
> "UGLI!" Joe exclaimed. "Undercover Global League of Informants!"
> Frank gave a low whistle. "This is really big! UGLI is the most powerful espionage ring in the world."
> "And hostile to democratic countries," added Joe.
> The boys exchanged grim looks. If their father had been kidnapped, he was in ruthless hands!
> "I think I know now why this is filed under school," said Frank.
> Joe nodded. "That's probably a camouflage word for SKOOL. Dad must be working for them."
> Both boys had heard of the famous supranational counterespionage ring which worked on behalf of democratic powers. The letters stood for Secret Knowledge Of Organized Lawbreakers [13–14].

In the era of *The Man From U.N.C.L.E.* Frank and Joe Hardy were keeping pace with their adult counterparts, working with acronymic agencies on behalf of the free world. If in the Twenties the Hardy Boys were juvenile knockoffs of hardboiled adult detectives, by the Sixties they were adolescent knockoffs of James Bond (minus the Bond girls).

Frank and Joe's mobility and range of operations increase dramatically in the later books. They spend more time flying cross country (even piloting their father's twin-engine plane) and less time riding motorcycles around Bayport or churning across stormy Barmet Bay in the *Sleuth*. In the early novels Frank and Joe primarily solve local crimes. Aside from trips to Blacksnake Island and Montana, many of McFarlane's first novels are set in and around Bayport — the tower mansion, the house on the cliff, an old mill on Willow River, Cabin Island, the local airport. Trips to Mexico and Canada are exceptions.

In the Seventies international travel becomes routine. The Hardy brothers (occasionally accompanied by chums) travel to Brazil in *The Masked*

Monkey (1972), Greece in *The Shattered Helmet* (1973), and Hong Kong in *The Clue of the Hissing Serpent* (1974). By 1975, Frank and Joe are truly global. *The Mysterious Caravan* (1975) opens with the boys vacationing in Jamaica, where they discover an ancient death mask on the beach, which leads them to North Africa. In the following novel, *The Witchmaster's Key* (1976), the brothers travel to England. *The Jungle Pyramid* (1977) takes Frank and Joe from Zurich to Mexico. In *The Firebird Rocket* (1978) they follow up leads in Australia. In addition to understanding Spanish, Frank and Joe speak high school German and pick up a few phrases of Arabic and Swahili.

The Secret Agent on Flight 101, 1967.

The novels of this era reflect greater diversity and present more favorable depictions of other cultures. The books often include a novel-specific chum of another nationality. Frank and Joe have a Chinese-American friend named Jimmy Foy in *The Mystery of the Chinese Junk* (1960). In *The Shattered Helmet* they attend film school with a Greek exchange student. They befriend a Jamaican teenager in *The Mysterious Caravan* and a black youth named Leroy in *The Sting of the Scorpion* (1979).

Although the depiction of ethnic groups changes markedly in these books, the role of female characters alters only slightly. Callie Shaw and Iola Morton remain marginal figures. In many of the novels they do not appear at all. Frank and Joe, however, for the first time in the series, notice girls and initiate contact, though the interactions rarely go beyond a soft drink date in a public place or a dinner with the girl's family. Chet goes out on dates with a girl who becomes enamored enough to discuss getting engaged. Exotic-looking foreign girls appear briefly but no relationships or direct contact occurs. When encountering a beautiful woman, Frank and Joe note her appearance with the objectivity of a naturalist studying a rare species.

The travelogue theme continues, along with tie-ins to selective current events. In 1969 (the year America reached the moon) the Hardy Boys travel to Iceland in *The Arctic Patrol Mystery* to locate a missing person and become involved in the rescue of a lost astronaut. The novel contains numerous bits of planted dialogue as Icelanders educate the visiting Americans about their nation's language, geography, history, and culture. When an official suggests the boys place an ad in a local paper to aid their search, Frank is amazed that a city of seventy-five thousand has five daily newspapers. "'Icelanders like to read,'" he is told. "'In fact,'" the official informs him, "'there is no illiteracy in our country'" (37). A guide explains that moon-bound American astronauts train on Iceland's volcanic soil because it resembles the lunar surface.

The moon landing is the only major historical event of the Sixties and Seventies depicted in the novels. There is no mention of the Viet Nam War, the assassinations, race riots, the civil rights movement, or counter culture in the Hardy Boys. All of these events could have provided the syndicate with interesting plots, especially in a juvenile series. But like World War II, the political and social events of the era are ignored.

Terrorism and Identity Theft

The novels published in the early Seventies, though avoiding the issues of their own day, oddly presage twenty-first-century concerns. *The Bombay Boomerang* was published in 1970, the same year as the invasion of Cambodia and the Kent State University shootings, when anti-military sentiments, especially among the young, were extremely high. The plot, in which Frank and Joe work with a Pentagon admiral, runs counter to the mood of the times. Yet the mystery involving a terrorist attack and a weapon of mass destruction makes the book more relevant and realistic thirty-five years later. The novel opens with Fenton Hardy calling on his sons to help him solve the theft of mercury shipments. As the case progresses, the Hardy boys realize that they are not tracking down a common criminal gang but a terrorist organization. In addition to stealing the mercury, the gang acquires a missile. With Al Qaeda–like inventiveness, the gang intends to create a weapon of mass destruction. They use mercury fulminate to design a "super warhead" that is so powerful that it can "crack the crust of the earth for miles" (173). They plan to fire the stolen missile into a nerve gas storage facility in Colorado. A gang member explains their goal is to create massive civilian casualties and destabilizing terror: "'The missile will home in on a heating unit we've set up in Colorado right under the nose of the military. We'll get the underground defenses one after the other. The gas will be all over the state in a matter of minutes, with a terrific toll!'" (173). The resulting loss of life will cause social unrest. A gang member tells the Hardys, "'That nerve gas will knock out enough people to start riots from coast to coast. The government will be overthrown'" (172). In 1970 such a plot would strike adults as simplistic and far-fetched. After September 11, 2001, however, the idea of terrorists attacking a nerve gas depot would be seen as a credible threat.

In the following novel *Danger on Vampire Trail* (1971) Fenton Hardy introduces his sons to a new criminal enterprise — identity theft. He explains the modus operandi of an ingenious gang of criminals who stole information from a credit card company: "'The swindlers apparently got hold of Magnacard's master file — important data on all the clients, including copies of their signatures. They duplicated the credit cards perfectly, then forged identification papers — drivers' licenses and the like. They purchase goods which are then billed to the owner of the charge card'" (3). Frank and Joe then investigate a crime that would not captivate the public until the end of the century.

As in the previous novels, Frank and Joe Hardy are agents of social stability. They help defeat terrorists and white collar criminals. Though young, they are trusted by authority figures, from Pentagon admirals to local sheriffs. In most cases they are recognized as being young but given the respect of full adulthood. When doubt arises, they introduce themselves as being the sons of Fenton Hardy, which generally dismisses any lingering doubts about their skill and maturity.

The streamlined novels lack the colorful asides of the McFarlane era. Unlike the riotous comedy of the fake bomb in Rocco's fruit stall in *The Tower Treasure*, the later books feature at best rare bits of humor. In *The Masked Monkey* Chet Morton, who seems to take up a new hobby or business venture in each novel, uses a suction machine to retrieve golf balls from water hazards at local country clubs. In one scene Chet, accompanied by Frank and Joe, is driving a pickup truck full of golf balls when the tailgate opens:

> As they went through the main intersection, a wild uproar broke out behind them. Horns blew. People shouted.
> "What's wrong?" Chet muttered. "I didn't go through a stoplight!"
> Joe, looking back, cried out, "We're paving the avenue with golf balls! The tailgate's open. We're losing them!"
> Their cargo was streaming out of the pickup into the crossing. Pedestrians went into frantic contortions as the golf balls rolled under their feet. Cars jolted to a halt. Traffic was snarled in four directions [17–18].

The scene harkens back to the snowball fights of the McFarlane era when the chums benignly rebel against authority represented by oafish Con Riley. In this scene, however, the boys are obedient and compliant, the writer making sure this bit of humor is quickly followed by the chums demonstrating proper respect for authority and social responsibility:

> Chet pulled over to the curb. "We're in for it now," he groaned.
> "You can say that again," Frank muttered. "Here comes the traffic cop."
> "And he's not too happy about running the obstacle course we just set up," Joe added.
> "Everybody out!" the officer commanded the three youths. "Start picking them up!"
> Frank, Joe, and Chet meekly climbed out of the truck and began gathering the golf balls. A group of youngsters pitched in for the fun of it. When the balls were back in the truck, Chet double-checked the tailgate before driving off.
> "Lucky I didn't get a ticket," he sighed.
> "And fortunately nobody got hurt," Frank said [18].

Frank and Joe's fidelity to adult authority is further demonstrated when they agree to help a wealthy industrialist locate his missing son. The father admits there is a "generation gap" between himself and his son, whom he states "'had some weird ideas I didn't go along with'" (2). He recognizes that because the Hardys are teenagers themselves, they will be able to "'speak his lingo'" and "'get through to him'" (3). The Hardy boys appear as adolescents upholding and reaffirming adult values, operating almost as undercover agents for an older generation.

The Sting of the Scorpion mimics the 1977 movie *Black Sunday* with its tale of terrorism and airships. The book makes several references to the 1937 crash of the *Hindenburg*, building on, perhaps, the 1975 film starring George C. Scott. As in many of the previous novels, Frank and Joe stumble onto a local mystery connected to a larger investigation conducted by their father. On page 1, Frank and Joe hear an engine roaring over their house and rush out to see the gleaming airship *Safari Queen* flying over Bayport. Described as the largest dirigible built since the *Hindenburg*, the ship is bringing a load of animals from Africa to a nearby wildlife park. As the boys watch, there is a powerful explosion and an elephant tumbles from the airship. The animal plunges through the sky then blows up. Convinced the elephant was a dummy, they debate whether the whole thing is a bizarre publicity stunt to advertise the Wild World animal park. Puzzled by the strange sight, they decide to investigate and head to the airship's nearby base.

The Quinn Air Fleet, operator of the *Safari Queen*, is owned by Lloyd Quinn, an ambitious entrepreneur who extols the use of mammoth airships. These aircraft, he tells the boys, can cheaply carry 300 tons of cargo long distances and reach remote regions because they do not need airports. Recently, his company has been threatened and his giant airship sabotaged.

Fenton Hardy then informs Frank and Joe that he has been hired by the federal government to round up a group of political terrorists known as Scorpio who will "'use any form of terror to hurt American companies and individuals they don't like'" (36). He suspects that the Quinn Air Fleet is the next target of the gang, which accuses the firm of being an "imperialist tool" used to "loot the resources of new African countries" (37).

As Fenton Hardy tracks down the terrorists' headquarters in New York City, Frank and Joe, along with a newly acquired black chum, investigate leads involving the Wild World animal park and a rival airship line. With the roundup of the terrorist gang and the head of the rival airship company, who sympathized with the unnamed foreign power financing Scorpio, the skies of Bayport are again safe for dirigibles.

An Ending and New Beginnings

The Sting of the Scorpion appeared without the standard "throw ahead" preview to the next novel in the series, breaking a tradition established by Edward Stratemeyer fifty years before. This was the last of the original series, and the last Hardy Boys title to be issued in hardcover. The syndicate had published fifty-eight Hardy Boys novels with Grosset & Dunlap that had sold over fifty million copies. The series book had all but died out with Raggedy Ann dolls and radio dramas, but a popular television show in the late Seventies with its stream of merchandising kept the Hardy Boys (and Nancy Drew) books alive and well. Now depicted wearing bell bottoms, platform shoes, and sideburns, Frank and Joe were being read by children whose grandparents received *The Tower Treasure* or *The Secret of the Old Mill* as Christmas gifts in the 1920s.

The syndicate decided to end its long relationship with Grosset & Dunlap to pursue an opportunity with another publisher. Simon & Schuster would carry the Hardy Boys into the twenty-first century in a number of paperback formats. Grosset & Dunlap continues to print the original fifty-eight titles. *The Tower Treasure*, first published in 1927, is now read by children born after 9/11.

Chapter 7

Race

> At first Tom Wat was not inclined to translate the note. With loyalty to his race he did not want to explain anything to the white boys.
> —*Footprints Under the Window*, 1933

The early Hardy Boys novels, like motion pictures, best sellers, Broadway musicals, radio shows, and comic books, reflected the prevailing attitudes of their times. Stratemeyer's historical fiction was patriotic, bordering on jingoistic pronouncements of American superiority. Overall, however, his series books had fewer of the vicious stereotypes and ethnic slurs found in supposedly better-written juvenile novels such as Booth Tarkington's *Penrod*. McFarlane's Hardy Boys books use ethnic characters as villains and for comic relief, relying on standard stereotypes found in Hollywood films until the Second World War.

The Hardy Boys, however, differ from the standard series fiction of the Twenties by making an early, though highly flawed, stab at ethnic diversity.

Jews and Italians

The original outline Edward Stratemeyer provided Leslie McFarlane included a list of Frank and Joe's chums with a few notations:

Chet Morton, school chum. Mr. Morton real estate dealer. Live mile outside Bayport. *Chet,* full of fun and jokes.
Perry Robinson, "Slim," school chum, likes to box.
Jerry Gilroy, Phil Cohen (Jew), *Tony Prito* (Italian) at school.[1]

The inclusion of a Jew and an Italian mark a striking departure from the all–American world of series fiction in which nearly all the heroes and those associated with them have solidly WASPish names — Hardy, Swift, Scott, Martin, Sherwood, Drew. Stratemeyer was interested in volume sales. His target market was middle-class, middle-America. His books avoided politics and social criticism, edging on patriotic xenophobia when it came to his series heroes traveling overseas or encountering foreigners at home.

The inclusion of a Jewish and an Italian character in the Twenties is notable. Warren G. Harding's "Return to Normalcy" was a time of resurgent nativism and isolationism following the First World War. In his 1920 bid for reelection, Senator James Phelan, former mayor of San Francisco, used the phrase "Keep California White" in campaign posters. That year John Rankin was elected to Congress, where he would openly rant against Jews (frequently using the word "kike" in speeches) for the next thirty years. Another Congressman would introduce legislation making it a federal crime to join the B'nai B'rith Anti-Defamation League.[2] The Ku Klux Klan was then at its height of popularity and influence. It claimed four million members, including members of Congress and local officials throughout the South and Midwest. In the Twenties the Klan opposed not only African Americans but also Jews and Catholics. Al Smith's 1928 presidential campaign sparked a flurry of cross-burnings and anti–Catholic cartoons.

Hostility to Jews and Italians was intense. Two million Jews, many from Russia and Eastern Europe, had arrived in the United States between 1880 and 1920. During the same period twice as many Italians entered the United States, the largest number of immigrants from a single country to arrive in a com-

The Mark on the Door, 1934.

parable period. They clustered in distinct communities, and their appearance, language, and religion troubled nativists, who believed their nation was imperiled by this invasion of aliens. Books like Lothrop Stoddard's *The Rising Tide of Color* (1924) and Martin Grant's *The Passing of the Great Race* (1916) inflamed anti-immigrant sentiments. Grant's book, which was reprinted throughout the Twenties and sold over a million and a half copies, specifically labeled Jews and Italians as threats to America's future. Grant highlighted New York City, the largest metropolis near the Hardys' Bayport, as bearing the worst of the immigrant flood. "New York," he argued, "is becoming a *cloaca gentium* which will produce many amazing racial hybrids and some ethnic horrors that will be beyond the powers of future anthropologists to unravel."[3]

Beginning in 1918 many major universities, including Cornell, Columbia, Harvard, and Yale, instituted quotas restricting the number of Jews they would admit, especially to medical and dental schools. A noted exception was Middlesex University outside Boston, which blamed its failure to receive AMA accreditation, in part, on its refusal to limit Jewish enrollment. Other restrictions against Jews were commonplace and deeply entrenched. The Borscht Belt resorts of the Catskills began largely because middle-class Jews found it difficult to obtain vacation accommodations elsewhere. Hotels, restaurants, country clubs, apartment houses, and whole towns were restricted. Even in Hollywood, where Jews presided over major film studios, country clubs refused membership to non–Gentiles. The Hillcrest Country Club was created to serve Jewish entertainers and executives excluded from existing organizations. Buyers of Model T's frequently received a copy of Henry Ford's anti–Semitic book *The International Jew* as a premium item courtesy of the Ford Motor Company. Henry Ford implicated Jews as major forces behind bootlegging, white slavery, Hollywood tripe, and jazz in his newspaper, the *Dearborn Independent*, which republished *The Protocols of the Elders of Zion*. Harry Truman's diary contained disparaging remarks about Jews. Even though he supported the recognition of Israel in 1948, he explained to a Jewish interviewer years after leaving the White House that his wife would not receive Jews in her home.

The intensity of anti–Semitism in the Twenties shocked even African Americans. Bayard Rustin, an organizer of the March on Washington in 1963, campaigned for Al Smith in 1928. He accompanied a Jewish friend to distribute Smith flyers and buttons at a country club, where they were "terribly abused." Rustin was struck by the fact that "nobody spit at me, or spit on me or called me a bastard, but they did him. That was when I discovered that very often Jews were treated even worse than blacks."[4]

Leslie McFarlane did little with the Phil Cohen character. He did not openly identify the Hardy chum as a Jew until the third book where he is introduced as being "a diminutive, black-haired Jewish boy who was one of their friends" (*The Secret of the Old Mill*, 20). In some novels Phil Cohen makes only marginal appearances, his name listed alongside other minor chums like Perry Robinson and Biff Hooper attending a celebratory feast or high school outing. When Phil Cohen appears in the novels of the 1970s, there is no mention of his religion, but he remains something of a chum apart. He is the only chum who plays the piano. While all the other boys play all–American football for Bayport High, Phil is described as being a "lightweight" who plays tennis (*The Mysterious Caravan*, 3). The same novel notes that Phil Cohen is planning a medical career, a stereotypical Jewish profession. Although Phil never plays a role as large as Tony or Chet, his mere inclusion represents a striking departure from the all–Gentile world presented in juvenile series fiction. For many American children, especially those in the South and Midwest, Phil Cohen may have been the first Jew, real or fictional, they came into contact with. The fact that a Jew was accepted by the all–American Hardy Boys without question marked a degree of uncommon tolerance, particularly in the novels published in the Twenties and early Thirties.

Tony Prito becomes, after Chet Morton, the most significant of the Hardy chums. He rises from the role of extra to supporting character in the later novels. In the Twenties, Italians were perhaps just behind Jews in facing discrimination and suspicion. For many Americans of the era, including demographers and sociologists, Italians were deemed "non-white." When a mob attacked Italian-Americans in West Frankfort, Illinois, in 1920, newspapers dubbed the clash a "race riot."[5]

Italian immigrants clustered in the Little Italys of major cities. They were Catholic. Often excluded from established Catholic communities, Italian immigrants built their own churches, which took on a distinct, ethnic flavor. The widespread practice of sending their children to parochial schools further estranged Italian-Americans — or "Italo-Americans" as they were called — from mainstream society. For many native-born Americans, particularly in the South, Italians were "colored people" and subject to semi-segregation.

The hostility to Italians was cruel and pervasive. When a jury failed to convict nine Italians accused of killing the police superintendent of New Orleans in 1890, a mob, led by members of the local bar, stormed the jail where the defendants were being held pending trial on lesser charges. Eight Italians were shot, and three others were taken out and lynched. The action of the vigilantes was hailed not only by the local press but also by a *New York Times* editorial, which opened with a stinging denouncement of Italian immigrants: "These sneaking and cowardly Sicilians, the descendants of bandits and assassins, who have transported to this country the lawless passions, the cutthroat passions and the oathbound societies of their native country, are to us a pest without mitigation. Lynch law was the only recourse open to the people of New Orleans."[6] The well-known Italian personalities of the time were generally negative. Aside from Marconi and Caruso, most Italian names appearing in newspapers were associated with crime, violence, extremism, and decadence. This was the era of Sacco and Vanzetti, Mussolini, Al Capone, and Valentino. Italians were associated with both anarchism and socialism, leftist trade unions and fascism.

Conservatives were alarmed by the role Italians played in leftist and revolutionary movements. Newspapers and magazines called sit-down strikes "Italian strikes." Louis Fraina (portrayed by Paul Sorvino in *Reds*) was a leading figure in the American Communist Party. Italian-born anarchist Luigi Galleani edited the Italian-language newsletter *Cronaca Sovversiva* (*Subversive Chronicle*) which advocated "propaganda by the deed" and the violent overthrow of the United States government. Addressed to Italian radicals, his newsletter printed names and addresses of business leaders, strike-breakers, and other "enemies of the people," creating a virtual hit list. For twenty-five cents, readers could purchase a bomb-making manual sold under the title *Health is in You!* Galleani's followers sent mail bombs to thirty prominent Americans in April 1919. Two months later, the Galleanists detonated eight bombs in several cities on a single day, targeting judges, businessmen, an immigration inspector, and a church. Carlo Valdinoci, a close Galleani associate, was killed when the bomb he was placing on the porch of Attorney General Mitchell Palmer's home exploded prematurely. When Galleani was deported to Italy in 1919, his American followers responded with waves of bomb attacks that continued off and on until 1932. Galleanists were suspected of the Wall Street bombing in 1920 that killed thirty-eight and injured over four hundred.[7]

Liberals were troubled by the Italian American infatuation with Mussolini. By the early 1920s thousands of Italian immigrants had joined Fascist organizations in New York City. Smaller *Fasci* were organized in other major cities. Established Italian organizations like the Sons of Italy were suspected of promoting fascism, as were Italian language schools. San Francisco alone had nine such schools. In Chicago enthusiastic crowds of flag-waving Italians greeted the arrival of Fascist air marshal Balbo when his fleet of twenty-four seaplanes landed on Lake Michigan during the Century of Progress World's Fair in 1933. In San Francisco's Italian community Mussolini was an ethnic hero: "Mussolini had been their champion, the modern strongman who would make their old nation a power, a world model.... The matrons of North Beach proudly sent *Il Duce* their gold wedding bands. He would melt them down to fund the glory of *La Nuova Italia* and send back copies of the rings, made by Italian craftsmen in steel."[8] After Pearl Harbor, thousands of Italians (including many language school teachers) would be interned along with the Japanese, and government posters would discourage the speaking of Italian, which was branded "the enemy's language."

Prohibition brought immense wealth and power to organized crime figures in the Twenties, many of whom had Italian names—Capone, Nitti, Genna, Belcastro, Accardo, Luciano, and Torrio. Crime itself had an Italian tinge as terms like *Mafia* and *La Cosa Nostra* began to appear in print. Popular culture followed suit. Books like W. R. Burnett's *Little Caesar* (1929) popularized the stereotype of the "dark oily" spaghetti-eating gunmen with names like Rico, Tony, Vettori, and Otero. The fact that Italian judges, police officers, and professionals would serve as pallbearers at a gangster's funeral or attend his daughter's wedding out of community fidelity led to conspiracy theories and charges of secret allegiances. The code of silence—*omerta*—suggested that even law-abiding Italian immigrants had dangerous ethnic loyalties that resisted assimilation and threatened American society.

Rudolph Valentino, America's first motion picture sex symbol, was held responsible for the decline in public morals, especially among the young. Clergymen found the outright sexual adoration of a film star by women, many of them married, distasteful and threatening. Valentino was charged with both inflaming female passions and perverting masculinity. A *Chicago Tribune* editorial blamed the star of *The Sheik* for the "effeminization" of the American male. His funeral took a bizarre political turn when, as a publicity stunt, a number of men in Fascist uniform appeared, claiming to be an honor guard sent by Mussolini.

Richard Ben Cramer would credit Joe DiMaggio's popularity with Italian Americans in the late Thirties with their hunger for a hero after the invasion of Ethiopia tarnished the image of *Il Duce*:

> He wasn't from Mussolini, or for Mussolini. Joe was everything the papers said and more.... He played that clean American game ... in God's own sunshine, on pristine grass. He was strong, but shy — a regular Joe — from a big family, working people, who'd made their way by honest labor. He played for a team whose very name stood for America. By his natural grace, he'd made them champions.... DiMaggio was their American story. He was the face they could show in their new world.[9]

But in 1926 when Stratemeyer outlined the Hardy Boys series, Italians were still commonly associated with conspiracies, vendettas, feuds, violence, blackmail, and subversion.

The influx of Jewish and Italian immigrants alarmed nativists and prompted calls for immigration restrictions. The Immigration Act of 1924 established quotas for each nation. Designed to halt the immigration of "undesirables" from Southern and Eastern Europe (i.e., Jews and Italians), the act had a dramatic impact. From 1900 to 1910 about 200,000 Italians immigrated to the United States annually. The new immigration act limited the number of Italian immigrants to 4,000 a year.

For a businessman catering to middle-class tastes, Stratemeyer took something of a risk in 1926 by casting Phil Cohen and Tony Prito as chums who are unquestionably accepted as equals by Frank and Joe Hardy.

This stab at diversity, however, was not without its blemishes.

The Tower Treasure contains the most elaborate scene of ethnic humor in the series. It plays on common stereotypes and current events of the 1920s. Fenton Hardy faces a dilemma. He wants to get to New York to interview the dying Red Jackley before the bumbling Bayport cops interfere. The boys conspire to sidetrack the police and call upon their chums for help. Among the gang is Tony Prito, introduced as an Italian-born immigrant, who speaks with a pronounced accent:

> "What's the mattah?" asked Tony Prito. Tony was the son of a prosperous Italian building contractor, but he had not yet been in America long enough to talk the language without an accent, and his attempts were frequently the cause of much amusement to his companions. He was quick and good-natured, however, and laughed as much at his own errors as any one else did [130].

The boys propose and reject various schemes, leading Tony Prito to muse, "'If we were in Italy we could get the Black Hand to help'" (132). The other chums become excited at the idea. When Tony points out there is no Black Hand society in Bayport, the chums decide to create one.

The boys fashion a fake bomb by wrapping up an old alarm clock in a box. They place the bomb under a fruit stand located near the Bayport police station. The stand owner is an Italian named Rocco, described as "a simple, genial soul, who believed almost everything he heard and, like most of his countrymen, he was of an excitable nature" (133–134). True to the stereotype, Rocco talks with his hands, reciting his fruit prices "with much explanatory waving of arms" (134).

To set up the bomb plot, Chet objects to Rocco's prices, arguing that a fruit peddler on the next street has cheaper oranges. Rocco explodes with Latin outrage:

> "He no can do!" shrieked Rocco. "My price is da low." Then, angered by this reflection on the prices of his wares, he burst into a lengthy explanation of the struggles confronting a poor Italian trying to get along in a new country. He grabbed Chet by the coat collar, dragged him to a corner of the fruit stall, bade him inspect the fruit, gabbled off prices, and generally worked himself into a state of high indignation. In the meantime, Tony Prito made good use of his time to shove the mysterious package under the front of the stall. Then he joined the other boys who had screened his movements by gathering about Rocco.
>
> "You'll have the Black Hand after you if you keep on charging such high prices — that's all I can say!" declared Chet, as the boys moved away.

"Poof! W'at do I care for da Blacka Hand. No frighten me!" said Rocco bravely, but he gulped when he said it and there was no doubt that the shot had gone home [134–135].

A half hour later Phil Cohen stops at the stand, buys a banana, and chats with Rocco who proclaims, "'I sella da good fruit at da good price'"(135). Phil knocks an apple to the ground then bending over to retrieve it, remarks "'Oi! What's this?'" as he retrieves the fake bomb Tony had planted. The ticking package has the effect the boys anticipated, and Rocco goes ballistic:

> Rocco, in his white apron, was dancing about in the middle of the street, yelling, "Bombs! Police! Da Blacka Hand!" Then, suddenly fearing that the supposed bomb might explode at any moment, he whirled rapidly about and raced down the street away from the stand, in the general direction of the police station [136].

Just as Chief Collig and Detective Smuff are leaving to catch their train, a distraught Rocco implores them to save him from the Black Handers, screaming "Da bomb, she go 'teek-tock'" (137).

The cowardly Collig and Smuff take cover and order Patrolman Riley to pour water on the bomb. After the dumb Irish cop pours innumerable buckets of water over the package, a trembling Detective Smuff unwraps the crumbling parcel and the alarm clock clatters to the street, leading the chums to laugh in delight. The train to New York has left, giving Fenton Hardy a free hand to interview the dying criminal.

For Italian immigrants in the 1920s, a Black Hand bomb was no laughing matter. The Black Hand terrified Italian-Americans, especially small merchants. Although rumored to be a highly organized, national criminal enterprise, the Black Hand, in most instances, consisted of small independent gangs using similar tactics and symbols to terrorize their victims and potential witnesses. The size and influence of the Black Hand may have been exaggerated because police and reporters often ascribed unsolved crimes involving Italians to the work of the secret underworld organization.[10]

Black Handers extorted money from prosperous Italians, sending them threatening letters demanding payoffs embellished with sinister images of knives, daggers, skulls, or a black hand. Typically, a letter would order a merchant to drop a sum of money at an intersection at a specified time or risk death, the kidnapping of a child, or an attack on his business. Bombs were a favorite weapon.[11]

A 1913 article in the *Chicago Daily News* provides insight into the extent of Black Hand activities and the media's derisive attitude toward Italian-Americans:

> In the first ninety-three days of this year, 55 bombs were detonated in the spaghetti zone. Not one of the 55, so far as can be determined, was set for any

reason other than the extraction of blackmail. A detective of experience in the Italian quarter estimates that ten pay tribute to one who is sturdy enough to resist until he is warned by a bomb. Freely conceding that this is all guess work, then 550 men will have paid the Mano Nera since January 1. The Dirty Mitt never asks for less than $1,000. If a compromise of $200 was reached in each case of the 550 cases, "Black Handers" profited by $110,000 in 93 days. That's an average of $1,111 a day, which is fair profit for the expenditure of five two-cent stamps, a dollar's worth of gun-powder and 15 quarts of wood alcohol chianti, that being the usual ration. Perhaps these figures are inaccurate in detail, but they are conservative enough en masse. Well informed Italians have never put the year's tribute to the "Black Hand" at less than half a million dollars.[12]

Rocco could hardly be blamed for assuming the ticking package was a bomb. In Chicago alone in the 1920s over 700 bombings were attributed to the Black Hand, which was often used by organized crime figures to force barbers and other small businessmen into gang-run unions or trade associations.[13]

McFarlane uses an Italian to plant the bomb and a Jew to discover it. Having the dumb Irish cop dutifully pour buckets of water over an old alarm clock completes the ethnic farce.

Though tasteless by twenty-first-century standards, the ethnic humor reflected in this scene fits the pattern established in Hollywood films and popular books of the era. Rocco is excitable. His dialect is pure Chico Marx. But he, like the other ethnic minorities in the book, is not depicted in a sinister or vicious manner.

Tony Prito manages to lose his accent in volume two, published the same year as *The Tower Treasure*. His Standard English remarks conclude *The House on the Cliff*: "'Once I wanted my father to buy an automobile and he bought a motorboat instead. Now he wants to sell the boat and buy an automobile. Just let him try it! That boat gave me more fun in one day than I'd ever had since we came to the States'" (212). In later books Tony appears increasingly assimilated and is no longer introduced as being from Bayport's "Italian colony." In *The Great Airport Mystery* (1930) Tony announces plans to attend college rather go into the building business with his father. In the postwar novels, when Tony Prito often plays a major supporting role, he is presented without any ethnic appellation. The only hint of his ancestry is the spelling of his last name. His near total assimilation is demonstrated in 1956's *The Clue in the Embers* when he takes Frank and Joe home for a dinner of spaghetti and homemade apple pie.

By 1972 Tony and Phil are given only hints of being different than Frank and Joe: "They arrived at the Hardy house to find their pals Phil Cohen and Tony Prito waiting for them. Phil was the sensitive, studious type, but could be counted on when Frank and Joe were on a dangerous mission. Olive-skinned Tony, the son of a Bayport contractor, was another friend who frequently helped the Hardys solve mysteries" [*The Masked Monkey*, 18]. It takes a near death experience for Tony to reveal his ethnic roots. In *The Clue of the Hissing Serpent* (1974) when their small plane flies into a vicious storm, Tony blurts out to Joe, "'*Mama mia!* ... The wings are coming off!'" (80).

Asians

If the stereotypes of Jews and Italians are patronizing, the images of Asians in the early novels are blatantly racist. The first Asian referred to in the series is a dope smuggler called Li Chang. When Fenton Hardy and his sons are captured by the smugglers in *The House on the Cliff* (1927), one of the gang suggests to the leader Ganny Snackley that they rid themselves of the detectives by handing them over to Li Chang. Snackley is delighted with the idea, noting, "'Leave it to Li Chang. The old villain would just like to have three white men in his power. He'll attend to them'" (171). When captured, Li Chang is described as "a small, wizened little fellow with a villainous countenance" (206).

The image of the sinister Chinaman returns in full force in *Footprints Under the Window* (1932) which features Louie Fong, a villain of Fu Manchu proportions. The Hardy Boys encounter their Asian nemesis in a Bayport laundry. Dropping off shirts at the local laundry, they are not greeted by "quiet, friendly, and smiling" Sam Lee but his replacement, who appears from the back of the shop and accuses them of eavesdropping:

> There was a sharp exclamation in Chinese, then a silence. A swift pattering of slippers on the floor heralded the approach from beyond the counter of the most villainous-looking Oriental the boys had ever seen. He had a long, lean face with high cheekbones. His head was pointed and almost bald, while a cruel mouth was partly concealed by a drooping wisp of mustache. His eyes were as cold and glittering as those of a snake.
> "Why you listen?"
> "Where's Sam Lee?" demanded Frank.
> "Sam Lee gone. Far away. Back to China. Me Louie Fong. What you want? Why you listen?" snarled the man.
> "If that's the way you talk to customers you won't get much business," remarked Joe. "We have some laundry here. We want it done by tomorrow."
> "No can do," returned the Chinaman impatiently. He ripped a laundry check from a pad on the counter. "Thlee-fo' day. Not befo.'"
> "All right," sighed Frank. "Here's the laundry."
> Louie Fong seized the soiled linen, tossed Frank the check, and retreated.
> "You go 'way now," he snapped. "No listen."
> The boys went out onto the street.
> "Nice man, eh," grinned Chet.
> "I'd hate to meet him in a dark alley," admitted Frank. "He's an ugly one" [6–7].

That evening the boys go to the dock to pick up Aunt Gertrude and are met by Sidney Pebbles, who informs them their aunt slipped on a plank and will be taking a later boat. Pebbles also tells them a similar tale of a vanishing Chinese laundryman:

> "We had a laundryman named Joe Sing who was very popular. One morning he disappeared and there was a new Chinaman in the laundry. He didn't know anything about Joe Sing, he said. About a week later I was returning home late at night and I met Joe Sing on the street.
> "'When did you come back, Joe?'" I asked the Chinaman.
> "He shook his head and said: '"Me not Joe. Me Charlie Wu.'"
> "Well, I was positive he was Joe Sing but I didn't argue the matter. Two days later I went into the laundry and there was Joe Sing behind the counter, as large as life. I asked him if he hadn't met me on the street but he said he had just returned from New York that morning. Next day I passed the place and found the laundry closed. Both Joe Sing and the other Chinaman had disappeared and no one in town ever saw them again" [17].

The mystery is compounded when Sidney Pebbles turns out to be an imposter, who slipped Aunt Gertrude a doped drink on the boat to knock her unconscious and use her absence as a ruse to be invited to the Hardy home. After his departure, the brothers discover some of their father's papers are missing and search around their house for clues. They discover footprints under a window, and Chet Morton retrieves a scrap of paper with a message in Chinese characters.

Joe suggests taking the note to Louie Fong, but the others doubt if they can trust him to provide an honest translation. Frank admits they will have to "'look around for a more dependable Chinaman'" (48). When the brothers decide to return to the dock, Chet reminds them that just the night before there had been a fight among Chinamen along the waterfront. "'If the police hadn't shown up in time,'" he tells them, 'there would have been corpses all over the place'" (48).

When Frank asks the cause of the fight, Chet tells them that even one of the hospitalized victims has refused to speak: "'They're a secretive crowd,' he said. 'They like to settle their little quarrels in their own way without getting mixed up with the law. I doubt if the police will ever know just why the battle began'" (49).

The image of secretive rival Chinese gangs plays on a common theme in the 1920s and early 1930s when various tong wars raged in Chinese communities throughout the United States. Popular culture depicted America's Chinatowns as dens of vice, crime, sinister gangs, and bloody feuds. In San Francisco's Chinatown the tongs operated brothels, gambling operations, and opium dens. Rival gangs fought over territory, leading to shootings, murders, and street battles. The tong wars were not confined to major cities. In the 1920s the Chinatown of Pittsburgh was dominated by two fraternal societies—

Hip Sing (Help-Success) and On Leong (Peace-Fraternity) — who engaged in violent confrontations that claimed five lives between 1924 and 1927.[14]

By 1932 the tong wars were actually in decline, but their memory fueled the public's perception of Chinese secrecy, separateness, and viciousness. The image of the villainous and conniving Chinaman was also conveyed in the motion pictures of the era, such as *The Mysterious Dr. Fu Manchu* (1929), *The Return of Fu Manchu* (1930), *The Daughter of Fu Manchu* (1931), and *The Mask of Fu Manchu* (1932), based on the character created by Sax Rohmer. Rohmer's novels, first published in 1913, relate the evil doings of a satanic criminal bent on destroying Western civilization and the white race. He disdains Western weapons such as guns and relies on knives, serpents, and poison to kill. Louie Fong lacks the international scope of Dr. Fu Manchu but evokes his image, down to the bald head, moustache, and evil reptilian eyes.

When the Hardy Boys reach the dock, they find Con Riley on duty. Here there is double ethnic humor. Just as the dumb Irish cop was clueless about the Black Hand bomb in Rocco's fruit stand in *The Tower Treasure*, he is equally obtuse about the mysteries of Chinese gangs:

> "From what I can learn," said Riley with a severe glance at Chet, "the whole business was a food."
> "A what?" said Frank, puzzled.
> "A food. One of them foods among Chinamen. You know."
> "Like chop suey?" inquired Chet, interested.
> "A food, I said," declared Riley. "A battle. A war. A food."
> "A feud!" exclaimed Joe.
> "What were they fighting about?" asked Chet.
> "Nobody knows," Riley replied [53–54].

Riley's attempt to summarize his knowledge of the fight descends into a "Who's on First?" routine as the chums play on the Irishman's thickheaded consternation:

> "Another Chinaman came down to the dock and picked a quarrel with one of the fellows who was here already. So then he went away —"
> "Which Chinaman?" asked Chet.
> "The second Chinaman."
> "Which one was that? The one who was here first?"
> "No," spluttered Riley. "The second Chinaman was the one who had the row with the first Chinaman. He got here second."
> "The first one?"
> Constable Riley flushed.
> "I'm tellin' this story," he said darkly [54].

The Hardys learn that the Chinaman stabbed in the fight is Tom Wat, a "quiet little fellow" who works in a Bayport restaurant. Mr. Wat's stabbing evokes no sympathy from his countryman, Louie Fong. When the boys return to the laundry to collect their clothing they again run into the sinister Asian:

> ...when the boys stepped inside the evil face of Louie Fong popped up from behind the counter like a jack-in-the-box.
> "Hullo! You come fo' laundly. No got," he said sharply.
> "What's the idea?" demanded Frank.
> "Solly. Not got. Tomolla, mebbe." ...
> "Did you know the man who got stabbed, Tom Wat? How is he getting along?"
> "In hospital. Him get all betta soon. Too bad."
> "Too bad he got hurt?"
> "No. Too bad he get all betta," said Louie Fong unsympathetically. "He look fo' tlouble."
> "How was he looking for trouble?"
> Louie Fong's eyes narrowed suspiciously, and he did not reply [73–74].

If Rocco is an excitable Italian fruit peddler afraid of "Da Blacka Hand" in *The Tower Treasure*, he is balanced by a more assimilated and positive countryman in Tony Prito. Tony has a sense of humor about his mangled English and is accepted as one of the chums. He is also solidly upper middle class.

In *Footprints Under the Window*, however, the stereotypes are more intensely racist and unbalanced. Louie Fong's evil nature is associated with his Asian features. He has an "evil, yellow face" (130). In addition to being compared to a snake, Fong is described as being as "quiet and sinister as a cat" (133). Other Hardy adversaries are generally identified as being villainous through a few references to having a "gruff nature" or "snarling" and dropping their final "g's" in dialogue. Louie Fong, however, is given lavish descriptions of his strange, alien, and "sinister" features. When captured by the Hardy Boys, Fong is not even recognizable by the chums as a human being:

> Suddenly he spied Louie Fong in the car.
> "Great suffering hoptoads!" he yelped. "What have you got there? A mummy?"
> Tony Prito's eyes bulged.
> "Is it real?" he squeaked.
> "Of course it's real," said Frank, getting out of the car [183].

The other Chinese in the book remain a race apart. There is no Chinese chum. In other adventures the Hardys can easily separate the guilty from the innocent. But Joe has to ask Sam Lee several times if he is truly opposed to Louie Fong. The Chinese are depicted as exotic, inscrutable, driven by hidden agendas, and seemingly possessed with magical powers. Joe chases after Sam Lee, thinking at first it would be easy to "overtake the old Chinaman," only to discover he has vanished from the street, leading Joe to speculate that he "'must be able to make himself invisible'" (161). Later, Louie Fong escapes from the Hardys when the "wily Oriental" wrenches off his handcuffs and summons his dog Chan for help (190). Tom Wat, though an innocent victim, remains an alien figure. In one scene he turns "white with fear" (100). In another, his eyes are "round with fear" (158). When the boys ask him to translate the note found by Chet Morton, he hesitates, reluctant to betray a fellow Chinese, even one trying to kill him. For Tom Wat racial loyalty overrides self-preservation.

When Wat does speak, he talks with such a stereotyped dialect that the dialogue is formatted to provide readers with a running translation:

"You say you just got out of the hospital a few minutes ago. What sent you there in the first place?"
"Me got hurt. One — two nights ago," replied Tom Wat. "Chinaboy try killee me."
"Tried to kill you?" asked Pebbles in surprise. "Why should anyone try to kill you?"
"Big fight," returned Tom Wat.
"But what was the fight about?"
"No savvy. Fella no likee me. Come up with big knife. I get hurt."
"And you don't know why you were stabbed?" asked Pebbles incredulously.
"Me gettee square," promised Tom Wat solemnly.
"You'll get square? With whom?"
"Louie Fong gang."
The Hardy Boys started. So Louie Fong was involved in the battle on the wharf!
"What has Louie Fong been doing?" asked Pebbles. "How will you get square with him?"
"Land in jailee klick. Me tell police. Smuglee."
"You'll land him in jail for smuggling!" [86].

When Tom Wat is nearly killed by a knife thrown by Louie Fong outside a roadhouse, the "little Chinaman" is fearful, knowing that "even Louie Fong's arrest would not save him from revenge and death at the hands of the leaders, and a cruel, heartless death it would be" (104). The Hardy Boys offer to help Tom Wat despite Sidney Pebbles' warning that "'Chinese feuds are good things to leave alone'" (104).

What follows is one of the most perverse scenes in the entire Hardy Boys series, one that plays on both ethnic and gender stereotypes and is laced with white male supremacy. The boys decide the only way to hide Tom Wat from the clutches of Louie Fong is to disguise him through cross dressing:

"We can dress him up as a girl. He's just the type."
Tom Wat took alarm at this suggestion. He shook his head violently.
"No dlessee me up allee same like girl," he objected. "No likee" [106].

Sidney Pebbles suggests that one of the maids at the roadhouse might be willing to help. Much is made of the fact that the Chinese male is about the same size as a white female, emphasizing his diminutive stature. Pebbles asks an employee about her wardrobe:

> "Have you an extra outfit you'd like to sell?"
> "We'll buy you a new one," volunteered Frank quickly.
> "No girl would miss a chance of getting a new outfit," said Jean, dimpling. "What sort of clothes do you want?"
> "Just a plain dress, shoes, silk stockings and a hat," said Pebbles.
> "Our friend here," and he indicated Tom Wat, "has decided that he'd like to dress as a girl."
> Jean looked at the wretched Chinaman and she began to giggle [108].

Tom is given women's clothes and told to change. Unable to master the ways of Western female fashion, he returns tottering on high heels with the dress on backwards and still wearing his trousers.

The girl, Pebbles, and the Hardys roar with laughter at the sight. A chambermaid spots the strangely dressed Wat, mistakes him for a "female tramp" and runs away in fright. The grumbling Tom Wat is sent back to try again:

> "I'll go and lend him a hand," said Frank.
> A little later, when he emerged with Tom Wat again, the disguise was more than passable. The dress fitted his slight figure perfectly, the hat drooped coyly over one eye and the stockings were trim and neat. Jean clapped her hands.
> "Why, that's simply perfect!" she exclaimed. "Now a little touch of make-up—"
> She fled toward her own room and returned quickly with powder, rouge and lipstick. She advanced on the embarrassed Tom Wat.
> "No likee. No likee," he said hastily, backing away.
> Frank and Joe snickered.
> "Whether you like it or not you're going to be disguised properly," said the girl firmly as she grasped his chin. "Hold still, now."
> Expertly she dabbed rouge and powder on his cheeks, applied lipstick, penciled his eyebrows and then stood back to survey her handiwork.
> "There!" she announced proudly. "What do you think of him now?"
> "He's a knockout!" exclaimed Sidney Pebbles jubilantly [111].

The forced cross dressing takes Tom Wat from being a "passable" transvestite through a complete transformation into an Asian "ladyboy" so that "he stood before them as a neat, shy and rather pretty girl, his delicate features and clear complexion adding to the effect" (111–112). The disguise works so well that Callie Shaw and Iola Morton are jealous when they learn Frank and Joe have been spotted with a "swell-looking girl" in their roadster. The language of this transsexual episode is strikingly suggestive: "Submissively, the Chinaman donned the girl's outfit, powdered his nose and completed the various details of his disguise" (151).

Later in the novel when Frank decides to wear a disguise, he uses the same makeup his father used when he went underground to investigate a tong war in New York City's Chinatown. Frank, of course, dresses himself as a Chinese male. Only Tom Wat has to be transformed by both race and gender to escape Louie Fong.

Captured by Louie Fong, the Hardys are tormented by the Oriental villain who exhibits a greater degree of sadistic glee than expressed by white car thieves and kidnappers: "There was a burst of maniacal laughter. The boys looked up. There, behind a tiny grating in the wall, they saw the sinister yellow face of Louie Fong. His teeth were bared in a hideous grin as he gloated over their plight" (208). They escape when Frank manages to unlock a door and allow the still cross-dressed Tom Wat to flee. His disguise is so perfect that even veteran detective Fenton Hardy mistakes him for a girl.

A more positive image of the Chinese occurs in *The Melted Coins*, published twelve years later. The word "Chinaman" appears just once. Otherwise, Wu Sing, a merchant and coin collector, and an unnamed laundryman are referred to being "Chinese" or "Oriental." Wu Sing is treated respectfully by Frank and Joe who call upon his numismatic expertise. When they are waylaid in Bayport's unsavory waterfront district, an observant laundryman calls Wu Sing "a respected and powerful figure in the life of Bayport's Chinese community" (104). Wu Sing summons the police who free the Hardy Boys from the clutches of a piratical tattoo artist. The helpful Asians remain humble and mysterious, bowing and vanishing before anyone could thank them (107).

Sixteen years later, the image of the Chinese improves markedly in *The Mystery of the Chinese Junk* (1960). In this novel the usual chum cast of the 1920s — Chet Morton, Biff Hooper, and Tony Prito (who is no longer introduced as being an Italian-American) — is rounded out with one-book chum Chinese-American Jim Foy. Foy tells them that his cousin works for a firm in Staten Island that is selling a second-hand Chinese junk for a fraction of its value. It is June, and the boys decide to start a ferry service on Barmet Bay for a summer job. They agree to share the cost of the junk and take a bus to Staten Island the next day.

When Frank calls Jim Foy outlining their plans, the Chinese-American boy is delighted and speaks in only stilted formal English with no trace of pidgin dialect: "'My good parents say I may go. I will phone my cousin at once and have him place an option on the junk. When shall I meet you fellows?'" (7). The Hardys retrieve two hundred dollars of their reward money from their father's safe then go downstairs to call Chet Morton. Hanging up the phone, Frank sees a "fearsome-looking Oriental face" pressed against the window, the "man's teeth bared in an evil grimace!" (9). Frank discovers that the scary face belongs to Jim Foy who jokingly calls himself "the Oriental Avenger" when he contorts his features.

The novel contains generally positive images of the Chinese. The boys sample Asian food in a Chinatown restaurant, admire the exotic goods in a Chinese shop, and learn a bit about Chinese culture. They are told, for instance, that Chinese junks have glass eyes affixed to the bow because, according to an old proverb, "'*Boat with no eyes cannot see!*'" (18). There is also a bit of humor. When Jim Foy arrives on the junk, Joe Hardy bows in an Asian fashion, leading the Chinese-American chum to remark, "'Boy, that's corny enough for a Grade D movie about China!'" (46).

Chinese villains, however, are depicted as evil in part because of their Asian features. After purchasing the junk, Frank and Joe are approached by four Chinese, all having "cruel, calculating expressions," who offer to buy the boat from them (19). When they are refused, they become indignant. The four men later approach the Hardys in a Chinese restaurant. While the brothers enjoy their egg rolls and almond cakes, a Chinese man "glided out of the shadows to their booth." He is described as being tall with "a long melon-shaped head and jutting ears" (26). Introducing himself as Chin Gok, he offers again to buy the junk. When his offer is declined a second time, his face goes "pale with rage."

Overall, the level of ethnic stereotypes in this novel is markedly diminished from *Footprints Under the Window* published thirty years earlier. There is no suggestion that the Chinese have clannish loyalties or alien agendas. Jim Foy is as assimilated as Phil Cohen or Tony Prito. There is even a Chinese detective, Ti-Ming, who informs the Hardys that they are entitled to a reward for finding a hidden map to a lost fortune.

African Americans

Frank and Joe Hardy first encounter African Americans during their trip to Montana in 1928's *Hunting for Hidden Gold*. Discovering that they are locked in their train compartment, they pound on the door until they hear "a shuffling of feet in the corridor" and a knock:

"Something foh you, gemmen?"
"Yes—let us out of here!"
The porter tried the handle of the door.
"By golly," he observed, "you done lock yo'selves in."
"We didn't lock ourselves in. Somebody locked *us* in. Haven't you got a key?"
"Jes' a minute" [67].

The boys then hear the porter "shuffling away" in search of a key. If the shuffling porter is reminiscent of Step 'n' Fetchit, the next encounter the boys have with blacks is right out of *Amos and Andy*, complete with rattletrap car.

Waylaid by toughs on a back road, Frank and Joe are struggling against a group of armed men. The boys are outnumbered and about to be overpowered "but for a surprising interruption":

> Down the roadway came a clattering and roaring, and around the other car came plunging an ancient and decrepit Ford with an enormous negro at the wheel. Beside him sat another colored man, and the pair gazed at the struggle before them, with mouths agape and eyes staring. Then the negro driving the car brought it to a stop and clambered down, picking up the car crank as he went.
>
> "You's the speeders what run oveh mah chickens!" he roared, bearing down on the two toughs who were grappling with Frank....
>
> The two colored men rushed into the battle with enthusiasm. The three toughs in the other car had, it appeared, deliberately driven their automobile into a flock of chickens at the side of the road near the negro's farm farther down the road. Revenge, therefore was sweet [77].

The toughs take off, leaving the boys grateful for the intervention of the angry black farmers, who speak in stereotyped dialect:

> "Ef dey runs oveh any moah of mah chickens, Ah'll folley 'em fum heah till Doomsday," declared the big negro.
>
> "You certainly showed up in the nick of time," said Joe, brushing off his coat. "They had us beaten two to one."
>
> "White trash!" declared the other colored man. "Ah knows 'em. Dey jes pool room toughs" [78].

The two black men offer to take the Hardys back to the train station, the driver promising, "dey won't ha'm yoh no moah — not so long as yoh is in dis autymobile" (79). When a grateful Frank and Joe tip him five dollars, the driver beams "with gratification and delight" (81).

Far more racist and sinister stereotypes appear in *The Hidden Harbor Mystery* (1935) in which African Americans appear as secretive and conspiratorial villains rather than bumpkin rescuers. The story involves a complex feud between two Southern families. Taking a train, Chet Morton and the Hardy Brothers encounter Luke Jones, a "burly, thick-set negro, very loudly dressed and with a swaggering, arrogant manner" (83). When the conductor objects to him propping his feet on a seat, he dismisses the conductor's request to obey the rules. "'Fools rules!'" he objects "disdainfully" stating, "'Luke Jones don't stand for no nonsense from white folks! ... Ah pays mah fare, an' Ah puts mah shoes where Ah please!'" (84).

The son of a butler employed by one of the feuding families, Luke Jones is the most offensive depiction of African-Americans in the original Hardy Boys series:

The more he saw of Luke Jones the more he disliked the fellow, who was dressed in a suit of extreme collegiate cut, and wore a pink shirt with a violet necktie. A diamond ring twinkled on his finger, and his patent leather shoes shone.

"Yo' white boys bettah git away from heah, Ah's warnin' yo,'" he said. "You'll git into plenty ob trouble hangin' 'round de Blackstone place. Ah knows who yo' is. Ah knows lots mo' dan you' thinks Ah does, but Ah'm not tellin' nuthin'" [140–141].

Luke's father blames his son's brusque manner on adopting Northern ways:

The old man sniffed contemptuously.
"Wastin' yo' time when yo' talks to *him*. Evah since he's been up No'th with Massa Blackstone he thinks he's smart. Fine new clothes, big diamon' ring, an' he swaggers 'roun' heah lak he own de place."
Jones eyed his son with disfavor. It was evident that he was worried over Luke's apparent prosperity, as well as his unseemly conduct since coming back from up North [141–142].

Luke is referred to as a "colored boy" and called a "black rascal" by Joe. His loud clothes, the diamond ring (stolen from his master), and disrespectful manner are stereotypes of the crude, abrasive black man who "does not know his place." The repeated comments about Luke's behavior changing from exposure in the North play on a stereotyped complaint of the Jim Crow South that blacks became restive or "uppidity" from spending time in the more tolerant North. He is no longer the respectful servant like his father but assertive and independent.

Luke Jones is an Uber-villain like Louie Fong. It turns out that he not only steals from his master, but also is the "'lowdown person'" who vandalizes the Hardys' campsite. He digs a tunnel with the intention of planting explosives under a house and engineers incidents the feuding families blame on each other.

In one scene Chet Morton and the Hardys witness Luke Jones leading a "strange procession" of black men and boys to an initiation ritual, depicted as a kind of Mystic Knights of the Sea Lodge meeting and Ku Klux Klan rally. Luke Jones addresses the group in tones suggestive of *Amos and Andy*:

"Membahs ob dis secret society!" he orated. "We is gathered heah tonight to initiate a new person into our club."
"Heah Ah is, Luke," cried a big Negro, shuffling forward. He was a huge, broad shouldered, bullet-headed youth, very dark, and rather stupid looking.
"Everybody heah knows Jed," continued Luke. "Anybody whut don't want him to join our secret society, jes' step up heah an' say why dey don' want him."
"All right by me"—"Jed's all right"—"Initiate him"—"He make a good membah," shouted several voices....
"Good!" said Luke. "Come on into de clubhouse an' we'll hold de fust part ob de initiation."

The gang trooped off into the old boathouse. Soon lights could be seen flashing beyond some of the windows. After a while there was a wild yell of terror, presumably from the luckless Jed, who was being initiated [179–180].

The secrecy, the hint of barbarism, the reference to a "stupid-looking" black "shuffling" evokes the most offensive racist stereotypes, which are almost nineteenth century in their viciousness. Another stereotype, often used for comic effect in films of the era, occurs in the next scene when Chet falls from a tree into their midst. Instantly, a "colored youth, with a bleat of fear, yells, 'It's a ghost!'" and flees in terror (182).

The group manhandles Chet and decides to cast him adrift in a boat. Rescued by the Hardys, he is left with a "wholesome fear of the heartless fellows" (187). When the Hardy Boys set off to free a member of one of the feuding families, Frank knows "that every second counted" because there "was no telling what that wild society, under the influence of the callous Luke, would do to Ewald Rand" (190).

Luke Jones rivals Louie Fong in absolute villainy. Confronted by the Hardy Boys, his "natural cowardice" asserts itself, and he begins to plead and whine. He admits to robbing his master. When asked about stirring up trouble between the Blackstones and Rands, Luke is defiant:

"You' bet Ah has!" he declared viciously. "Ah done plenty ob t'ings dat each ob 'em blamed on de oder."

Since childhood the vicious fellow had furthered the feud between the rival white families. Desiring to gain prestige with his master, Mr. Blackstone, he had deliberately caused the Rand horses and dogs to come onto the Blackstone property and do some damage. Then he had faked rescues, until finally he had become a favorite servant [199].

These revelations lead Frank to proclaim, "'Luke Jones, you're the worst scoundrel we have ever come across, and we have run into some pretty bad customers'" (199–200). Like *Footprints Under the Window*, *The Hidden Harbor Mystery* was substantially revised in the 1960s to remove dialect and offensive stereotypes.

An African American appears in the following novel, *The Sinister Signpost*. The truck driver of a missing racehorse is a black man who speaks in dialect and comes across as a less vicious but still patronizing stereotype of the docile, uneducated darky. Held against his will in a remote house, he begs his captors to release him saying, "'Ah wants to go home ... I'se gettin' tired of stayin' in dis yeah place'" (110).

In *The Secret Warning* (1938) Joe Hardy goes in blackface to disguise himself. Taking off his makeup, he tells Frank, "I think I've been a colored boy long enough" (94).

Stereotypes of African Americans appear in postwar novels, though the depictions are more benign. In *The Secret of the Lost Tunnel* (1950) Frank and

Joe travel south to locate a lost Civil War treasure buried by a Confederate ancestor of an army general. The general has a black servant named Claude, who is portrayed as the typical butler figure, humble, obedient, respectful, and helpful. When Frank and Joe ask if anyone is alive who remembers the war, Claude directs them to his pastor, who in turn, informs them of an elderly black man who grew up on the lost plantation. Benjamin Bradley speaks with a pronounced dialect:

> "No. I disremember any tunnel, but I knows my grandpop was scared o' the woods along the run."
> "Why?" Joe was first with the question.
> "He once saw Mr. Beauregard swallowed right up by the earth. Grandpop figgered they was some sort o' hole that nobody but ol' Massa Smith knew about."
> "That may be just what we're looking for!" Joe burst out. "Where was the place, Ben?"
> "That I don' know zactly" [192–193)].

African Americans vanish from the Hardy Boys until 1975 when the Hardys befriend a Jamaican in *The Mysterious Caravan*. William is the first black character to be introduced to readers as an equal to Frank and Joe. He speaks Standard English, and like earlier versions of Tony and Phil, is presented favorably with only a hint of ethnicity to distinguish a difference in background rather than in intelligence, class, or social acceptance: "Framed in the entrance stood a tall, well-built black youth, about the same age as the boys from Bayport. He had a handsome face, lit up now by a broad smile. Like the others, he wore cut-off jeans and a tee shirt. Around his neck dangled a small trinket carved in the shape of an African native" (10). William not only assists the chums in their sleuthing but also aids in their education. Joe is described as having "developed a special interest in William's hobby of African lore and his great admiration for King Mansa Musa. He had even learned a few words of Swahili, which William was studying" (11). Through William, readers are introduced to a smattering of African history, culture, and language explained in respectful and positive terms, a distinct departure from the patronizing tone of the earlier depictions of African Americans. During their investigation, Frank and Joe learn that Mansa Musa, the black Muslim king of Mali, set out on the *hadj* in 1324 with a caravan laden with gold, which he distributed along his pilgrimage to Mecca.

The small African trinket becomes a lucky talisman for Joe. In parting with his new friends, Williams gives Joe the necklace. Planning to drop off a precious death mask he found on the beach with the police before leaving Jamaica, Joe is pursued by treasure hunters. Seeking help, he dodges into the back door of a restaurant and is collared by an immense black cook, who recognizes the necklace and demands to know where Joe obtained the African symbol. When he informs him it was a gift from William, the cook immediately casts aside his suspicions and hides Joe from his pursuers.

William remains a valuable asset to the Hardys. After they return to Bayport, he wires them to alert them that their adversaries had followed them on the next plane. He later calls with more information and travels to the United States to help the chums solve the mystery of the ancient death mask. When William is taken captive, the Hardy brothers respond with the same anxious concern they previously showed when their father was abducted. After his rescue, William accompanies the chums on a trip to North Africa, where his knowledge of Arabic and African customs proves valuable.

There is a humorous scene which echoes Joe's blackface disguise in *The Secret Warning* almost forty years before. In pursuing a suspect in Morocco, Joe falls next to dye vat and is splattered with the dark substance. Told that he must wash immediately or be stained for a year, Joe thoroughly scrubs himself with soap and water. His arms remain dark, and William breaks "into a white-toothed smile" and says, "'Joe, now we are brothers! Can you lend me a dollar?'" (154).

The final African American character in the original series appears in *The Sting of the Scorpion* (1979). When Frank and Joe arrive at a wildlife park seeking a clue hidden in a hollow tree, they are greeted by Leroy Mitchell, a park attendant, who instantly recognizes them:

> Leroy Mitchell's eyes widened. "Man alive! Don't tell me you're one of *those* dudes?"
>
> "Which dudes?"
>
> "The ones who solve all the mysteries — the sons of that famous detective."
>
> "You guessed it. That's us," Frank said. "I'm Frank, and this is my brother, Joe."
>
> Leroy broke out in a friendly grin as he shook hands with the boys. "Wait till I tell everyone about meeting you two!"
>
> "How about the tree," Frank asked, glancing around. "If I read this map right, it must be near here."
>
> The black boy studied the diagram for a few moments. "Yeah, it's got to be that big old hollow oak." He pointed to a tree about a hundred yards off, on the right side of the road leading away from lion country.
>
> "Okay if we get out and take a closer look at it?"
>
> "Sure, I guess so. Nothing dangerous around there. But watch your step" [18–19].

Frank and Joe follow Mitchell's directions and examine the tree, breaking a park regulation by leaving their vehicle. Spotting the young detectives, a burly security guard growls at the brothers, demanding to know why they ignored the rule. Noticing that the boys are in trouble, Leroy Mitchell rushes to intervene:

"Take it easy," the black youth said to the officer. "I told them it would be all right to get out their car just this once. They wanted to take a look at the tree."
"Don't you know it's against regulations for visitors to leave their cars?"
"Sure, but they only wanted to get out for a couple of minutes. And there's nothing dangerous around here." ...
"It's still against regulations," the officer said roughly.
"Okay. If I've done anything wrong, report me," Leroy said. "Don't hassle these guys" [21–22].

Aside from his use of words like "dudes" and "hassle," Leroy Mitchell speaks Standard English and exhibits Hardy-like virtues of cool mindedness, diplomacy, maturity, and social responsibility. He plays a small role in the investigation and becomes, briefly, a chum. Later in the novel, the Hardys invite Leroy and his girlfriend to join them on a picnic.

The Seventies characters of William and Leroy contrast sharply with the shuffling porters, *Amos and Andy* farmers in their battered flivver, and the villainous Luke Jones McFarlane depicted in the Twenties and Thirties. Like the rest of popular culture, the Hardy Boys series dramatically altered its depiction of African Americans.

Hispanics

The Mark on the Door (1934) followed *Footprints Under the Window* and again dealt with another "foreign" element. But this book's treatment of Mexicans is markedly different than the previous novel's depiction of the Chinese. Although Mexican characters are repeatedly noted as looking "foreign" with "swarthy" features and "olive skin," they do not speak in dialect. Their dialogue is presented in Standard English with a notation that the character has an accent.

On the track of a missing witness, Fenton Hardy and his sons board a plane to Texas. En route, a stowaway is found, a ragged Mexican teenager. The Hardys take him under their wing, and he plays an important role in the adventure. Unlike Tom Wat, Juan Marcheta is not an object of ridicule or pity. He is a well spoken and highly educated youth from an upper-class Mexican family who was kidnapped and taken to New York City. He provides valuable advice to the Hardys about Mexico. Unlike either Tom Wat or Sam Lee who appear only as victims, Juan takes an active role in the case, saving the Hardys' lives during a cattle stampede. Whereas China is depicted as a land of smugglers, gangs, and coolies, Mexico is called the "romantic country across the Rio Grande" (50).

Accompanied by Juan, Fenton Hardy and sons fly to Mexico, marking Frank and Joe's first trip outside the United States. They stay with Juan's family in a large and "luxuriously furnished" hacienda then set out seeking the kidnapped witness.

Much of the book reads like a travelogue as the Hardys marvel over the diversity of the Mexican landscape. The Hardys wear the "costume of the country, with wide-brimmed sombreros to shade their eyes from the sun" (84). Juan teaches them about desert life, including how to get water from a cactus. The brothers follow his lead, acting like guests in a new country.

The only character in the novel who speaks with a stereotyped Spanish accent is a bandit leader, described as "the man with the scar" who says, "'The Americanos do not weesh to come weeth us? ... You weel do as I say'" (129–130). Like Louie Fong, his criminality is linked to his nationality in phrases like the "wily Mexican." Pedro Vincenzo, like Louie Fong, is a dime novel villain. Threatening the Hardys with the "Ceremonial of the Fire" in which he brands his mark on victims' foreheads, his features are "ugly with malice and cruelty" (174). Like other ethnic villains, he exhibits a streak of sadism absent in white criminals, who, though sinister and surly, rarely resort to threats of mutilation.

Unlike *Footprints Under the Window*, however, *The Mark on the Door* presents a more balanced view of another nationality. Fenton Hardy speaks Spanish. The Hardy Boys rely on Mexican soldiers to track down and capture the bandits. The Marchetas are described by the Hardys as "friends" or equals in a way that Tom Wat is not.

The Hardy boys venture south of the border to Guatemala in *The Clue in the Embers* (1956) and *The Mystery of the Aztec Warrior* (1964). In these novels, Frank and Joe speak Spanish fairly fluently, showing a familiarity with a foreign culture and society not shown other nationalities they encounter.

The Mystery of the Aztec Warrior is notably respectful of Mexican history, culture, and especially Mexican society and government. At the time, when other popular media portrayed Mexico as a land of sleepy peasants, cigar-chewing bandits, corrupt policia, and lazy officials, this novel depicts a nation that is almost a mirror image of American honesty, productivity, and efficiency.

The novel includes a strong educational component, explaining to readers the Spanish and Native American influences shaping Mexican culture. As the chums pass a "huge" library, they admire the "beautiful, intricate mosaic" mural which depicts a "gigantic figure — half of it representing the Indian background of Mexico, the other its Spanish influence" (60).

This lesson is amplified later when the chums watch costumed children engage in intricate dances. Frank's conversation with a Mexican provides additional information about the nation's culture:

> A bystander heard Frank's admiring comments and said, "Children in Mexican schools have regular instruction in native dances at an early age. Many become professional dancers."

Frank asked whether schools taught only the Spanish-dominated period in the country's history. The man shook his head. "Our pupils learn the history of Mexico from prehistoric times. Many of them can speak the various Indian dialects, and through legends handed down in their families, know a lot about the great civilizations that were here in ancient days" [82–83].

Other passages portray Mexican authorities as responsible, efficient, and eager to assist the chums in their investigation. Hoping to determine whether some American tourists are imposters, Frank calls the Mexican tourist authority. An official takes his request and immediately calls back with a report (140).

Throughout the series Mexicans are granted more favorable descriptions than Asians or African Americans.

Native Americans

Native Americans do not appear in the books until 1934, though the image of the "wild Indian" is invoked to describe abandoned behavior in *The Tower Treasure* (1927) which depicts the chums "shouting and yelling like wild Indians" (47). When the boys encounter a deranged Captain Royal in *The Secret of the Caves* (1929) the old man "was yelling and shrieking like a wild Indian" (170). In *While the Clock Ticked* (1932) people investigating mysterious goings on in the Purdy mansion are terrified by a chilling scream. The terrifying scream was produced by a river thief named Indian Tom. Detective Smuff tells the Hardys, "'Having Indian blood, it was easy for him to give that particular kind of war-whoop.... It's called the Indian death yell'" (151).

The first Indian character appears in *The Mark on the Door* (1934), set in Mexico. Yaqui, a full-blooded Yaqui Indian, is depicted as the noble savage — intelligent, soft-spoken, and in touch with forces the suburban Hardys cannot comprehend. He is introduced as "a magnificent figure in the sunlight; a tall, broad-shouldered Indian with coppery skin" (93) who is wise and speaks without dialect:

> The camp was, of course, deserted. Yaqui dismounted and examined the tracks in the sand made by those who had left.
> "Their burros are heavily loaded," he said at last. "They will travel slowly. Perhaps we may be able to overtake them before they reach the edge of the desert" [116–117].

Parts of the novel reads almost like a children's travel book. As the Hardys watch, a Mexican strews cactus leaves on the river and pounds on them. "'He's fishing,' Joe explained. 'That's a species of cactus that acts like a sleeping powder'" (146). McFarlane then notes, "The Hardys, although they did not know it at the moment, were witnessing a method of fishing that has been used by Mexican cliff dwellers since prehistoric times" (146).

Later depictions of the Mexican Indians are more stereotyped. A dance sequence is reminiscent of Hollywood depictions of African tribes with costumed natives dancing around a fire. The natives have fallen under the sway of the Mexican bandit Pedro Vincenzo, who adds the branding of victims to the ceremony.

In *The Secret of Skull Mountain* (1948) Indian graves are violated and Native American skulls are tossed about or planted as warning signs to scare off those encroaching on squatters. Neither Frank nor Joe, who show some sympathy toward the impoverished mountain dwellers, make any comments about the violation of the Indian burial site. This is marked contrast to the respect they show when they accidentally unearth the grave of a Confederate soldier in *The Secret of the Lost Tunnel* (1950). Thinking the CSA carved on a stone is a marker for buried treasure, they begin digging. When they hit something wooden, they realize they have discovered a coffin and that the marker is actually the headstone of an anonymous Civil War soldier:

> "A soldier's grave," Frank said solemnly.
> "Bingham's? The spy?" Joe suggested.
> Frank shook his head. "I think not. This rock marked C S A is probably the headstone for an unknown soldier of the Confederate Army."
> Joe reverently started to push the dirt back into the hole. "We won't disturb him."
> The brothers finished filling the ancient grave and tamped the ground with their feet. Then Frank rolled the stone into place. The boys saluted and silently walked away [198].

In *The Sign of the Crooked Arrow* (1949) another noble savage appears on Ruth Hardy's New Mexico ranch. Cousin Ruth introduces Pye or Pymatuno as being "'the best Indian in all of New Mexico'" (109). Pye is described as having a "leathery face" that is "as weather-beaten as a mountain rock" but indicates a "keen sense of humor" (109). Like Yaqui, Pye exhibits a keen knowledge of the natural environment and animals. Riding, he moves with his horse "in perfect rhythm" so that it appears "he and the little animal had been born riding together" (115). He puts his ear to the ground to detect the approach of others. Pye speaks in dialect — "Me see plane many time.... All time he fly low by trees" (117), but there is no element of deprecation or ridicule. Frank and Joe are impressed by Pye's knowledge of horses and archery skills.

Pye's ingenuity saves Joe's life. Riding through the forest Pye and Joe are startled when a young lamb falls to its death from a cliff. Without explanation, Pye picks up the dead lamb and places it on his saddle. When they are attacked by a pack of wild dogs, Joe sees no way of escaping the dogs snapping at the heels of their ponies. But Pye's face lights up and "like lightning," the "wily Indian" severs parts of the lamb and tosses them to the dogs who pause temporarily to fight over the meat. Racing up a steep butte, Pye tosses the last piece of lamb over the edge and the hungry dogs race up the embankment and skid off the bluff (190–191).

The Crisscross Shadow (1953) introduces a Native American theme with a parody of Indian culture when Chet Morton surprises the Hardy Boys by appearing in costume and speaking in pidgin English:

> The Indian raised his hand commandingly. Then a deep but strangely familiar voice intoned: "I am Chief Wallapatookunk."
> "Chet!" whooped the Hardys, roaring with laughter as they recognized the voice.
> "Where in the world did you get that Indian costume?" Frank asked.
> Chet himself was struggling to maintain a dignified and fierce look.
> "This Indian warrior's suit," he replied solemnly. "Chief say you his prisoners." He pointed to Iola. "Bring um white girl to Wallapatookunk."
> Iola now was giggling but pretended to be alarmed and shrank toward Joe.
> "I will defend this maiden to the last arrow!" Joe said [46].

The impromptu skit humorously plays on stereotypes of Indian barbarism, especially that directed against white women. In going along with Chet's gag, Iola and Joe enact gender and ethnic stereotypes of the innocent, helpless white female and the brave, protective male needed to rescue her from violation by non-whites. When Chet explains that the costume belonged to his great-grandfather, he hastily adds that Ezekiel Morton was actually "honorary Chief Wallapatookunk of the Pashunks," not an ethnic Native American. When the Hardys and Chet plan to search for an Indian tribe, they joke about coming back with a scalp, another stereotyped allusion to Indian barbarism.

Once Frank, Joe, and Chet embark on a journey to an Indian village, the novel presents a more serious depiction of Native American life. Heading through a forest, the chums are approached by a man with long black hair dressed in fringed suede who warns the "paleface boys" to stay away. He speaks with a "strange accent," sounding like a Hollywood Indian, "'I give warning. You, paleface boys. You walk to bad country'" (99). After the figure runs off, promising to inform the tribal chief of their presence, Frank voices skepticism, stating that these days Indians are "just as peaceful as everyone else" (100). He points out, "'No real Indian talks like that these days. I'm sure he's a phony'" (100).

Frank's view is confirmed minutes later when they encounter an Indian youth dressed in modern clothing. Only his "coppery skin and straight black hair" indicate that he is a Native American. He is pleasant and speaks in Standard English. Introducing himself as Ted Whitestone, the youth tells the chums that his father, Oscar Whitestone, is tribal chief. The blend of European sounding first names and an almost British surname suggests assimilation and acceptance.

As Ted Whitestone escorts the chums to the Indian village, he answers Chet's questions, proving further insight into modern Native American life: "'No, we don't live in wigwams,' the Indian boy replied with a smile. 'Just regular houses like everybody else. And we don't dress up in feathers and big war bonnets, either. I hope I'm not disillusioning you fellows,' he added with a grin" (105). Instead of wigwams, the Indians live in "neat houses," attend school, and work in a small leather factory. The chums watch Indian youths play lacrosse, displaying the same skill and dexterity Frank and Joe exhibited playing football for Bayport High in the opening chapter. Chief Whitestone is described as having a "booklined study." Though isolated in a deep forest, the Native Americans are shown living in a civilized community that parallels Bayport.

Chief Whitestone tells the Hardy Boys the history of his tribe, which symbolizes the larger Native American experience. For 1953, this passage is strikingly sensitive to the status of indigenous Americans, giving children raised on cowboy and Indian movies an alternative view of their nation's history:

> "We Ramapans are an old tribe. Like most Indian tribes nowadays we were once a great and powerful nation, a leader among the Indians in this part of the country.
> "But as the years passed, and the white men spread out, our territories grew smaller. Our people became fewer in number as tribal warfare and sickness took their toll. Gradually, the Ramapans' power was so weakened that we were forced to move north. This was many generations ago.
> "Then, gradually, the chief continued, "the wars stopped, and modern medicine cut down our death rate. We became prosperous, but still we were small and missed our former greatness," he said with a faraway look in his eyes" [112].

The Chief explains that the tribe faces the loss of its land unless a missing deed can be located. Frank deciphers a riddle that had perplexed the Ramapans for sixty years and helps dig up the missing deed. Thus, the Hardys help a Native American tribe maintain its land against the chicanery of duplicitous white men.

The sensitive portrayal of Native Americans, however, applies only to Indians living in the continental United States. When the Hardy Boys venture out of the lower forty-eight states, they encounter Native Americans who are portrayed as uneducated, easily manipulated, or semi-savage.

In *The Clue in the Embers* Frank, Joe, Chet, and Tony travel to Guatemala. Frank suggests that "with his black hair and olive skin" Tony Prito could "pass" for a Native American (159). When Tony points out that he does not speak any Spanish or Indian dialect, Joe suggests he could "act like an antisocial Indian and say nothing" (159). When Tony dons native garb, he is spat and cursed at by a "Spanish-looking Ladino" (165).

Tony masters the local dialect and costuming so effectively that some Indians assume him is a shaman and grab him and ride off to their village. Assuring Chet that Tony is in no danger, Frank explains that a shaman is a combination of priest and poet who performs a ritual called "telling the mixes" to determine whether it is a propitious day for an individual to embark on a venture. He suggests they follow the Indians, joking that by the time they arrive at their village, the natives will have elected Tony chief. Frank assumes that the Indians will quickly release Tony when they realize their mistake.

Arriving in the settlement of thatched adobe shacks, the chums receive a harsh reception. Frank attempts to question the "poker-faced" Indians, who respond with "cold stares" (179). The chums approach a large building with a long porch that resembles a store. When Joe asks permission to go inside and look around, Indians scowl with disapproval. When he reaches for the doorknob, two Indians attack Joe, striking him across the face with "the butt of their hard, bony hands" (180). A fight ensues, and more Indians join in to subdue Frank, Joe, and Chet. The chums are dragged inside the building, which turns out to be not a shop but "some kind of ceremonial hall" (181). Indians carry in armloads of mahogany and pile it in the center of the room. When an old man starts a fire, Chet is terrified, assuming the Indians are going to burn them alive. Surrounded by a circle of forty "glowering" Indians, the chums fear the worst.

Bound and helpless, the boys can only watch as the Indians begin to chant. Two drummers beat out an accompaniment to the singing, which introduces a primitive ritual: "The singing became an angry, wild outcry that sounded like war-dance music. Snakelike, the circle came to life as the men, one by one, slowly rose to their feet and started stamping, sending clouds of dust off the dirt floor into the smoke-blue atmosphere" (182). With the appearance of a quartet of "weirdly painted" dancers, the ceremony becomes more agitated and frightening: "With a savage throbbing of the drums, these half-naked Indians, brandishing long spears, leaped through space into the moving circle of stamping fanatics. As they whirled past the boys, the prisoners could see the milk-white and scarlet streaks of paint on the dancers' faces and the eerie blue lines daubed along their sweating shoulders" (183–184). The chanting becomes a "half scream" as the drummers beat so fast they threaten to "tear the skins off their instruments" (184). Suddenly the frenzy stops, and an old man speaks some "gibberish" then rakes out hot ashes from the fire and marks the foreheads of the chums.

At that moment Tecum-Uman, "a handsome elderly Indian," arrives and walks "stately" toward the chums. Taller and more dignified than his fellow tribesmen, he orders the boys to be released. Tecum-Uman explains that he is the chief of three Indian villages victimized by a "dishonest Ladino." He apologizes for their mistreatment, telling the boys that the Indians were engaged in a ritual used to break a curse. His loyal people, he assures them, meant no harm. Reunited with Tony Prito, the chums continue their venture and discover long lost treasure with assistance from Tecum-Uman.

Two years later in 1958's *The Ghost at Skeleton Rock*, Frank and Joe again venture to Latin America. When the chums land on a small island, they are attacked by "a horde of wild-eyed natives" who wave knives and clubs and greet the boys with "blood-chilling yells" (141). The boys flee, but later Frank and Joe are captured by the natives. When Joe tries to explain their presence, he mentions "skeleton rock," which makes their captors "go wild." "Babbling in mixed Spanish-Indian dialect," the natives seize the brothers and throw them to the ground (150). Dragged to the sea, Frank and Joe fear they are going to be thrown to the sharks. Instead, the natives brusquely warn the boys to leave the island and never return. The scene depicts Indians as primitive people who are easily manipulated and given to violence.

In *The Mystery at Devil's Paw* (1959) Frank and Joe venture to Alaska and are introduced to Indians who are not as assimilated as those in the Northeast. They greet outsiders with reticence. Warned by their pilot that the Alaskan Indians may not be talkative, the Hardys step from a helicopter and notice the natives' response:

> Instead of running to meet their visitors, the Indians gathered to watch from a distance. Their dark, slanted eyes, set in coppery faces, stared impassively at the newcomers.
> "They don't look very friendly," Joe muttered.
> "Do they speak English?" Frank asked the pilot.
> "Most of them do, although they may not admit it. Often they use the Chinook trading jargon in talking to strangers" [54].

When the Indians merely shrug their shoulders and shake their heads in response to their questioning, Frank and Joe decide to walk about the village, hoping the Indians "open up a bit" after becoming used to their presence (55). The Hardys note that although the houses are "crude," they are "stoutly built." The brothers are "intrigued" by the caches, small log structures built atop stilts behind each home to store food out of reach of wild animals.

As the boys wander through the village, a few children begin to follow them. A teenager named Fleetfoot steps forward and introduces himself. Speaking in dialect, he offers to help the Hardys in exchange for a ride in a helicopter, which he calls a "big funny bird" (57).

The Alaskan Indians are presented as a people apart, steeped in ancient traditions that sometimes border on hostility. On their river trip Frank and Joe pass an Indian ceremony in which a woman is bounced up and down on a walrus skin. Fleetfoot rushes toward the Hardys with a "wide-eyed look of fear" telling the brothers, "'Quick! Do not let my people see you! ... Run for your lives!'" (110).

Fleetfoot hastily explains that his tribe is holding a wedding ceremony. The Kotzebue Eskimo bride must prove to everyone she will be a good *skookum* wife by demonstrating her ability to be tossed in the air and land on her feet. The trial takes skill, and novices risk breaking their necks in a fall. Fleetfoot warns them that tradition demands that visitors be subjected to the same test.

Heeding Fleetfoot's warning, the Hardys back off but are spotted before they can escape. Indians "swarm" around Frank and Joe and drag them "into the circle of yelling, whooping" natives. Frank protests, explaining they had no idea a wedding was taking place. Fleetfoot "jabbered excitedly in the Haida tongue, trying to persuade his fellow Indians to let the white youths go," but a brave insists the visitors take part in the ceremony. Frank continues to protest in vain as "the Haidas had reverted to the savage customs of the Alaskan wilderness!" (112). After Frank survives the test, the boys are invited to partake in the wedding feast. After taking hesitating bites of raw salmon to avoid offending their hosts, the Hardys enjoy nuts, vegetable, fruit, and coarse bread made from rice lily bulbs.

Arabs

The Hardy Boys encounter Arabs in Morocco in 1975's *The Mysterious Caravan*. In this most multicultural of the novels, Frank, Joe, and Chet travel from Jamaica to North Africa, accompanied by a black chum, William. A Eurasian girl acts as their guide. Frank and Joe travel through Arab neighborhoods past mosques and open-air markets. Frank haggles with a merchant for a dagger. The haggling process is described in neutral language with no patronizing commentary or suggestions that the Arab shopkeeper is dishonest or deceitful. The chums also meet blue-eyed Berbers who, they learn, are non–Arab Caucasians. Their simple homes are described as having "crude" beds, but the people are depicted in fairly complimentary terms.

Erin Go Bragh: The Hardy Boys Discover Their Roots

As paragons of all–American youths, Frank and Joe Hardy are given no ethnic identity until 1976. In *The Witchmaster's Key* Fenton Hardy tells his sons that their ancestors came from Dublin sometime after the Salem witch trials, making them both Irish and old-line Yankees. Arriving in the late 17th or early 18th century, the original Hardys were most likely Protestant, a breed apart from the poor and Catholic famine Irish who flooded America after 1850.

When Frank and Joe prepare to fly to Britain to solve a mystery, their father tells them to "check on the genealogy of the Hardy family" (83). While in Dublin, Frank goes to the library with Pat, an Irish friend, and examines "several enormous tomes" in "hushed concentration" (125). Frank apologizes for not knowing much about his ancestry, confessing, "'Sorry to say we lost track of the old timers'" (125). As he studies the library records, Frank discovers that the Hardy family immigrated in 1800, a full century after the Salem witch trials. He also discovers that Fenton "'is an old family name among the Hardys of Ireland'" and notes, "'So that's where my father's first name comes from. He'll be interested to hear that'" (125). Pat compliments Frank on his heritage, noting, "'Your chaps are a distinguished clan'" (125). Leaving Trinity College, Frank and Pat pass statues of Edmund Burke and Oliver Goldsmith and men raising tankards and singing drinking songs in pubs.

It is noteworthy that the Hardy Boys series waited until 1976 to reveal the brothers' Irish heritage. In the Twenties the outstanding Irish character in the novels is oafish, cowardly Con Riley. He is followed by Mary, a dialect-speaking Irish laundress in *The Twisted Claw* (1939), who says she is "lavin" the Hardy home because its excitement is not suited for "dacent folks." Possibly the syndicate decided that by the late 1970s it was safe to link Frank and Joe to the Emerald Isle a half-century after the last No Irish Need Apply signs were taken down.

Chapter 8

Class

> "You High School kids think you own the earth."
> —*What Happened at Midnight*, 1931

The Hardy Boys operate in a solidly upper middle-class world. The series opens with Frank and Joe owning motorcycles. Over the years they acquire a roadster, a speedboat, and eventually use of their father's airplane. Their chums appear to come from affluent households as well, having no difficulty coming up with money for cross country trips and other adventures. Chet Morton lives on a farm, but his father is a realtor. Tony Prito is the son of a successful contractor. Even during the Depression nearly all the teenage chums own a car, a motorcycle, or a speedboat. The only true proletarian "chum" is Perry Robinson, who makes brief appearances as the son of Hurd Applegate's caretaker. The Hardy Boys jet around the world, taking trains, and paying for hotel rooms as if on an open-ended expense account. When Frank and Joe's car is burned in a garage fire, Fenton Hardy surprises his sons with a new convertible. Only when they are robbed in New York City in 1931's *What Happened at Midnight* do Frank and Joe share the plight of millions of Americans in the Depression. Left with only fifty cents, they are forced to dine on sandwiches and sleep on park benches.

Throughout the series, there are only a few glimpses of wealth or poverty. Like youths living in a comfortable suburb who only see the mansions of the wealthy on a Sunday drive or slums of the poor from a freeway overpass, Frank and Joe have little contact with economic extremes. Only a handful of non–middle class characters make appearances, evoking common stereotypes.

Rich Eccentrics

Bayport is home to a number of rich eccentrics. *The Tower Treasure*'s Hurd Applegate lives with his maiden sister in a towered mansion resembling "some ancient feudal castle" (53). Their palatial home was first constructed by Major Applegate, "an eccentric old army man who had made millions by lucky real estate deals" (53). The Applegate family, however, has dwindled over the years, leaving only the celibate siblings Hurd and Adelia to inhabit the rambling mansion. Hurd is a "stooped man, eccentric in his ways" who devotes his time to his stamp collection. The only visitors to the tower mansion are philatelists from New York eager to see his latest acquisition from "some remote part of the world" (54). Adelia, who is "as eccentric as her brother," dresses in rainbow colors and rarely leaves the mansion except for infrequent shopping excursions into Bayport stores where she orders employees about in a high "cracked" voice, carting off more multi-colored garments. Though reputably wealthy, "these eccentric people" keep few servants and live simply.

The Mystery of Cabin Island (1929) features another eccentric stamp collector. Described by Joe as a "'queer old codger,'" Elroy Jefferson lives in a "gloomy mansion" with a "gloomy" entrance hall (31–32). He allows the chums to camp out on his island, staying in the cabin he built for his wife and son, now both dead.

The chums learn more about the eccentric Elroy Jefferson when they buy provisions from local grocer Amos Grice:

> "Yes, I know Elroy Jefferson real well. He's a fine fellow, too, but very queer."
>
> "He's a bit eccentric," agreed Frank.
>
> "Yes, he's a queer old chap, but a better man never wore shoe leather. How was he when you was last talkin' to him?"
>
> The boys decided to humor the lonely old storekeeper....
>
> "He was quite well. He let us have the cabin for our outing."
>
> "Yes, that's just like Mr. Jefferson. Got a heart of gold, specially where boys is concerned. But queer — mighty queer in some ways," said Amos Grice, again wagging his head. "Do you know" — and he leaned forward very confidentially — "I really think he married Mary Bender because of her postage stamp collection" [86–87].

Grice tells the boys that Jefferson, an antique collector, was set on purchasing the Bender stamp collection. When Bender declined to sell his stamps, Jefferson married his daughter. After Bender's death, his daughter inherited the stamps and gave them to Jefferson, whereupon the treasured collection vanished. At mystery's end the Hardy Boys recover the stamp collection. Like Applegate, the eccentric Jefferson is delighted with the return of his lost treasure and rewards the brothers with four hundred dollars and use of Cabin Island.

Much of the action in *While the Clock Ticked* (1932) takes place in an empty mansion built by Jason Purdy, another wealthy Bayport eccentric. The house was constructed with a vault-like inner room without windows and a steel door secured by a time lock. Here the miser shut himself up for hours on end, "gloating over his wealth, clipping coupons, hatching out new schemes for making money" (29).

Another strange Bayport residence, constructed by yet another rich eccentric, appears in *The Secret Panel* (1946). John Mead, a partner in a large New York hardware firm, retired and built a large home without a single lock or keyhole to remind him of his former business. The mansion has an ornate oak door on each side of the structure with no visible knob, keyhole, or lock. After manipulating various raised figures carved in the doors, the brothers locate a hidden keyhole and gain entrance into the thickly carpeted and ornately furnished mansion. The house's massive dark furniture produces "a weird, gloomy effect" (76). As the brothers search the residence, they notice that window locks and other hardware are hidden from view. On a subsequent visit they locate a secret room behind a panel opened by a magnet. The strange house also has an eerie way of distorting the brothers' sense of time. Frank discovers a book about locksmithing, which he finds so fascinating that when Joe tells him they should leave, he asks for a minute, "but the minute dragged into five, and might have even been longer, but for the fact that the lamplight suddenly went out" (78). When Frank and Joe inspect the ornate paneling looking for a secret panel, Frank glances at his watch and is "startled to find he and his brother had been in the house two hours" (169).

The rich, elderly eccentrics of Bayport live out the fantasies of children, building castle-like structures with secret panels and hidden rooms. Like children, they create their own inner worlds, shielded from the prying eyes of outsiders.

Capitalists

The Hardy Boys series includes a number of small business owners — grocers, laundrymen, storekeepers, and farmers — who are generally portrayed in positive terms. But there are a few entrepreneurs and corporate leaders. *Footprints Under the Window* (1933) presents Orrin North, a "big, burly, broad-shouldered man with a coarse, red face, clumsy hands and a stubborn, obstinate chin" (60). A self-made man, North is the son of a poor fisherman "who worked long and hard until he bought a boat of his own" (61). Up to this point he appears to be emblematic of the American Dream, rising from humble origins to commanding his own enterprise. North, however, was not satisfied being a small time operator with a single boat:

From that, by his own ruthless efforts, he had gained control of a small fleet of vessels. In the course of years he had become wealthier and it had been hinted that not all his riches had been honestly earned. In middle life he had bought the fleet of a bankrupt trading company, and by business methods which were not above a suspicion of shadiness he had throttled competition and added to his fleet until he was now one of the most powerful men in the state [61].

Accustomed to getting his way, North is intemperate and impatient. He demands to see Fenton Hardy. When Frank and Joe explain their father is out of town and cannot be reached, North explodes in rage. The Hardy Boys dislike his "domineering manner" and are reminded of the "many stories of his cruel, scheming and unscrupulous nature" (62). North is engaged in smuggling with the evil Chinaman Louie Fong and hoped to hire the famous detective to demonstrate his legitimacy. Fenton Hardy sees through his ruse and keeps the shipping magnate under surveillance.

In the final novel of the original series, *The Sting of the Scorpion* (1979), Frank and Joe aid Lloyd Quinn, an enterprising proponent of lighter-than-air transport, who operates a giant cargo dirigible that has been sabotaged. He is a plain-speaking man who works out of a simple office. In contrast, his rival Eustace Jarmon rules a business empire from a "huge modern desk" in a penthouse office. Unlike the casually dressed Quinn, Jarmon is the "perfect picture of a hard-driving business executive" (76). Like Orrin North, Eustace Jarmon initially contacts the Hardys asking for their help when in fact he is involved in illegal activity. Working on behalf of a foreign government, Jarmon plots with terrorists to destroy Quinn's airship service.

In both novels capitalist greed is linked to sinister foreign elements that threaten the national security of the United States.

Bumpkins

Bayport is surrounded by farms, and repeatedly the Hardy Boys stop to ask farmers if they have seen a car or a missing chum. Occasionally, a horse-drawn hay wagon gets in the way of their speeding roadster. Invariably, the farmers are depicted as hayseeds who drop their final "g's," drawl, wear straw hats, and look for excuses to engage in long-winded conversations to avoid work.

Bumpkins first appear in the third chapter of *The Tower Treasure* when the boys are in hot pursuit of Chet's stolen roadster. Spotting men in a hayfield, they stop to see if anyone saw the stolen car:

> Frank scrambled over the fence and went over to talk to the farmhands, who watched his approach with curiosity.
> "Didn't see a yellow roadster pass here within the last hour, did you?" ...

"A roadster, eh?" asked one.

"A yellow roadster," Frank told him.

One of the men removed his hat and mopped his brow.

"Seems to me," he observed, "I *did* see a car come by here a while ago."

"A yellow car?"

"No — twan't a yeller car. It was a delivery truck, if I remember rightly."

Frank strove to conceal his impatience.

"It was a roadster I was asking about. A yellow roadster."

"Not one of them there coops, hey?" asked the oldest man in the group doubtfully.

"No, not a coupe. A roadster."

"Roadster, eh," remarked the old farmer. "That's one of them there autymobiles with just two seats and a little cupboard in the back, eh?" [19–20].

Bumpkins figure into one of Chet Morton's early pranks, in which he uses a bit of twentieth-century automobile technology to trick a farmer plodding along in his horse-drawn wagon. Spotting a "lean and solemn farmer perched on the front seat, half asleep," Chet Morton gets an idea. "'That's Lem Billers — the laziest man in nine counties,'" he tells the Hardy Boys, "'Watch me have some fun with him'" (39). Chet hops onto the back of the hay wagon with a car horn. He sounds the horn, and as was the custom for slow-moving farm wagons, Lem Billers yanks the reins, leading his horses to the side of the road to allow the car to pass. When no car drives by, he turns around and gazes at the empty road behind him in bewilderment. Tugging the horses back onto the road, he continues on until the horn sounds again. He pulls his team to the shoulder of the road, but again no car passes. "'My ears must be goin' back on me,'" he mutters to himself and moves on. Chet repeats the trick until Billers refuses to yield to any more non-existent vehicles. When the chauffeur of a luxury sedan pulls up behind the wagon and honks to pass, Billers ignores the horn and plods on. The driver becomes enraged and calls out to Con Riley to arrest the dim-witted farmer. An argument ensues with the Irish cop trying to mediate between an angry chauffeur and Lem Billers who now thinks his eyes rather than his ears are failing him. With the wagon and sedan blocking the road, traffic backs up, sparking a "chorus of automobile horns."

The whole scene leaves Chet with "tears of laughter running down his face" (44). The Hardys laugh all the way home and "during supper that evening their spasmodic outbursts of chuckles puzzled their parents extremely" (44).

A similar comic bumpkin appears in *The Secret of the Old Mill* (1927). Planning a Saturday hike, Frank and Joe decide to drop by a local farm to ask about the current cherry crop. Frank, Joe, and Chet set off on their outing, pausing to swim in the Willow River, and engage in a few boyish pranks before heading to the Stummer farm.

Carl Stummer is described as a "lanky, shambling old farmer with drooping shoulders, a drooping mustache and a drooping pipe" (42). Stummer is something of a local oddity, known for his ability to "chew a straw and smoke a pipe perpetually at the same time" (42). Bayporters had seen him without the straw or without the pipe "but no one had ever seen him without one or the other" (42). Chet Morton claims "as a grave fact that Carl Stummer slept with his pipe in his mouth and a supply of fresh straws constantly by his bedside and that he changed them in his sleep" (42).

Like the farmers in *The Tower Treasure*, Stummer speaks with an archaic country dialect, greeting the chums with a "Lo, boys!" saying "kin" for "can," "dunno," "ain't," and "fair to middlin'." With hands "plunged deep in the pockets of his faded overalls" and the straw waggling "beneath the drooping moustache," Stummer warns the chums to avoid the old flour mill along the Willow River, noting that the long abandoned building is now occupied by three "fellers" who are "onpleasant lookin' chaps" (45).

When Frank and Joe investigate an automobile left at a garage in 1949's *The Sign of the Crooked Arrow*, they cannot resist poking fun at the owner. Slow Mo, originally dubbed Slow Motion in his youth, is a grimy mechanic working out of a cluttered "two-by-four" office in a "musty-smelling garage" (3). Entering the humble room, Joe cannot resist teasing Slow Mo by feigning ignorance and asking the garage owner the location of his office:

"Why, gol hang it, boy," Slow Mo said, "I can see right now you're not the detective your father is. This is the office. He'd of knowed that right off."

"Sorry," Joe replied, keeping a straight face.

"Set down here," the proprietor offered, motioning toward a couple of kegs [3].

The Hardys also have fun showing up Slow Mo's dim-witted brother-in-law, who is the local chief of police. After the pompous chief, who blows his nose "like an elephant trumpeting for his mate," conducts a superficial search with an oversize magnifying glass, the Hardys locate several overlooked clues.

The bumpkin character reappears in 1975's *The Mysterious Caravan*. After a pursuit by adversaries, Frank and Joe's car is left hung up on a rock in a farm field. The brothers walk to a nearby farmhouse to ask for help. The farmer, sullen and ungrammatical, is disapproving but reluctantly assists the boys:

"Can you help us, please? We're stuck in your field and can't get out."

"I saw them cars a while ago," the farmer said. "What was that, some fraternity initiation?"

"Nothing like that," Joe replied.

"Well, whatever it was, it was plumb crazy!"

"We're high-centered on a rock, sir," Joe said.

"I ought to let you sit," the farmer grumbled. "Where'd this nonsense get you? Into trouble, that's where!"

"Perhaps we could use your tractor," Joe pleaded.
"It ain't working."
"Do you have a horse?"
"Yes, I got a horse. Two of 'em."
"Could we have them pull the car out?" Frank asked. "We'd be glad to pay you."
"I wouldn't take no money from no kids. Okay. I'll get the horses. But next time you're fooling around with your friends, don't play tag in my fields!" [86–87].

While the farmer is bitter and patronizing, Joe is deferential and diplomatic, offering to pay for assistance. Although the farmer is portrayed as unfriendly and uneducated, the Hardy boys do not ridicule him or make him a target for pranks.

The Crabb Corners Boys

What Happened at Midnight (1931) opens with a scene of class conflict. The chums are inspecting Bayport's latest commercial innovation, the automat. Several farm boys enter and demand the Hardys make way for them. "'You High School kids think you own the earth,'" one of them says, challenging the middle-class youths (4). The Crabb Corners boys are described as being "far from bad, but they were rough and boisterous, considerably given to horseplay" (12). They later show up at the Morton farm during a party. While the chums enjoy food and music, the farm boys stand along the fence, "looking hungrily at the gay scene" (17). Callie Shaw suggests taking them cake, and Iola plans to tell the farm boys to "go around to the back" so the cook can give them some ice cream. The high school girls show compassion to the hungry farm boys, but do not consider including them in the party and serve them apart from their middle-class guests in a form of condescending charity (18).

The Urban Poor

For crime fighters, Frank and Joe Hardy have little contact with poor people. Unlike adult detectives, their cases rarely take them down mean streets. Most of the poor they encounter are straw-chewing farmhands, lazy and comical. Urban poverty, with its associations of drugs, violence, and vice, is rarely depicted. The entire series gives readers only a few glimpses into slums or what Leslie McFarlane deemed "poor quarters."

In *The Tower Treasure* Perry Robinson's family is forced to leave the Applegate mansion and move to an unpainted cottage after his father is accused of theft. When Callie and Frank visit, Frank studies the neighborhood of "squalid shacks and tumbledown houses." Noting that the Robinsons have repaired a picket fence and cleaned their yard, Frank calls it the "neatest place on the whole block" (111). The working class Robinsons have values the truly poor lack. It takes no money to mend a fence and clean a yard. Evidently, other residents lack the Robinsons' concern for order and cleanliness.

The Short-Wave Mystery (1945) is the only novel that makes a connection between poverty and crime. Chasing a suspect, Frank and Joe encounter a puffing Patrolman Riley in pursuit of some young "pests" he believes responsible for a spate of petty thefts. In the following chapter, called "Boys of the Alleys," the Hardys encounter Jimmy Gordon and his pals. Dirty and neglected, the youngsters boast about missing summer school. Jimmy considers his criminal uncle "smart." Frank and Joe are moved when they see Jimmy's crumbling tenement and vow to help him avoid following in his uncle's footsteps. When Mickey, one of Jimmy Gordon's pals, is arrested for stealing buns from a bakery, Frank and Joe intervene with the judge, promising to mentor the delinquent. With their guidance, the alley boys come to see the virtues of following the right path, going to school, and being honest. Like the Crabb Corners Boys, the alley boys are poor, uneducated, and potentially bad but deserving of middle-class charity.

Frank and Joe, like characters in a sitcom or soap opera, live in secure comfort and never face economic deprivation — except when their wallets are stolen. In Bayport school and hard work pay off. The Great Depression, like World War II, never touches Frank and Joe's hometown. No one is laid off, downsized, or evicted — save for the wrongly accused Mr. Robinson in *The Tower Treasure*. His exile to the "poor quarters" of Bayport is temporary. At novel's end, he returns to the mansion with his old job back and a raise. The Hardy Boys series assures children that America is ever prosperous, stable, and always safe.

CHAPTER 9

Hardy Girls: Gender in the Hardy Boys

"I wish I were a boy," sighed Callie Shaw.
—*The Secret of the Caves*, 1929

In Stratemeyer's segregated series females played marginal roles in boys' books. Ever conscious of the need to guarantee the wholesomeness of his products, he maintained strict standards. The instructions he sent Leslie McFarlane in 1926 outlining the new detective series "intimated that relations between the Hardy boys and their girlfriends would not go beyond the borders of wholesome friendship and discreet mutual admiration."[1] It was made clear to McFarlane that he was to avoid "the knee-pawing, tit-squeezing stuff that was sneaking into so much popular fiction, to the disgust of all right-thinking people."[2]

The entire series, targeted to boys, avoids female characters. All the villains, nearly all the victims, and most of the witnesses are male. Unlike adult detective fiction, there are no seductive femme fatales trying to lure the hero away from his quest, few ingénue victims full of innocent vulnerability, and absolutely no gun molls. In the world of the Hardy Boys desperate criminals and heartless terrorists are as celibate as the teen detectives tracking them down. The closest scene of debauchery occurs in *The Great Airport Mystery* (1930) when Frank and Joe search a gang hideout and come across an empty liquor bottle and some cigarette butts. The evil men never hook up with evil women or take advantage of innocent females.

Scenes of even suggested sexuality are few and muted. *The Mark on the Door* (1934) contains an uncharacteristically graphic passage of sexual sadism.

Held hostage in a cave in Mexico, Frank and Joe meet a "dark-skinned, gypsy-like young creature with big eyes" (189). As the exotic girl approaches, the brothers are horrified when they see that she bears the letter P — the villain's initial — branded on her forehead. When Frank inquires about the mark, the girl panics:

> A look of terror crossed her face. She glanced over her shoulder as if fearful of being overheard.
> "Eet was Pedro," she whispered.
> "He branded you?" Joe exclaimed in horror.
> Although she did not understand his words she gathered their meaning. The girl nodded slowly.
> "Pedro — not please wit' me," she answered.
> Then she shrugged and gestured toward the mark again.
> "He branded you because he was angry with you?" Joe asked.
> The girl nodded her head vigorously [190].

The girl's "not please wit' me" clearly hints at sexual abuse. Joe's follow-up question shows that he is clueless about what prompted Pedro's anger. In *The Hidden Harbor Mystery*, published a year later, Frank observes an adult sexual interaction worthy of a Victorian novel:

> Frank edged forward and peered through the bushes. The detective and Miss Fox were walking slowly down a garden path. Suddenly Heator grasped the actress's hand.
> "Why are you so cold to me, Alice? You know I've been in love with you ever since I first saw you on the stage —"
> Miss Fox, however, was evidently in no mood for love-making. She drew away her hand.
> "Please don't be foolish, Mr. Heator" [139].

A Figure in Hiding (1937) includes a scene in which a female character tells the Hardy Boys that she shoved a holdup man from the running board of a car "because he was becoming too friendly" (208).

Though Frank is the older brother and shown to have more confidence in talking to Callie Shaw than Joe has with Iola Morton, he is indifferent and shy when he encounters a beautiful flirt. In *The Mystery of the Flying Express* (1941) Frank's attempt to catch up with Joe is stalled when the moving van he is riding in breaks down. Seeing a small plane touch down in a nearby field, Frank runs over to the young pilot and asks if he can fly him to a town called Bainville. The friendly pilot offers to help, adding that Frank might have to wait because he had planned to take his girlfriend for a ride:

> Frank's heart sank. A beautiful girl was hurrying toward them from the farmhouse, "Oh, hello," she said when she saw the Hardy boy.
> "This fella wants me to fly him to Bainville, Martha," the young pilot explained, "but I told him we had a date."

Despite his feelings of impatience, Frank smiled at the girl, who returned it. "I'm sorry," he apologized, "I shouldn't want to interfere with any plans —"

Martha laughed gaily. "Don't worry about me, Jimmy. You just go ahead and take this nice young man to Bainville. He seems very nice," she added coyly.

Frank felt himself reddening, at which both the others laughed outright.

"Say," chuckled the pilot, "before you two get any friendlier I guess I'd better fly this fellow to Bainville!"

Frank's heart leaped. His watch told him that he had an excellent chance of catching Joe through this unexpected opportunity [155–156].

Frank's duty to Joe is not shaken even by a pretty girl.

The only overt sexual exchange involving the chums occurs in *The Phantom Freighter* (1947) when Biff Hooper and Joe Hardy enter a seedy waterfront office and encounter a gum-chewing "stringy-hair blonde girl" who gazes "languidly" at the boys. The girl takes an "admiring" look at Biff, cooing "'Oooh! Such muscles!'" (41). Biff turns red with embarrassment. The girl continues to dart "admiring glances at the brawny Biff" (41). A "crimson" Biff flees the office, begging Joe Hardy not to tell anyone at school. "'For the love of Pete,'" he begs, "'don't tell anyone what the dizzy girl said'" (42). Joe promises to keep Biff's "conquest" secret.

The general sexlessness of Frank and Joe is revealed in *The Sign of the Crooked Arrow* (1949). Armed with the description of a female suspect, Frank and Joe cruise the streets of several small towns hoping to spot her. Joe remarks that people will think they are "batty" because they are "looking at all the women" (25). Frank laughs it off, suggesting it is after all "'in the line of duty'" (25). The idea that teenage boys looking at women would be viewed as unusual bespeaks of total innocence.

Stratemeyer's avoidance of sex comes partly from his nineteenth-century values. He was a church-going family man with two daughters. It also stems from his understanding of the adolescent mind, which made his books so popular. He knew the inclusion of girls would alienate younger male readers who would resent their presence in a "boy's book." He also knew that presenting both male and female characters in books might raise parental concerns.

The Hardy Boys have retained their virginity for eighty years, but they have not been without at least superficial female companionship.

Callie and Iola

Frank and Joe Hardy have pseudo girl friends who dimly register on their radar screens. Introduced in the first novels, Callie Shaw and Chet Morton's sister Iola play supporting roles throughout the series. Unlike Frank and Joe, Callie and Iola change in appearance over the series. Callie, Frank's love interest, is a "quick and vivacious" girl with brown hair and brown eyes in 1927's *The Tower Treasure*. In *The Missing Chums*, published the following year, she is described as a "dark-haired girl" with "small, even teeth of a dazzling whiteness" (26). In *The Yellow Feather Mystery* (1953) Callie is "blond and vivacious" (33). Seven years later *The Mystery of the Chinese Junk* describes Callie as "an attractive blonde" (49). Chet's sister, Joe's occasional date, undergoes greater change. Originally "plump and dark" in 1929's *The Mystery of Cabin Island*, Iola loses weight by 1950's *The Secret of the Lost Tunnel* to become "just as slender and good-looking as her brother was fat" (29). (In 1987 Iola Morton is blown up by a terrorist car bomb in the first Hardy Boys Casefiles novel *Dead on Target*.)

In the early novels Callie Shaw and Iola Morton are merely associated with Frank and Joe Hardy. Their relationships are limited to brief conversations, and, in the case of Joe and Iola, distant mutual admiration. By *What Happened at Midnight* (1931) they attend parties and are shown dancing together. In *The Mystery of the Chinese Junk* (1960) Callie is called "Frank's favorite date" who double dates with Joe and Iola (49). Though they have steady girlfriends, the boys remain sexually innocent. The only onpage kiss occurs when a grateful Callie and Iola thank Frank and Joe for saving them from certain death after they pass out from lack of oxygen in a cave:

> Callie, who was trying to smooth her rumpled hair, flashed a grateful smile at Frank. "We'd still be there — and maybe dead by this time — if it hadn't been for you Hardys. Thanks a million for saving us!"
> "She means you naturally," Joe quipped to his brother. Then he blushed as Iola said:
> "Well, I think *you're* wonderful, too! So there!" To back up her words, Iola planted a quick kiss on Joe's cheek, which left him gulping in surprise [*The Mystery of the Chinese Junk*, 67–68].

Callie and Iola play an important role in the wish fulfillment theme. Being desired or admired by the opposite sex dominates the lives of teenagers, motivating their choices in clothes, music, behavior, and lifestyle. Callie and Iola cheer the Hardy Boys on, fall victim and require rescuing, and affirm their manhood. The brothers win the girls' approval by solving mysteries the way other boys demonstrate their masculine prowess by scoring touchdowns at a homecoming game.

Frank and Joe exhibit contrasting attitudes toward girls. Frank, a year older, exhibits more confidence and comfort around female characters. He speaks easily with Callie, while Joe is bashful and awkward, especially in the early novels:

> "Let's go," muttered Joe, tugging at Frank's sleeve. He was incurably shy in the presence of girls, especially Iola.
> But Frank did not go just then. He chatted with Callie Shaw for a while, and

Iola tried to make conversation with Joe, whose answers were mumbled and muttered, while he inwardly wished he could talk as freely and without embarrassment as his brother. At length, Frank decided to go and Joe sighed with relief....

"Whew!" breathed Joe, mopping his brow. "I'm glad that's over."

Frank looked at him in surprise.

"Why, what's the matter? I thought you liked Iola Morton."

"That's just the trouble — I do," answered Joe mysteriously, and Frank wisely forbore further inquiry [*The Missing Chums*, 26–27].

In the early novels the girls provide moral support to the detective brothers and display the widely accepted sex roles of the times. In *The Secret of the Caves* (1929), the girls bemoan the restrictions gender imposes on them:

"I wish I were a boy," sighed Callie Shaw.

Iola Morton looked up from her ice-cream soda.

"Me, too."

"It's tough luck that you're not," said Joe Hardy. "We'd like to have you along on the trip with us."

"Boys have all the luck. Girls have to stay home" [43].

Frank and Joe's interest in the girls is muted with only a hint of attraction. When Chet Morton notes that the Hardys are lucky because they don't have sisters, Frank replies with the slightly incestuous suggestion, "'If we had sisters like Callie and Iola we wouldn't have any kick'" (45).

In *The Secret of Skull Mountain* (1948) Callie Shaw moves from supportive cheerleader to sleuthing chum, albeit for only a few pages. Suspecting that a plumber is hiding something, Frank suggests that Callie take care of the man's shop and keep the store's books in order. Callie then becomes a Hardy operative, much like Chet or Biff, and secures vital information. Although the plumber catches her copying a telegram and fires her on the spot, Callie memorizes the message and is able to provide Frank and Joe with a valuable clue. *The Wailing Siren Mystery* (1951) includes a half-page scene in which Callie and Iola follow a suspect then report back to the Hardy Boys. The girls are described as having "done sleuthing for the boys before" (60). In *The Crisscross Shadow* (1953) Callie and Iola work together again, in Nancy Drew fashion, and uncover an important clue while searching through books found in an attic. Significantly, the females work at home, indoors, with books. The clue they unearth in their domestic sleuthing leads the Hardy Boys and Chet to an outdoor adventure hundreds of miles from the safety of Bayport.

The Sexual Revolution Comes to Bayport

In the 1970s when Frank and Joe take a slightly more active interest in girls, Callie and Iola rarely appear. Though earlier described as their customary dates, they all but vanish toward the end of the original series. Perhaps authors sensed that references to "going steady" would imply sexual activity or alienate younger readers.

The more open atmosphere of the late Sixties and Seventies led to some, very slight and very passing glimmerings of sexual attraction in the series. In *The Arctic Patrol Mystery* (1969) Frank, Joe, Biff, and Chet fly to Iceland. Chet Morton, usually focused only on food, takes notice of Steina, the stewardess. As she takes their dinner trays, Chet whispers to Frank, "'She sure is good-looking'" (21). "But Frank's mind," the author tells readers, "was on the special equipment his father had supplied" (21). Brawny Biff, however, shows greater interest in the stewardess, which surprises the sexless Hardys when they discover their chum with the dark-haired beauty—"There was Biff Hooper chatting gaily with Steina the stewardess!" (85).

But even Biff's interest in Steina is limited to her value as a potential source of information. The scene of eighteen-year-old boys chatting with a stewardess is devoid of any explicit sexual attraction or even playful banter.

> Biff Hooper spoke to Frank in a low voice. "Do you think Steina might be able to help us? She probably knows lots of important people in Iceland."
>
> "Yes, she might," Frank replied and looked at the stewardess. "Steina, we'd like to contact a man named Rex Mar on the fishing trawler *Svartfugel*. Do you know how we can get in touch with him?"
>
> "Of course," the girl answered with a wave of her hand, as if the request were an easy one.
>
> Joe had his doubts. "You're not kidding, are you?"
>
> "No. My uncle Oscar will help you, I'm sure."
>
> "Your uncle Oscar?" Chet raised his eyebrows. "Who's he?"
>
> "Head of the Icelandic coast guard," Steina replied, cocking her head coyly.
>
> "Great!" Joe exclaimed. "Will you give us an introduction?"
>
> Without a word the girl rose, went to a wall telephone nearby, and dialed a number. After chatting in Icelandic, she hung up and returned to the boys. "Uncle Sigtryggsson is in his office. He's expecting you."
>
> "Thanks a million, Steina," Frank said. "Can we see him in half an hour?"
>
> "Sure. I must be going along now," the girl replied. Waving good-bye, she left in her small car which she had parked in front of the hotel [86–87].

Chet Morton's eye for females becomes sharper in 1971's *Danger on Vampire Trail* and leads to something of a sight gag in a Laundromat:

> He pushed through the door and looked around. Two women sat on folding chairs, watching their laundry tumble behind the glass doors of the machines. At the far end, a girl about Chet's age was bending over a half-filled basket of clothes.
>
> Chet got a packet of soap powder from a vending machine and approached a machine with its door half open. Paying more attention to the girl than to the clothes in his hand, he stuffed them into the machine, tossed in the detergent, and closed the door. The machine began to whirl.

> Suddenly the girl turned about. An expression of indignation covered her pretty face.
> "You can't do that!" she cried out.
> "Wh-what do you mean?" Chet asked. "Can't boys do laundry in this place?"
> "Not in *my* machine!"
> Chet looked bewildered as the girl chided him.
> "Half my laundry was in the machine you're using!" she told him rather sharply.
> Chet blushed. "Gee, I'm sorry. I didn't see it!" He was embarrassed and sat down on a bench, looking glum.
> "Oh, don't take it so hard," the girl said finally. "There's no harm done."
> Encouraged, Chet brightened and began to tell her about his friends and the camping trip. "You see, we're detectives," he said importantly. "And we're looking for a crook named Whip Lasher" [105–106].

The brightened Chet talks about their investigation to impress the girl, who, like Steina the stewardess, provides useful information. When Chet mentions they are seeking a man in a buckskin jacket, the girl tells him that she has seen several men in buckskin jackets. Now willing to forgive the washing machine mix-up, the girl offers to dry Chet's laundry. As in the scene with Biff and the stewardess, the loyal chum does not follow up the girl's helpful gesture beyond a thank you. As soon as his laundry is finished, Chet races back to inform Frank and Joe of his fresh lead.

In *The Shattered Helmet* (1973) Chet moves beyond a brief friendly exchange to actually dating a girl he encounters. In this novel Chet joins Frank, Joe, and a Greek student in a summer film course at a small college. Looking for a local camera shop, Chet notices a tall girl with a "winsome face, short auburn hair, and large hips" (36) who appears to be following them. Chet jokes with Joe, telling him that "'she's got a thing for you'" (36–37). Joe approaches the shy girl and introduces her to the chums. The girl, Thelma Sanger, tells the boys she lives on a farm, which peaks Chet's interest. Thelma then tells the boys she observed them filming near a waterfall, a place she has explored since childhood. She witnessed the boys being attacked and recovered Chet's camera after it fell into the falls. Opening her shopping bag, she returns the camera to Chet. In gratitude, he offers to buy the girl a chocolate soda.

Later that evening when Chet rejoins the chums, Frank asks about his date with the wide-hipped Thelma:

> "Did you enjoy your soda?" Frank said.
> "You bet. All three of them. And brother, can Thelma pack 'em away! She kept up with me!"
> "Yes, I would say she looks well-fed," Joe said. "Does she play tackle or guard on the high school team?"
> "Cut it out," said Chet. "She may be big, but she sure has personality. Besides she likes me!"

Banter about Chet's new girlfriend continued through the dinner hour [39–40].

This is the first time in the entire Hardy Boys series that Frank and Joe comment on a woman's body. While Frank and Joe exhibit the typical teenage male fascination with physical perfection, rotund Chet praises her personality.

The following evening Chet returns to the dorm looking "starry-eyed" which immediately leads Frank to assume he has seen Thelma. Chet announces that the girl is "'the greatest,'" telling the Hardys that the big girl beat him arm wrestling and had such great biceps that "'she'd be great working on a farm!'" (50). Frank and Joe interrupt Chet's starry-eyed reverie, urging him to come "'back to reality'" (50).

As with Biff and Steina, Frank and Joe seem both amused and troubled by a chum's association with a female who might distract him from solving the case. Chet himself is eager to get back on the job, telling Frank he was glad to be free from Thelma who wanted to get engaged.

This is the first time any of the Hardy chums is associated with any serious relationship with a girl that even hints at marriage. The potential engagement is presented as humorous, something Chet is anxious to escape by rejoining Frank and Joe's sleuthing.

The Shattered Helmet also contains a clear bit of gay humor. When the boys enroll at the film course, they spot Leon Saffel, a man they confronted during an airport scuffle. Noticing him as he "fussed with his scarf" Joe quips, "'Oh, boy!... Isn't he cute?'" Frank responds with a taunt, telling his younger brother, "'Don't be jealous'" (23). Attempting to smooth things over between Saffel and the Hardy brothers, an instructor tells them to "'kiss and make up'" (25).

Sirens of the Seventies

In the novels of the 1970s Frank and Joe encounter a number of "lithe" and "willowy" girls who exert an aura of subtle but noticeable sexuality. For the first time it is the Hardys themselves who observe and interact with the girls rather than their chums.

In *The Mysterious Caravan* (1975) the chums encounter a Steina-like character when they arrive in Casablanca and meet Christine, the Eurasian daughter of a physician friend of Fenton Hardy: "The door opened, and the boys turned to see a beautiful dark-haired girl enter. She seemed to be about eighteen years old, slim and lithe. Her slightly almond-shaped eyes flashed over the Americans and she smiled. 'Frank and Joe Hardy?' she asked in a lilting French accent" (122). The girl's exotic beauty makes little impression on the chums. No one makes a comment about her appearance, though some purely platonic socializing occurs as the young people relax over "frosty glasses of coke" and discuss local customs. Frank is cognizant of the lithe female with the almond-shaped eyes, but his observations are more anthropological than erotic. Introduced to her parents, Frank is surprised to see that her father is Vietnamese and her mother French. He reasons that this blend explains her "odd and beautiful look" (135). There is no open flirting, bantering, or even lingering glances on the part of the boys from Bayport.

Ironically, it is shy and reserved Joe who has the first interaction with a siren figure. In *The Witchmaster's Key* (1976) Frank and Joe travel to Britain where they rendezvous with Chet and Phil who are taking a cycling tour of Ireland. While on a ferry to the Isle of Man, the boys are greeted by a "willowy blonde with a big smile" (150). The girl introduces herself as Shirley Evans, a native of the island, who "politely" listens to Chet and Phil, while concentrating her attentions on Joe:

> But it was obvious that she had her eye on Joe. After a while, she directed all her attention to him. Joe did not mind at all. They chatted gaily for a while, then moved away from the others, discussing foreign politics of their respective countries.
> Chet shook his head. "What do you know? Joe's being swept off his feet before our eyes!"
> "Obviously he's in love," Phil added. "Just look at him. His face is one big grin!"
> Frank chuckled. "Shirley's very pretty. I would be grinning too if she'd picked me" [150–151].

The scene presents a role reversal of typical teenage behavior, depicting the girl as the initiator of an interaction, using an opening line to introduce herself to a group of the opposite sex, then selecting one for special attention. The chums, in contrast, are passive. There is no vying for the girl's attention, just quiet envy when the girl chooses Joe. The girl moves from introductory conversation to an invitation, suggesting that the boys come to her parents' home for lunch. Joe eagerly accepts and jumps to his feet. Shirley takes Joe by the arm, being the first to make physical contact and leads him to her home.

At lunch the chums discuss their case with Shirley's father, hoping to learn more about the witch covens they are investigating. After a long discussion, the boys thank their hosts and excuse themselves. Shirley Evans tells Joe to write her, adding "archly" that it would "'foster international understanding'" (153). The word "archly" is interesting, indicating that the girl's interest in Joe is stronger than his interest in her. This, too, reflects a role reversal in teenage behavior. Typically it is the girl who ends an introductory date with a polite goodbye, disappointing a boy hoping for greater intimacy. Afterwards, the chums tease Joe about his new girlfriend, but once back at their hotel, they dismiss discussion of the girl and concentrate on their mission.

In the following novel, *The Jungle Pyramid* (1977), both Frank and Joe go on a date at the invitation of a girl. While in Switzerland, the brothers meet a fellow American youth in the hotel lobby who tells them he is on vacation with his sister and two other girls. The brothers break into "grins after glimpsing three very attractive teen-aged girls" (48). They agree to join the foursome for sodas. While discussing their Swiss trips, two of the girls ask the Hardys to join them on a ski outing:

> Karen set her glass down on the table. "Joe," she said, "do you ski?"
> "A little," Joe answered. "So does Frank."
> "That's great!" Alice exclaimed. "We're leaving today. Want to join us for the weekend?" [48–49].

Again, females initiate a date. Again, the boys cut the encounter short. After a number of risky ski runs, the Hardys bid their new friends farewell and return to solving the mystery of a stolen gold shipment.

These dealings with girls represent the wish fulfillment of the bookish adolescent male who feels too shy and awkward to approach girls, wishing girls would approach him. These scenes liberate Frank and Joe from the teenage male dilemma of being exposed to rejection or ridicule by asking girls out.

But in depicting females as being more assertive, Frank and Joe appear almost feminized in their passivity and their apparent unwillingness to pursue any deeper relationship with the girls who ask them out.

Liberated Coeds

In *The Firebird Rocket* (1978) high school students Frank, Joe, and Chet travel to Princeton University. After spending a day investigating the mysterious disappearance of a scientist, the boys relax in a lounge, where Joe notices three attractive girls. He suggests meeting the "young ladies," and Frank invites them to the chums' table. Hedy Hollwig, "a pretty blonde," introduces her friends Pat and Jane to the boys. The boys ask the girls to dance, and later the three couples engage in a lively discussion. Intrigued by the boys' detective work, the girls bombard them with questions. Disinclined to discuss details of their case, Joe changes the subject by asking the girls how they like Princeton. The brief conversation that follows gives the Hardy Boys series a fleeting homage to feminism, followed by a description of a wholesomely sexless "fun-filled evening" worthy of a chaperoned barn dance of the Twenties:

> "It's great!" Hedy said. "I'm glad they let coeds in."
> Pat nodded vigorously. "This is one thing Women's Lib did for us. Princeton used to be for men only. But no more!"

"Personally, I wouldn't want to go to a school that excludes girls," Chet said, eyeing Jane appreciatively. He smiled at her. "Would you like to dance?"

The young people had a fun-filled evening, and when they finally said goodbye to each other, the Bayporters thanked the girls for their pleasant company. Then Hedy, Pat, and Jane went to their dorm while the Hardys and Chet walked up to their room [40].

Feminine Fragility

Overall, the Hardy Boys series depicts women as caring, compassionate, fragile, and submissive.

In *The Tower Treasure* (1927), for example, Callie Shaw shows great empathy for the Robinsons when the arrest of their father forces them to leave the tower mansion for a slum cottage. While Frank feels reluctant to visit them in their "reduced circumstances," Callie Shaw is deeply moved by the family's plight: "It was evident that she had been profoundly affected by the change that the Tower Mansion mystery had caused in the lives of the Robinsons. Naturally sympathetic and tender-hearted, she felt keenly the injustice of it all, and she realized even more than Frank what it had meant to Mrs. Robinson and the girls to move from their comfortable home in the Mansion to the squalid and distant part of the city in which they now lived" (114).

The concern for comfort and security motivates women to refrain from danger. While males are enthusiastic for adventure, females urge caution, preferring seclusion and safety to action. In *The Secret of Wildcat Swamp* (1952), a Bayport High teacher nicknamed Cap is attacked and beaten in his home to dissuade him from searching for a valuable fossil. Cap and the Hardy Boys are still eager to make the trip, while the teacher's wife expresses feminine concern for her husband's safety:

"I take it you fellows are still interested in making the trip?" Cap asked with a grin.

"More so than ever," Frank cried. "The further you get into a case like this, the more it gets under your skin."

"All I ask," Mrs. Bailey interrupted with a worried glance at her husband, "is that you all take care of yourselves. I'm afraid that these men may be very desperate characters" [22].

This feminine concern for security echoes Laura Hardy's in *The Wailing Siren Mystery* published a year before. Learning that someone had been spying on the Hardy house, Mrs. Hardy is worried. With her husband absent, her elder son provides masculine reassurance: "Returning upstairs, the brothers were met by their mother. 'Do you suppose that Peeping Tom will come again?' she asked anxiously. 'Oh, dear, I wish your father were home!' 'Don't worry, Mother,' Frank said quickly" (30–31).

Women are depicted as helpless without their husbands. In *The Secret of Wildcat Swamp*, a widow is pressured by criminals to sign a document. "The woman mourns, '"I wish my husband were still alive!... He'd know what to do"' (197).

The notion that women are helpless is repeated in the following novel, *The Crisscross Shadow* (1953), in which Frank and Joe rush home from a football game after Aunt Gertrude tells them of a suspicious salesman. Because their father is out of town the brothers feel "a protective responsibility toward the two women at home" (3). Again, adolescent boys are depicted as the protectors of adult females who are presumed to be both weaker and more vulnerable to not only physical assault but also a con man's ploys.

The difference between the genders is illustrated in how men and women react to a common event. When Frank and Joe are pushed in front of a train, the reaction of the people on the platform divides on gender lines: "Men shouted. Women screamed and covered their eyes" (92). Men call out to warn or summon help. Women voice emotion and hide from unpleasant danger.

The idea that women need to be shielded from danger is demonstrated in *The Mystery at Devil's Paw* (1959). When Frank and Joe are forced off the road by a truck, Fenton Hardy warns his sons, "'Better not mention the attack to your mother or Aunt Gertrude'" (12). Teenage Frank and Joe join their father in a male conspiracy of silence and deception, protecting women from the truth for their own good.

Chapter 10

Hardy Family Values

> Literature these books were not but, by God, they were Moral.
> — Leslie McFarlane, *Ghost of the Hardy Boys*

Part of the appeal of juvenile fiction is the escape to a dream world of adolescence where young people triumph over the restrictions of school, homework, chores, after-school jobs, parents, teachers, and adult authority in general.

The appeal of the Hardy Boys lies in their independence and freedom. Though they are high school students living with their parents, they transcend the limitations faced by their readers. For one, they are depicted in near constant motion. At fifteen and sixteen, Joe and Frank Hardy roar down Shore Road on motorcycles, zip across Barmet Bay in speedboats in summer and iceboats in winter, race down highways in roadsters, and eventually defy gravity by taking to the air in planes. Like adults, they travel cross-country in train compartments and stay in hotels in cities like New York and Chicago. With the development of air travel following World War II, the Hardy brothers travel overseas to Guatemala, Puerto Rico, Jamaica, Britain, Ireland, Iceland, Brazil, and Hong Kong — without parental supervision.

Unlike most of their readers, Frank and Joe Hardy are economically independent. Having earned thousands of dollars in reward money, they have the cash to finance their ventures without having to accept a demeaning parental allowance or work after school for minimum wage. When the boys do work, they do so as entrepreneurs, managing their own businesses, often competing successfully against resentful adults. When they run short of funds or their car is destroyed, gracious Fenton Hardy stakes his sons with expense money and a new car — without a lecture.

Throughout the series, Frank and Joe Hardy remain teenagers who live at home with their parents. *The Tower Treasure* introduces Frank and Joe as having a typical child/parent conflict on page three, as the boys manage to converse above the roar of two motorcycles. Both express frustration with their parents' lack of support for their interest in becoming detectives like their father:

> "But whenever we mention it to dad he just laughs at us," said Joe Hardy.
> "Tells us to wait until we're through school and then we can think about being detectives."
> "Well, at least he's more encouraging than mother," remarked Frank. "She comes out plump and plain and says she wants one of us to be a doctor and the other a lawyer."
> "What a fine lawyer either of us would make!" sniffed Joe. "Or a doctor, either! We were both cut out to be detectives and dad knows it!" [3].

This establishes the basis of the parent/child conflict that runs through the early novels. Eternally teenagers, Frank and Joe continually struggle to establish their independence and win the approval of their father, demonstrating over and over again their ability to outsmart both menacing adult criminals and condescending adult cops. Hoping for a mystery of their own in the first chapter of the first novel, Joe asserts "we'll show that Fenton Hardy's sons are worthy of his name" (4).

Within a few adventures the boys become junior partners with their father, often rescuing him from kidnappers, demonstrating skills and maturity while remaining obedient sons.

Fenton Hardy

Although the Hardy Boys rebel against their elders, it is a highly respectful rebellion. Unlike other children who rebel because they want to pursue something their parents consider unacceptable, Frank and Joe rebel because they want to be just like their father. Though eager to establish their independence, they nevertheless take direction from their father, who often challenges them, provides lessons, and tempers their adolescent impulses.

Fenton Hardy is the dream dad. Handsome, athletic, successful and respected, he provides his sons a perfect role model and serves as a mentor. In several novels Frank and Joe rely on their father's name and reputation to gain access to witnesses and assistance from police departments across the country.

In *The Tower Treasure* when Frank and Joe inform their father that witnesses have given conflicting descriptions of the holdup man's hair color, Fenton Hardy provides a lesson in close observation, echoing Sherlock Holmes' ability to astound Dr. Watson with his keen perception:

"For instance, I'll give you a test. You have each seen Superintendent Norton of Bayport high school — well, how often?"

"About two or three thousand times, I guess," answered Frank.

"Over a period of three years. Well, what color is his hair?"

Frank looked blankly at Joe.

"Why, it's — it's — "

Joe scratched his head.

"Brown, isn't?"

"I think it's black."

"You see?" said Mr. Hardy, smiling. "Your powers of observation have not been trained. A good detective has to school himself to remember all sorts of little facts like that, until it gets to be a habit with him. Both of you have been looking at Mr. Norton for about three years and you don't know the color of his hair. And if I asked you whether he was in the habit of wearing laced shoes or buttoned shoes you would be stumped altogether. As a matter of fact, Mr. Norton is bald and he wears a chestnut wig. You never noticed that? He always wears buttoned shoes, he belongs to the Elks, and his favorite author is Dickens" [35–36].

In the following chapter Joe follows his father's advice and accurately notes a distinctive tire tread that leads to the discovery of Chet Morton's stolen roadster.

After the Tower Mansion is robbed, the brothers decide to get a list of the stolen gems to check local pawnshops. Learning their father has already contacted the pawnbrokers, the Hardy Boys feel deflated. Realizing his sons are out for the thousand dollar reward to solve the robbery, Fenton Hardy challenges Frank and Joe, calling them the "opposition."

The boys are eager to win the reward and prove to their father their crime-solving abilities, but when they discover a valuable clue they cannot pursue on their own, they turn to Fenton Hardy, knowing that he will deal fairly with them and give them full credit for their share in the investigation. Frank and Joe are forced to accept their limitations. Although they discover the thief's discarded wig and clothing, they lack the technical knowledge and access to police resources to follow up the lead. They give the evidence to their father who goes to New York City to speak with wigmakers and follow the trail leading to Red Jackley. Trying to escape, Jackley is injured and lies dying in the hospital.

Fenton Hardy is presented with a dilemma. The bumbling Chief Collig and Detective Smuff have gotten wind of the suspect and announce their intention of interrogating the dying criminal. They will take credit for solving the crime, depriving the Hardys from the reward. Worse, the incompetent pair will likely cause Jackley to "clam up" and fail to obtain the confession needed to clear Perry Robinson's father. "Collig and Smuff will have first right to talk to him, for they are officials and I'm only a private detective," Fenton Hardy admits to his sons.

While Frank and Joe depend on the father's mature professionalism, Fenton Hardy has to rely on his sons' adolescent innovation to make sure his rivals miss the train to New York so he can obtain a deathbed confession without interference. The brothers, along with their retinue of chums, hatch a number of schemes, including kidnapping until they come up with a fake bomb, creating one of the most beloved comic scenes in Hardy Boys fiction.

Thus, the father/son conflict is resolved by a cooperative rivalry that demonstrates mutual dependence as a requirement for success. It is the teenage sons, not the veteran detective, who discover the stolen treasure. After obtaining the dying man's confession that he hid the loot in the "old tower," Fenton Hardy is stumped, admitting that he had "exhausted every line of action in the case." The boys savor their triumph over the police, not by defying law enforcement officials but by beating them at their own game. The metamorphosis of curmudgeonly Hurd Applegate into a "good old scout" scribbling out reward checks and hosting a celebratory feast for the boys is pure wish fulfillment.

But even in victory, Frank shows remarkable maturity when Joe wishes for another mystery, noting, "'We can't expect to get a reward for every case we work on — and we can't expect to solve 'em all, either" (209).

Laura Hardy

Laura (sometimes named Mildred) Hardy is loving, supportive, and eternally innocent. Having a "gentle nature that instinctively shrank from any discussion of crime," she is "distressed" that her husband's profession leads to the incarceration of the felons he brings to justice. Her unwillingness to hear about "terrible things" reduces her status within the family. Fenton Hardy shares knowledge with his sons, so that as teenagers they are more informed than their adult mother, who remains naively supportive.

For Frank and Joe, their mother's concern presents a moral dilemma, an obstacle to investigations that require them to take risks. In the third novel, *The Secret of the Old Mill* (1927), Frank and Joe want to spy on suspected counterfeiters at night but face the problem of their mother's expected "lecture":

"How can we get out to-night? Mother won't let us go. She'll be afraid we'll get hurt."

"I hate to do anything underhand, but it's our only chance. We'll go out for a motorcycle trip this evening, and as soon as it gets dark we'll head for the mill ..."

"If we get the goods on the counterfeiters we'll be heroes. If we don't we'll catch a lecture for staying out late" [169].

After being "conspicuously studious" for hours, the boys express a desire for some fresh air. Fenton Hardy urges them to go out, saying, "'Yes, you've been in the house all evening. Go ahead'" (170). In contrast, their mother warns them, "'Don't be too long'" (170).

By the fourth volume, *The Missing Chums* (1928), Laura Hardy is depicted as having a change of heart. Though still viewing their desire to become detectives "with considerable apprehension" she has "now almost resigned herself" to her sons following their father's footsteps, given their string of successes. When Frank and Joe announce they are heading to Blacksnake Island to search for Biff and Chet, their mother is supportive, trusting their judgment and maturity: "She knew her sons well enough to realize that they would not run into needless dangers, and when she kissed them good-bye her only request was that they would not stay away any longer than was necessary" (87–88).

Frank and Joe remain respectful of their mother and sensitive to her concerns for their safety. In later novels, however, she is depicted as being easily manipulated because of her feminine naiveté and compassion. In *The Wailing Siren Mystery* (1951) when Laura Hardy tells Frank that Chet had called stating his mother needed twenty-five hundred dollars, her son instantly suspects a hoax: "'Mother, you didn't fall for a line like that!' Frank exclaimed. 'Chet's mother would never ask for a loan of that much money!' Mrs. Hardy looked at her tall son in amazement as he continued (141)." Frank comforts his mother, accepting her gullibility as a maternal trait, telling her, "'I know you're generous and sympathetic'" (142).

Although Frank and Joe rack up continual successes, winning approval from grateful adults and praise from the FBI, they still remain teenagers requiring parental permission. Presented with a new mystery in *The Secret of Wildcat Swamp* (1952), the boys are excited but admit "'first we'll have to get Dad's and Mother's okay'" (7). By the Fifties their mother is deferential to her husband. In asking permission, the boys discover "their quiet, pretty mother" will leave the decision to their father. In 1963's *The Viking Symbol Mystery* she exerts enough influence over the boys to make them go to bed rather than pursue a hot lead. The boys follow her suggestion without an argument: "'You can look for that evidence in the morning,' their mother announced quietly. 'It *is* late.' Admitting that it had been a long day, the brothers said good night and went to bed. They were sound asleep almost instantly" (16–17).

Although the boys obey their mother, they remain protective, not wishing to worry her when they are placed in danger. They do not even ask her for help when they are stranded in New York City with only fifty cents. They decide to call home and have their mother wire them money until they discover the cost of the phone call will be seventy-five cents. When the switchboard operator informs them they can easily reverse the charges, the boys are initially elated but reject the suggestion to spare their mother anxiety:

"Say, that's an idea!" exclaimed Joe. "We can do that!"

Frank shook his head.

"No," he said in a low voice to his brother. "To let Mother know we are broke, or almost broke, in New York, would only worry her. Of course she'd let us reverse the charge all right, but I don't want her to worry."

"I don't, either," Joe said [143–144].

Aunt Gertrude

Perhaps more memorable than either Hardy parent is Aunt Gertrude, the boys' peppery, dictatorial maiden great aunt whom many children came to love. She makes her first appearance in *The Missing Chums* (1928). Described as a "maiden lady of middle-age" with no fixed home, she descends on relatives to live for weeks or months at a time, announcing her visit with the air of a royal command. Her relatives "had discovered that the best plan was to suffer her visits in silence and pray for her speedy departure" (51). She is an exaggerated stereotype of the stern, suspicious, patronizing authority figure: "The worthy lady had a habit of regarding them as though they were still in swaddling clothes and she invariably showed a tendency to dictate as to their food, their hours of rising and going to bed, their companions, and their choice of literature" (51). Learning that the brothers are planning a boat trip, Aunt Gertrude launches into one of customary tirades, which many readers recall as one of their favorite scenes, full of doom and dire predictions:

> "Boat trip! Boat trip! No! That settles it!" declared Aunt Gertrude, coming into the house and banging the umbrella decisively on the floor by way of emphasis. "I shan't allow it. The very idea! Laura," she said, turning to Mrs. Hardy, "I'm surprised at you. Ab-so-lute-ly astonished! The very idea of letting these children go out in a boat! Don't you remember what happened to my Cousin Peter? He went out on a boat, didn't he? And what happened? The boat upset. He might have been drowned if the water had been deep enough. Thank goodness he was only a few feet from shore. But it only goes to show what *can* happen. If these boys go out in a boat they'll be drowned. They shan't go on any boat trip. That settles it!" [58].

Forever predicting doom and disaster and extolling old-fashioned bits of wisdom, Aunt Gertrude provides the Hardy Boys with a pseudo-family figure they can dismiss, deride, outwit, and ridicule without being disrespectful to their mother. In contrast to Aunt Gertrude, Laura Hardy becomes more like an older sister, conspiring to help the boys get away: "'Run!' she said, smiling. 'I'll take care of Aunt Gertrude. Run along while you have the chance.' They kissed their mother good-bye and hastily departed, wondering how she was to explain their flight to the terrible Aunt Gertrude, in view of that lady's melancholy predictions concerning their fate should they venture out in the boat" (60–61).

At mystery's end, Laura Hardy welcomes back her successful husband and sons, now fully accepting their choice of profession, despite Aunt Gertrude's protestations about allowing "men-folks to go gallivantin' around the country and never stayin' at home":

> "Well," smilingly replied Mrs. Hardy, who had entered the room with Aunt Gertrude, "with three first-rate detectives in the family, I'm afraid I can't expect anything else. And they always come home again."
> Aunt Gertrude sniffed.
> "I'll guarantee that if I visit here much longer I'll see that those two boys haven't much chance for more detecting!" she announced. "I'll cure 'em, so I will. It's no business at all for boys."
> Mrs. Hardy smiled serenely.
> Fenton Hardy winked gravely at this sons, so Aunt Gertrude's threat did not greatly disturb them [213].

Having won their parents' respect, trust, and approval, the Hardy Boys collaborate with their parents almost as equals or at best younger siblings. Aunt Gertrude serves to dramatize the generational conflict that frustrates most children. She provides the constant criticism, lectures, threats, and injunctions children hear from adults who declare them to be helpless, naïve, and untrustworthy. In contrast, Fenton and Laura Hardy are not so much disciplinarians but mediators on their sons' behalf, praising their maturity and responsibility.

The typical mother/child conflict is entirely absent in the series. Laura Hardy remains the supportive and safety-conscious mother, forever making sandwiches and warning the boys to be careful. She never lectures, confronts, grounds, or says no to her sons. The boys' conflict with the older generation is directed against their father's maiden sister. The easy, trusting relationship between parent and child is another element of the wish-fulfillment theme.

The notion of deflecting generational conflict away from parents onto other mature figures follows a pattern established by Stratemeyer in his early stories. Deidre Johnson notes Stratemeyer's plot device of having adolescent heroes rebel against guardians or other adults rather than their mothers and fathers: "the protagonist's struggle with and final victory over his guardian or authority figure can be seen as the child breaking free from his parents, overthrowing his subordinate role to become an adult. Stratemeyer, however, sidesteps the issue of filial disrespect or disobedience by replacing the natural parents with a substitute figure, one who is [clearly] misusing his authority."[1]

Aunt Gertrude remains a staple character in the novels, though in later mysteries she takes a supporting role in the boys' adventures. While she still warns them of danger and predicts disaster, she often aids the boys by relaying important messages, usually by telephone or radio. *The Crisscross Shadow*

(1953) describes Aunt Gertrude as the "boys' favorite relative," whom they "respect for her insight into human nature" (3). In *The Secret of Pirates' Hill* (1957), Aunt Gertrude goes into action. Discovering Frank and Joe unconscious in the basement of the Bayport Historical Society, Miss Hardy seizes an antique cutlass and attacks their assailant:

> With a flailing motion, she slapped the man's back with the broad side of the cutlass. He shoved her back.
> "Oh, no, you don't!" she cried out.
> *Thwack!* She hit him again. Terrified, the man dropped the five cutlasses with a din heard in the meeting room upstairs and leaped to the sill. As he started to crawl through the window, Aunt Gertrude whacked him again! [58].

By the Sixties Aunt Gertrude is depicted in milder terms. In *The Mystery of the Aztec Warrior* (1964) she "adores" her nephews but thinks "they were not cautious enough in their sleuthing" (13). The novel points out that on "a few occasions her dire predictions of danger had come true" (13).

Trust

Teenagers live under a cloud of permanent suspicion from adults. Parents, teachers, police officers, shop owners, and employers warily eye adolescents as potential troublemakers. Television commercials, talk show hosts, therapists, and experts continually urge parents to watch their children for signs of drug use and inappropriate behavior. Adolescents dislike intrusion and seek to establish zones of privacy, resenting parental monitoring of their email, clothing choices, viewing habits, diet, and grades.

Frank and Joe Hardy, however, enjoy an open and trusting relationship with their parents. Laura Hardy expresses concern for her sons and urges them to be cautious but never demeans them by reminding them they are children or challenging their judgment, skills, maturity, or manhood. She never suspects her sons of doing anything illicit or immoral.

The degree of trust the boys enjoy is demonstrated in *The Great Airport Mystery* (1930). While searching for clues in a small cabin, Frank picks up an empty pack of cigarettes. Joe chides him, saying, "If mother finds that package in your pocket she'll think you've been smoking." Frank's reply that "Mother knows us well enough to know we don't smoke" (79–80) voices a level of parental trust most children would envy.

Religion

The early novels offer only a few hints of the role religion plays in the lives of the Hardys. Their respect for the Sabbath is demonstrated in *What*

Happened at Midnight (1931) when the chums agree that a party will end at twelve "since the next day was Sunday" (213). Actual references to church attendance don't appear in the books until the Sixties. In *The Mystery of the Chinese Junk* (1960) Frank tells Jim Foy he and Joe will meet him the following morning "after church" (37). Although Fenton Hardy is kidnapped in the opening chapter of *The Secret Agent on Flight 101* (1967), Frank and Joe wait to meet a security official "after church" (20). The benefits of religious life are alluded to only briefly. In *The Mystery of the Spiral Bridge* (1966) the Hardy Boys learn that a suspect, now dead, had reformed in prison and "become very religious" (48). The only overt demonstration of religion does not occur in the series until 1974's *The Clue of the Hissing Serpent* when a panicked Tony Prito crosses himself when a small plane is caught in a storm.

Alcohol and Tobacco

The first dozen Hardy Boy novels were published during Prohibition so that drinking was not only a moral but also a legal issue. The only characters who drink are criminals. Fenton Hardy never toasts a victory over a cocktail or sips an evening brandy while contemplating a course of action. Except for the scene describing the elder Hardy puffing on a pipe in his library in *The Tower Treasure,* he appears not to be a regular cigarette smoker.

Alcohol and tobacco are entirely absent from the majority of the novels. Unlike heroes in dime novels, Frank and Joe do not follow clues through smoky taverns, bars, nightclubs, or even restaurants serving cocktails. None of the chums lights a cigarette or alludes to drinking. Occasionally rural characters, like the farmhands in *The Tower Treasure* take "hearty chews" from a plug of tobacco (19).

The theme of intoxication occurs only in a few novels. In 1929's *The Secret of the Caves* Frank and Joe discover the car thief Carl Schaum on a beach "senseless from the effects of the liquor he had drunk" (138). Determining that Schaum is "dead drunk," Frank suggests they tie him up. Once they secure the stuporous drunk, Frank and Joe toss hatfuls of cold sea water into his face to wake him up. The Hardys take delight in their captive's helpless state: "As he sat on the beach, with his wet hair down over his eyes, his clothes completely soaked, he was a ridiculous object, and his expression of mingled wrath and surprise made it difficult for the lads to restrain their laughter" (140-141). The scene in uncharacteristic in the series. The Hardy Boys are rarely depicted gloating over a victory or tormenting an adversary. McFarlane may have sensed that was acceptable in this instance because Schaum was drunk.

The Great Airport Mystery starts with a replay of the opening of *The*

Tower Treasure. This time, instead of being nearly run down by a speed demon, Frank and Joe are almost killed by a drunken mail pilot who crashes his plane next to their roadster. Giles Ducroy stumbles from the wreckage and threatens the Hardys, blaming them for his wrecked plane. When Frank tells him he should sober up, Ducroy explodes with rage. A farmer, who witnessed the crash, sides with Frank and Joe, confirming their view that the pilot is intoxicated. Later Frank and Joe read in the newspaper that Ducroy was fired by postal authorities and had his pilot's license canceled for drinking. When Frank and Joe spy on Ducroy and his confederates plotting a crime in a remote cabin, liquor is present and the men are drinking: "There, in the dimly lighted interior of the building, they saw Giles Ducroy, Ollie Jacobs, and Newt Pipps seated about a rude table, with a bottle and glasses for them.... 'Nothing venture, nothing gain,' said Ducroy, taking a swig from the bottle" (53). Suspecting that someone might be listening, Newt Pipps announces he will look around. Frank and Joe are frightened because there is no place to hide. They duck behind some small bushes that offer only partial cover so that they "were so poorly hidden that they could plainly see Newt Pipps as he came around the corner" (55). But Frank and Joe are not discovered because "Pipps had been drinking" and gives the area only a drunken cursory glance. Back inside the cabin, Newt Pipps continues the discussion with Giles Ducroy and Ollie Jacobs, who finishes the bottle as the meeting breaks up.

Afterwards Frank and Joe speculate the meaning of the conversation they overheard. When Joe asks why Ducroy would select such a remote location for a meeting, Frank references the alcohol: "'It may have been because of the liquor. It's against the law to have it.... Perhaps we were only listening in on a drinking party after all'" (64). When they search the cabin for clues, Frank and Joe find the empty bottle and numerous cigarette butts.

In the following Prohibition-era novel, *What Happened at Midnight*, Frank and Joe tail a suspect to New York City. They follow him into a restaurant and attempt to eavesdrop when an angry customer demands they leave his favorite table. The waiter apologizes profusely, explaining the man is "'an ugly customer when he is drinking'" (129). On another occasion, the Hardys follow the suspect to a restaurant where they listen as illegal liquor is served:

> True enough, they could hear voices from the next booth. They heard a clinking of glasses and they saw one of the waiters enter the booth furtively with something concealed beneath a napkin. One of the men laughed loudly.
> "That's real service, Luigi. Not afraid of the prohibition agents, are you?"
> "Ssh!" cautioned the waiter. "Strangers in the next booth" [133].

With the end of Prohibition, McFarlane included fewer references to alcohol. Later novels rarely allude to drinking, even by criminals.

Modesty and Honesty

The Hardy Boys are pillars of all-American values of truth, honesty, and democracy. In *The Wailing Siren Mystery* (1951) money literally falls from the sky. Aboard the *Sleuth* on Barmet Bay, the boys hear the approach of an aircraft and see an object drop to the water. Frank manages to grab the item before it sinks below the waves and discovers that it is a wallet containing two thousand dollars. The brothers never discuss keeping the money for themselves and place an ad in the newspaper hoping to locate the owner. Fearing the money may be stolen, they take the wallet to the police station for safe keeping.

The extent of Frank and Joe's fair-mindedness is exhibited in *The Crisscross Shadow* (1953). When two assailants lock the brothers in a tenement closet, Frank rams his body against the door. Joe warns him to knock first, saying, "'We don't want to pay for a broken door'" (29). The idea that someone trapped in a slum closet would worry about damaging the door in order to escape exhibits a level of respect for property not shown in adult detective stories.

Respect for property is highlighted in several other instances. In *The Clue in the Embers* (1956) the Hardy Boys and their chums unearth a long-buried palace in Guatemala. Marveling at a golden throne inlaid with emeralds and rubies, the boys never consider enriching themselves. Surveying the wealth of artifacts, Frank Hardy announces, "'These treasures are certainly government property!... No one must be allowed to steal them. We must notify the Guatemalan government at once'" (199). Not only do the boys leave the treasure intact, they refuse taking a gold souvenir offered by the President of Guatemala as a reward. When the boys learn that the president insists they take a souvenir from the palace, Frank selects a gold bracelet for his mother and Joe chooses a small gold idol for Aunt Gertrude. A similar scene occurs in *The Mystery at Devil's Paw* (1959) when Frank and Joe locate a valuable treasure in the British Columbia wilderness. Joe recalls that their father "impressed on his two sons their responsibility for safeguarding any valuables which they turned up on a case," and they consider what to do with the artifacts. If they leave them behind, there is a chance they may be stolen. On the other hand, if they attempt to carry the valuables, they might be robbed. "'Besides,' Frank pointed out, 'I doubt if we have the right to carry such treasure out of British Columbia, even if we planned to turn it over to the Canadian authorities later'" (142). A similar concern is expressed in *The Mysterious Caravan* (1975) when Joe discovers an ancient death mask on a Jamaican beach. The boys ask an Arab antique dealer to examine their find. After verifying the mask's authenticity and estimating its value, he offers to buy the artifact. Frank objects, saying to the shopkeeper, "'You know we can't. It belongs to the government of Jamaica'" (37).

The Mystery of the Aztec Warrior (1964) depicts a similar scene demonstrating the boys' modesty. When Frank and Joe Hardy present the curator of a Mexican museum with a valuable artifact, they refuse to take credit for their find, pointing out that they had merely "picked the stone up" that had been "discovered" by a missing archaeologist (106).

Although Frank and Joe are heroes and clearly the leaders of the chums, they are not autocratic. In *The Wailing Siren Mystery*, for example, they bow to the concerns of their pals when they receive threats while camping:

> After Chet heard the whole story, he said, "Two warnings are enough for me. I vote we leave this place."
> "I think Chet's right," Biff said. "Let's shove off."
> Tony agreed with Chet and Biff.
> "What's more," he said, "my dad's expecting me home to drive for him."
> Outvoted, the Hardys agreed to go, but begged the others to stay until morning.
> "Look fellows," Frank said, "Joe and I will do some work alone. You fellows stay here and swim" [111].

Social Responsibility

Closely associated with their modesty and honesty is a strong sense of social responsibility. In *The Clue of the Screeching Owl* (1962) Frank, Joe, and Chet escape injury when a wooden bridge collapses. Immediately, they are concerned about the danger the bridge poses to others:

> "We'll have to do something," Joe declared, "to warn other drivers."
> Crossing to the opposite bank, Frank and Joe set up a temporary roadblock by rolling some logs down from the wooded hillside. Meanwhile, Chet arranged a line of good-sized rocks to close off the bridge on the other end.
> "We must report this as soon as we come to a phone," Joe remarked [47].

Later when the boys travel on a remote road and spot a stalled vehicle, they stop to assist the stranded drivers. The chums' final good deeds of the novel include rescuing a boy who becomes lost in the woods searching for a missing dog and reuniting him with his pet. This attention to animals is not restricted to lost pets. Although the chums had been threatened by a puma used by villains to protect their hideout, they are concerned about its welfare after the gang is arrested, and Joe insists the animal be donated to a zoo.

Social Consciousness

Frank and Joe typically use their investigatory skills to solve crimes against the rich or at least the comfortable. They protect entrepreneurs harassed by conspirators and save governments from rebels and terrorists. In a few situations, however, they are shown acting on behalf of the poor.

In *The Sinister Signpost* (1936) Frank and Joe attend a county fair. The "gay scene" includes a merry-go-round, vendors, shooting galleries, and a race track. Standing in line at a refreshment stand, they observe a "timid little woman" take a five-dollar bill from a "worn purse" and purchase an ice cream cone for her small son. The vendor briskly counts out her change, then turns to serve to Frank and Joe. Ever alert, Frank notices that a "trick had been perpetrated" on the timid woman. The vendor had deftly made change for only four dollars, keeping the extra dollar for himself. Watching the confused woman counting her change, Frank confronts the man behind the counter:

> "You owe the lady a dollar, I think," said Frank.
> The vendor scowled.
> "You mind your own business, young fellow," he said impudently. "She got her change."
> "We'll check it for you, ma'am," said Joe. "Look — one dollar, two-three-three-ninety. One dollar short, and we saw you give him a five-dollar bill."
> Frank regarded the fellow with level eyes.
> "Come on!" he said. "Give the lady the extra dollar."
> "Funny. Guess I must have made a mistake," grumbled the vendor, reluctantly handing over the money.
> "Perhaps we'd better tell one of the fair-grounds constables to keep an eye on you," Joe suggested.
> "Thank you ever so much," exclaimed the woman. "I had only five dollars, and if I'd lost a whole dollar it would have meant less food for my family this week. It was mighty kind of you to help me."
> "That's all right," they assured her, and drifted off into the crowd, regardless of the vendor's baleful glances [13–14].

This scene of helping a woman save a dollar needed for groceries resonated no doubt with readers during the Depression, when many stenographers earned sixteen dollars a week and department store sales ladies took home as little as seven dollars.[2]

Hard Work

A key Hardy Boys virtue is hard work. Joe Hardy announces in *The Mystery of the Spiral Bridge* (1966) that "'There's no mystery that can't be solved, if it's worked on long and hard enough'" (68). Again and again, the boys learn that to solve cases they must engage in arduous and sometimes boring labor to achieve their goals. In *The Secret of Wildcat Swamp* (1952) Frank and Joe learn from their science teacher that searching for ancient fossils requires hard, manual labor: "Swinging the heavy picks, they soon loosened the top layer of sandy soil. But when they had cleared away the soil they had loosened, the harder work began. 'This is really packed down,' Frank grunted as he swung the business end of a pick into hardpan and penetrated only a few inches. 'If we do very much of this stuff, we'll have shoulders like that guy Turk!'" (64).

In *The Crisscross Shadow* the boys discover a clue, an R design imprinted on a leather key case. Hoping to discover the maker of the leather goods, the boys spend several days calling on "every possible place" and visiting "all the leather goods shops in Bayport and examined key cases, wallets, handbags, and luggage" (32). But even their search through local shoe stores yields no information. None of the merchants report having ever seen the symbol. Although the search is fruitless and turns out to be a blind alley, the boys are not discouraged and continue their investigation. Detective work, readers learn, is often hard and boring. The same novel shows the brothers also hard at work at football. Frank and Joe's gridiron prowess is not automatic but requires hard work and adult direction: "During the next two hours they worked hard, running, tackling, trying out signals under the watchful eye of Coach Devlin. Finally, when the sun was setting over the empty stands, he dismissed the squad, telling them to take one lap around the field before hitting the showers" (79). The momentary thrill of adulation the boys receive when Joe scores a winning touchdown is only possible because of their long practice before "empty stands."

School

Although Frank and Joe Hardy are not bookish, they are serious students. While the novels conveniently arrange the mysteries on summer vacations, weekends, and holidays, school is continually mentioned as a priority. Throughout the Fifties and Sixties the back covers of the Hardy Boys books advertised the series, emphasizing the fact that crime solving for the school-age brothers is only an avocation: "Sons of a famous American detective, the Hardy boys help solve many thrilling cases after school hours and during vacations, as they follow up the clues they unearth in their quest to bring criminals to justice." In *The Secret of the Old Mill* (1927), which was part of the breeder set trilogy, Leslie McFarlane interrupts the Hardy brother's hunt for counterfeiters by having the brothers do schoolwork. Although the boys resent being made to study, they dedicate themselves to learning what the adult world mandates:

> Hard work in school occupied the attention of the boys for the rest of the week, for examination time was near, and even Jerry Gilroy was obliged to dismiss baseball from his mind in a frantic attempt to catch up with his geometry

and Latin, that somehow appeared to keep perpetually ahead of him. Frank and Joe sweated over the ablative absolute and grumbled over the heroic exploits that could be resurrected from the deathless lines of Caesar and Virgil if one could but distinguish verbs from nouns, and wondered, as schoolboys have wondered from time immemorial, why they should be obliged to concern themselves with things that happened two thousand years ago and more when they might better be outside playing ... [33].

A week went by, a week in which the Hardy boys and their chums again wrestled with refractory Latin phrases and geometrical problems, as the examinations drew near. There was little time for fun, even outside school hours. The boys were all overcome by that helpless feeling that comes with the approach of examinations, the feeling that everything they had ever known had somehow escaped their memory and that as fast as they learned one fact they forgot another [71].

Even when the brothers are deep in a mystery, they hit the books. When Joe remarks that he would rather be hunting down suspects, Frank agrees, noting however that he has to study algebra. Math comes before adventure.

Fortunately for Frank and Joe, life seems to consist of extended summer vacations. When a mystery cannot be solved within the limits of Christmas break, Bayport High conveniently closes for repairs. In *Hunting for Hidden Gold* (1928), a blizzard tears off the school roof, forcing a two-week holiday extension, giving Frank and Joe enough time to journey west to a gold mine and not miss any classes. Nearly fifty years later in *The Mysterious Caravan*, Bayport High's steam boiler breaks down, forcing another two-week holiday extension, allowing the Hardys and chums time to venture to Africa. The author points out, however, that this respite is not a reprieve from classes, which will have to be made up in an extended school year.

The Hardy boys use academic skills to solve mysteries. Libraries and librarians play key roles in some of the postwar novels. In *The Mystery of the Whale Tattoo* (1968) Frank, Joe, and Chet visit the New York Public Library to search old newspapers to locate background information on a missing whale exhibit. The scene provides a brief lesson in research practices and library etiquette. The chums locate indexes for New York newspapers from the 1920s, and begin to studiously peruse the records, "poring through the thick volumes" (108). The work is tedious, but the boys continue studying as "the large clock on the wall silently marked the passage of time" (108). After Chet locates a relevant entry, the boys request the "appropriate roll of microfilm and put it into the viewing machine" (110). Frank is described operating the viewer and the author notes that the boys "returned the microfilm to the librarian" before leaving.

A similar library scene occurs in *The Mysterious Caravan* where Frank and Joe become so engrossed in books about African history and a king's journey to Mecca that they lose all track of time (52). Three years later the chums pore over books about Australia in the Princeton library. Although interrupted by a suspicious character, the boys demonstrate library etiquette and carefully return books to their proper places before leaving.

Chores

Like all children Frank and Joe have family chores. Though they may find the work less interesting than solving crimes, they accept the assignments as a necessary family duty. Returning from a case in New York, the brothers are greeted by their mother who "wistfully" tells her sons she has felt lonely with both her husband and sons away. She also informs them "there are a lot of jobs around here that need my sons' attention" (*The Clue in the Embers*, 61). Frank and Joe help their mother without complaint and for "the next thirty-six hours the boys remained at home, cutting grass, weeding, running errands" (61).

Unlike their teenage readers, however, Frank and Joe can count on their chores being quickly followed by calls to adventure, out-of-town trips, or intriguing mysteries.

Chapter 11

Law and Order

> Would civilization crumble if kids got the notion that the people who ran the world were sometimes stupid, occasionally wrong and even corrupt at times?
> — Leslie McFarlane, *Ghost of the Hardy Boys*

As teen detectives, Frank and Joe Hardy strike a balance between the parental concern for respect and order and the adolescent drive for independence and freedom. On one hand, as investigators, the Hardy Boys are enforcers of security, stability, authority, and the status quo. In tracking down thieves, dope smugglers, counterfeiters, and enemy spies, they serve as agents for the adult world. They restore stolen property to its rightful owners. They ensure that wills, deeds, and legal documents are enforced. They protect America from hostile aliens. Unlike many adult detective heroes, however, the Hardy Boys never inflict punishments or use violence against their adversaries. Instead, miscreants are turned over to the authorities, be it the Bayport Police Department, the U.S. Coast Guard, or the Mexican army. On the other hand, as teenagers, they show self-reliance and initiative, confronting and defeating adult criminals and overcoming the deprecating remarks of adult skeptics by solving cases that baffled grownups. They often rebel against the local police, triumphing over uniformed adults who dismiss their suggestions or ridicule their efforts. Thus Frank and Joe Hardy are both social rebels and engines of conformity.

Law Enforcement

The Hardy Boys' relationship with the police undergoes an evolution. Leslie McFarlane, who believed that young people should be prepared to question authority figures, depicted the Bayport cops as vain, bumbling, incompetents in the original novels. Chief Ezra Collig is introduced in *The Tower Treasure* as a "burly, red-faced individual, much given to telling long-winded stories," who is usually found "reading the comic papers or polishing up his numerous badges" (26). Detective Smuff is depicted as pompous and stupid. Patrolman Con Riley is a stereotyped heavyset Irish cop, slow both in thought and action. The Hardys and the chums frequently poke fun at Riley, playing pranks on him and pelting him with snowballs in 1928's *Hunting for Hidden Gold*.

In *A Figure in Hiding* (1937) Chief Collig dismisses the Hardy Boys' concern for a missing chum, voicing a common adult suspicion about teenagers. When Frank and Joe report that Chet Morton has failed to show up at his parents' farm, the head of Bayport's police force refuses "to attach any importance" to Chet's disappearance: "'He *said* he was going straight to his house when he left here,' announced Collig, 'but that doesn't mean anything. Do you fellows always go directly home when you say you will?'" (63). His statement implies that the Hardys, like most teenagers, routinely deceive adults and therefore cannot be trusted. This reflects a common adolescent complaint, not only against law enforcement but adults in general. Teenagers are presumed to be untrustworthy and guilty of something. The readers of Hardy Boys books are repeatedly given a revenge fantasy in which either the mistrusted teenager is ultimately shown to be right or an adult authority figure is unmasked as a criminal or evildoer.

McFarlane's disdain for the police was not limited to the Bayport cops. At the end of *The Great Airport Mystery* (1930), the Hardy Boys and a pilot tie up a trio of mail robbers. When a country sheriff arrives with his shotgun to investigate what he calls "monkeyshines," the pilot "jubilantly" calls him over to take charge of their captives. But the "worthy sheriff," who is accustomed only to investigating "the occasional robbery of a hen roost," is reluctant to do his job. When he learns the identity of the captives, the sheriff is "one of the most astounded and bewildered men in the world" (197). Noting that "these fellers must be desperate criminals," he attempts to shirk his duty, not wanting to be responsible for their custody. The pilot has to insist that he hold the suspects until government authorities can take them off his hands. The "unhappy" sheriff is insecure, nervously covering the criminals with his shotgun "as though fearing they might break loose at any moment" (198). His demeanor changes when local citizens appear on the scene and begin asking questions. Then the sheriff, "becoming bolder, announced to all and sundry that he had just captured three mail robbers at great risk of his own life and called on his fellow villagers to help him take the trio safely to jail" (199).

McFarlane was writing in the 1920s and 1930s when police corruption was rampant and public respect for law enforcement, especially local police forces, was exceptionally low. The failure or refusal for police officers to enforce Prohibition and waves of police corruption trials in major cities tarnished the image of the law enforcement officer as public servant and hero. Chicago's chief of police Charles Fitzmorris admitted that "sixty percent of my police are in the bootleg business."[1] In New York City the Seabury investigations uncovered an extortion scheme run by crooked vice squad officers, court clerks, and judges in which hundreds of innocent housewives and working women had been framed as prostitutes and threatened with arrest and jail unless they paid for their release.[2] In many cities the police were used to break up strikes, engendering animosity among workers struggling for union recognition. In the South, sheriffs and police officers maintained segregation laws and rarely made arrests when blacks were lynched by white mobs.

McFarlane's cynical view of Bayport's finest also follows a long tradition in detective fiction, in which the private eye exhibits distain for his uniformed counterparts who are typically noted for corruption, incompetence, or slavish obedience. Conan Doyle's Sherlock Holmes views Scotland Yard's Gregson and Lestrade as "the pick of a bad lot" who are "quick and energetic" but "conventional."[3] In *The Study in Scarlet*, Holmes tells a "blundering fool" of a police officer who allowed a murder suspect to slip past him by feigning drunkenness, "'you will never rise in the force. That head of yours should be for use as well as ornament.'"[4] Holmes always stays one step ahead of the authorities not only in deductive skills but also in the use of technology. In one of his last adventures, he tells Watson, "'Since I ran down that coiner by the zinc and copper filings in the seam of his cuff they

The Hardy Boys Detective Handbook, 1959

have begun to realize the importance of the microscope.'"[5] Holmes' contempt for the police is echoed in *The Wailing Siren Mystery* (1951) which describes the Bayport police as being "well-meaning men, but not distinguished for their powers of imagination or deduction" (10–11).

This attitude toward law enforcement concerned Edward Stratemeyer. McFarlane received a cautionary letter following the publication of his first novels, urging him to tone down his Keystone Kops portrayals of Bayport's Finest. McFarlane was troubled by this request because he counted on the bumbling police officers as an ongoing source of humor guaranteed to delight his teenage readers. Why, he wondered, would Stratemeyer even name a lead detective Smuff if he wanted him to be taken seriously? "How could any lad with a scrap of intelligence stand in awe of a cop called Smuff?" he wondered.[6] McFarlane regretfully changed his approach in subsequent novels, so that "Chief Collig suddenly became the sagacious head of an efficient police department. Detective Smuff miraculously acquired wisdom in spite of his name. Constable Riley was strangely transformed into a lovable cop on the beat and a friend to all."[7]

McFarlane may have toned down his contempt for authority, but he did not wholly abandon his principles. Ironically, it was during World War II when popular culture stressed conformity and loyalty to officialdom, that he voiced his most hostile views toward law enforcement: "Fenton Hardy would never consider calling on the police to help him. He cooperated with them whenever necessary, but to ask their aid on one of his own cases was, to him, an admission of defeat. The Hardy boys, when helping him, tried to follow the same policy" (*The Flickering Torch Mystery*, 115).

The attitude toward the police changes substantially in the early Fifties after McFarlane left the series. The era of *Dragnet* had begun, and the police were portrayed as heroes in popular television programs. *The Crisscross Shadow* (1953) presents the police as respected equals. Chief Collig is no longer described as a comic-book-reading badge polisher but a "veteran" crimefighter and a "canny police officer" (126). "He and the Hardys," the novel notes, "had often worked together in rounding up underworld characters" (12). In this book, the usual opening exposition is not presented by the author but through dialogue. When a suspect resents being accused by the Hardys, a police officer tells him, "'I never question Frank and Joe's judgment.... they're sons of the famous detective Fenton Hardy. And they're right smart detectives themselves. Solved lots of cases, like *The Tower Treasure*'" (11). A role reversal takes place near the end of the novel, when Joe informs Chief Collig of their success in nabbing criminals. The chief congratulates the teen detectives, then is forced to admit that he has let the Hardys down:

"That's great work, boys."
"We want you to arrest Miles Kamp at once," Joe said.

There was a snort on the other end of the wire, followed by a long throat-clearing sound.

"Joe, I'm sorry to say Kamp gave us the slip," Collig confessed.

"What!"

"My men were covering him day and night as you and Frank wanted. Then, one evening, he just disappeared from his office like a puff of smoke" [199].

The Clue in the Embers (1956) depicts the Hardy brothers working alongside the Bayport Police. In this novel Frank and Joe have no reluctance in calling upon Chief Collig for assistance and protection. They ask for a police escort when transporting valuable curios to a museum for safekeeping. No longer dismissive of the Hardys, the chief readily agrees to come in person. Keeping watch with his men, the chief is now characterized as being "alert" and "genial," urging the boys to call him for help when needed.

By the next novel, *The Secret of Pirates' Hill* (1957), Chief Collig is more than genial. He is "amazed" by the boys' sleuthing skills, joking that "'We'll have you on the force yet!'" (44).

Federal Authorities

In contrast to the boys' smug attitude toward the Bayport cops in the early novels, they exhibit ongoing awe and respect for federal authorities, especially the Federal Bureau of Investigation. In part, the Hardy Boys novels reflect prevailing attitudes toward federal law enforcement. Beginning with its formation in the late 1920s, J. Edgar Hoover's FBI enjoyed an overwhelming positive reputation for honesty, efficiency, and resourcefulness. This image was fostered by newspaper stories, magazine articles, motion pictures, books, comic books, and hit radio shows such as *Gang Busters* and *The FBI in Peace and War*. Hoover personally supervised the use of the FBI name and image, requiring studios and networks to adhere to strict standards in their portrayal of his organization. The FBI maintained strong links to Hollywood. Suffering from criticism in the early Thirties for glamorizing gangsters in movies like *Little Caesar* and *Public Enemy*, studios were eager to reform themselves while exploiting the public fascination with crime. Stars, too, saw the FBI as a vehicle for improving their image. James Cagney, who had become famous playing gangsters in the early Thirties, played an FBI agent in *G Men* in 1935. Even the smug rapscallions The Dead End Kids were recast as federal agents in a short series in the Forties called *Junior G-Men*. Having personal ties to powerful media figures like Walter Winchell, Hoover was able to control the public image of his agency. FBI agents were universally portrayed as cleancut Anglo-Saxons who were incorruptible and efficient.

In the Hardy Boys books, federal officials are depicted as intelligent, honest, and resourceful. Whereas the Bayport cops treat Hardy victories with jealousy in the early novels, the FBI congratulates Frank and Joe and rewards them by sharing their latest technology. *The Short-Wave Mystery* (1945) ends with the boys receiving a "television walkie-talkie" with a note reading *"A personal gift to two fine young detectives"* signed by an FBI official. In some of the early books, the FBI was not mentioned by name. At the conclusion of *The Flickering Torch Mystery* (1943) the Hardys receive a congratulatory telegram from "high government authorities in Washington" (206).

Foreign Governments

The respect for federal authorities extends to those of other countries. Although Frank and Joe travel to Canada, Britain, and other democracies, they work most closely with authorities in Latin America at a time when these countries were dominated by corrupt dictators. In *The Mark on the Door* (1934) Frank and Joe round up a gang of criminals with the aid of the Mexican army. In *The Ghost at Skeleton Rock* (1958) Frank and Joe battle Cuban rebels trying to topple the "elected government" (actually the Batista dictatorship). Frank and Joe never question the motives or politics of foreign authorities and take at face value their depiction of dissidents as criminals and terrorists. For Frank and Joe, it seems, anyone in uniform behind a desk represents lawful and unquestionable authority.

The Criminal Type

The Hardy Boys novels, like nearly all detective fiction of the era, depict crime in purely personal and moralistic terms. Only one novel, *The Short-Wave Mystery*, draws a brief connection between poverty and criminal behavior when the boys intervene in a Big Brother fashion to mentor a poor "urchin" in hopes of preventing him from following in his criminal uncle's footsteps. The novel implies that the urchin has free will and that by altering his social circumstances and giving him positive options, he will be able to choose another path.

In all other cases, the books purport that crime is caused by evil-doers, villains, and occasionally the deranged. S. T. Karnack notes the characters' simplicity of motivation:

> One of the fine things about the Hardy Boys books is their cheerful avoidance of psychology. The purpose of psychology, after all, is to explain behavior, and — in literature as in the courts — that all too often means explaining away misbehavior. The Hardy Boys stories, by contrast, rely on normal motives we all

have experienced. It is the characters' moral values and conscious choices, not some irresistible psychological forces, that impel their actions. The protagonists are typically motivated by courage, common sense, and altruism; the villains by garden-variety vices such as greed, gluttony, sloth, and anger.[8]

In fact, the criminals Frank and Joe encounter appear almost genetically designed to be bad. They are marked by a distinct look and demeanor. Nearly every criminal adversary is sullen, ill-tempered, or unattractive. In the world of the Hardy Boys first impressions are telling:

> He was very tall and he wore a black felt hat, the wide brim of which obscured the upper part of his face. His countenance was tanned and weather-beaten, his lips were thin and cruel [*The House on the Cliff*, 121].

> Although they had only a momentary glance, the boys readily identified him as the man the tramps had mentioned. Disreputably clad, he was a thin man with a cruel mouth and hooked nose [*The Shore Road Mystery*, 64].

> "Agh!" crackled a guttural voice.
> To the boys' astonishment a heavy-set, scowling fellow in working clothes stood before them.
> "What are you doing here?" Joe demanded.
> The man clenched his fists for an instant, then seemed to gain control of himself. An unpleasant smile crept over his thick lips.
> "I? What — am I — doing here? I am waiting for money which is — owing to me." He spoke slowly in measured tones....
> The man muttered a word of thanks, focused his beady eyes on the boys for an instant, then turned and went out the front door....
> "There's something fishy about him, Frank" [*The Mystery of the* Flying Express, 2–4].

> The moon shone full on his face. It revealed a thin nose and jutting jaw, giving his face the sour demeanor of a man who is dissatisfied with the whole world [*The Sign of the Crooked Arrow*, 107].

In *The Crisscross Shadow* even the villain's lawyer bears the criminal stigmata. John Breck is described as being a "dark, burly man" with a "taunting smile" (5). When Frank and Joe turn Breck over to the police, he demands to call his lawyer:

> Ten minutes later Miles Kamp strode into the chief's office. He was a short, heavy-jowled man with a wide thin-lipped mouth that suggested a nasty streak in his character. He peered at them nearsightedly through thick-lensed glasses.
> Frank turned to Joe. "I don't like his looks, do you?" he whispered to his brother as the salesman shook hands with the lawyer.
> "No," the younger Hardy replied. "He looks even more suspicious than Breck."
> "Now, now what's going on here?" he said in an annoyed voice. "Why are you holding my client? I demand to know the meaning of this."
> The nearsighted little lawyer flailed his arms wildly [12–13].

When Laura Hardy falls victim to a phony rug buyer passing counterfeit money, she describes the con man to Frank and Joe in detail: "'He was a queer little fellow, very short and dark. He was a foreigner, you could tell by his appearance. He didn't speak very good English. He was dark and swarthy, with little, keen black eyes'" (*The Secret of the Old Mill*, 154–155).

In tracking down suspects, Frank and Joe Hardy often rely on appearances to identify criminal suspects: "Through a crack in the corral fence, the boys could see that one of the men was short, scrawny, beady-eyed Willy the Penman! The flat-nosed, fierce-looking man with the craggy brows must be Nick Snide, they surmised" (*The Secret of Wildcat Swamp*, 183).

This focus on the shapes of noses, lips, and brows seems almost Lombroso-like. Cesare Lombroso, the Italian physician and criminologist, championed the concept of the "born criminal," claiming that lawbreakers had specific physiognomic features that could be identified and measured. Criminals, he argued, had large jaws, sloping foreheads, hawk-like noses, fleshy lips, and shifty eyes. The pseudo science of phrenology influenced popular thinking of criminality well into the twentieth century. During the Leopold and Loeb trial in 1924, Chicago newspapers carried photographs of Nathan Leopold with arrows pointing out facial features "scientifically" linked to personality disorders and criminal tendencies.

What is noticeable is that Hardy Boys villains bear no truly distinct look but abnormality. They are either "very tall" or "short," "thin" or "burly." Their lips are either "thin" or "thick." They simply are out of the norm:

> A man with a thin unpleasant face lounged alongside the Crux Brothers diving barge....
> The lounger spat disgustedly and sidled away toward a patch of shrubbery behind the boathouse. "Pete?" he called in a low voice a moment later.
> "Yeah. Here I am." Another man, short and heavy-set, arose from behind a fir tree to meet his companion [*The Secret Warning*, 92].

Teenagers are notoriously conscious of their bodies and see physical imperfections as major character flaws. Therefore, anyone who is taller or shorter, thinner or heavier than the norm is subject to ridicule.

In addition, the villains invariably are brusque, rude, and ill-tempered — exactly the type of adult that intimidates children and adolescents. It is part of the wish-fulfillment theme that the authoritarian adult who threatens or chases the Hardys away turns out to be the villain Frank and Joe defeat in the end.

In addition to making bad first impressions, the rogues often become animalistic when confronted or captured:

> "Shut up," snarled Ollie Jacobs. "Shut up and take your medicine like a man. We're licked; but we would have been well away if it hadn't been for those Hardy boys" [*The Great Airport Mystery*, 194].

> Snarling like a couple of trapped animals, the suspects were led away to small cells in the rear of the building [*The Secret of Wildcat Swamp*, 38].
>
> When Ragu saw the Hardys, his face twisted into a snarl [*The Hooded Hawk Mystery*, 133].

Nearly all the villains have voices that match their looks. They don't speak but rather "snarl" or "growl" like animals.

In contrast, the Hardy Boys have "honest" faces, which signal their creditability to strangers, even security personnel. In *The Mystery of the Aztec Warrior* (1964), the brothers are waiting for a flight at Idlewild Airport when Frank spots an aviation mechanic with a tattoo that could be a valuable clue. Frank and Joe are teenagers with no security clearance, but their appearance alone serves as a kind of badge:

> They dashed through a corridor until they came to a gate near where the man was standing. "We're detectives!" said Frank to the guard. "Please let us go out and talk to that mechanic with the tattoo!"
>
> The guard looked at them and at first was not inclined to grant their request. But apparently the boys' honest faces convinced him that they were telling the truth, and he let them through the gate [40–41].

Criminals are also distinguished by their strange or sinister-sounding names and nicknames. The Hardys are run off the road by Red Jackley, capture Black Pepper in Montana, and contend with Duke Beeson, Taffy Marr, and Whitey Masco. Children familiar with comic books and radio dramas would immediately associate these names with criminals and villains, especially in contrast to the prosaic names of their heroes, Frank and Joe.

Respect for the Law

Frank and Joe are depicted as law-abiding youths who do not speed, even in emergencies. In *The Sign of the Crooked Arrow* (1949) they learn that their father has been shot and race to the hospital, driving "as fast as the law would permit" (36). Unlike the typical Hollywood detective making squealing turns and dodging pedestrians, Frank Hardy obediently waits at each traffic light. Later, the boys race to the hospital with their coupé's speedometer hovering "at the speed limit" (74). Twenty-five years later in *The Clue of the Hissing Serpent* (1974) Frank and Joe learn their father has summoned them using a code word indicating danger. The boys "bolt" out of the house and race to meet their father. In the car, however, they "hit the speed limit" (2). Even when tempted to speed to make up for time lost by a traffic delay, Joe sensibly "eased off the gas," explaining to Frank, "'If we get a ticket, we'll never get there on time'" (7).

Unlike adult detective heroes who characteristically violate the letter of the law to enforce justice, Frank and Joe never take the law into their own hands. Being minors, they step aside to allow adults to effect arrests and mete out punishment. As role models, they must always show responsibility, never exceeding the posted speed limits even in an emergency.

Chapter 12

Action, Not Violence

> No matter how ruthless and antisocial the criminals in a Hardy Boys book, nobody was ever shot, stabbed, blown up or bludgeoned to death.... We had our own code of nonviolence long before television.
> — Leslie McFarlane, *Ghost of the Hardy Boys*

Throughout the original fifty-eight novels, Frank and Joe Hardy confront a procession of violent felons, murderous terrorists, deranged criminals, and sinister enemy agents. Yet in all these adventures, which include capturing smuggling gangs and rounding up whole spy camps, they never kill an adversary and employ little violence to achieve their goals.

The Hardy Boys are detectives. Some of their mysteries are strictly investigatory, in which the brothers search for a missing person or lost treasure. Most of the books, however, involve locating criminals and bringing them to justice. This creates both great opportunities for drama and a dilemma for the writers of juvenile fiction.

As detectives, Frank and Joe can face an endless number of thrilling adventures. Each book can take the boys to an exotic locale, introduce a new theme or technology, or capitalize on a current event. Mystery stories by their nature involve countless possibilities for excitement — enticing clues, secret codes, threatening messages, car chases, kidnappings, risky escapes, searches through dangerous places, spying on gang hideouts, and following leads. The nature of crime stories propels the heroes into movement, giving Frank and Joe legitimate reasons to fly planes, take trains, ride motorcycles, drive cars, or take ships to distant places. The need to follow clues or help their dad justifies why the teenage heroes leave home and dash off to Hong Kong or North Africa. Each mystery can take the brothers down a distinctly new path, allowing writers to explore a limitless inventory of ever-changing locations and themes. Writers could capitalize on the excitement of flying in 1930, explore the new state of Alaska in 1959, and exploit the popularity of secret agents in the 1960s.

Detective stories, however, are ultimately tales of good versus evil, which necessitates personal confrontation and conflict. Unlike the cops and private eyes in adult fiction, Frank and Joe are child characters appearing in a juvenile series. They do not have powers of arrest. It is implausible that a fifteen- and sixteen-year-old can take on adult male adversaries. Above all, unlike their predecessors in dime novels, they cannot use the violence that made those stories so popular with teenagers. Unlike Deadeye Dick or Frank Merriwell, they cannot be depicted shooting, stabbing, or even beating up adversaries in rough-and-tumble fights.

Writers of the Hardy Boys had to devise plots with enough excitement to engage young readers without including scenes of violence that would upset adults and tarnish the wholesome image the series labored to project. For a crime series, there is surprisingly little "violence" and absolutely no gore in the Hardy Boys. There is little gunplay, no bloody fights, few corpses, and rarely even the mention of a homicide. In the entire series the brothers

THE BIG ICE-BOAT WAS BOOMING DOWN ON THE SMALLER CRAFT AT TERRIFIC SPEED.
The Mystery of Cabin Island

The Mystery of Cabin Island, 1929. Frontispiece from *The Mystery of Cabin Island* by Franklin W. Dixon is a registered trademark of Simon & Schuster Inc. All rights reserved. Used by permission of Simon & Schuster Adult Publishing Group.

never conduct a full-fledged murder investigation, the gold standard plot of adult detective fiction. Unlike Sherlock Holmes, Sam Spade, or the cops on *Law and Order*, Frank and Joe Hardy are never shown examining a corpse or even a murder weapon. Stratemeyer's formula was to tell exciting but sanitized stories, substituting "action" for violence.

The Tower Treasure establishes a pattern of action that runs throughout the series. The opening pages plunge Frank and Joe Hardy into danger as a speed demon nearly runs their motorcycles over a cliff into Barmet Bay:

> The auto brakes squealed.
> The driver of the oncoming car swung the wheel viciously about. For a moment it appeared that the wheels would not respond. Then they gripped the gravel and the automobile swerved, then shot past.
> Bits of sand and gravel were flung about the two boys as they crouched by their motorcycles at the edge of the embankment. The car had missed them only by inches! [9].

Here are all the elements of life-threatening danger and excitement guaranteed to grab the attention of a juvenile reader. The Hardy Boys face death, but the danger comes in terms of a speeding car, flying gravel, and squealing tires — not ricocheting bullets or shrapnel. This, in fact, is as close as the teen detectives ever come to their first adversary. The speed demon Red Jackley crashes his car, steals Chet's roadster, robs the Tower Mansion, and flees Bayport. Frank and Joe locate valuable clues, which they turn over to their father, who locates the thief and obtains a cryptic deathbed confession about the loot being hidden in an "old tower." The boys locate the loot, solve the mystery, and clear a wrongly accused man without the use of guns or a single fistfight.

The second novel, *The House on the Cliff*, in contrast, ends with several fusillades of smugglers' bullets, which departed dramatically from the tone of the rest of the series. Stratemeyer was troubled with McFarlane's emphasis on gunplay and reprimanded him in a letter. In most of the subsequent novels, Frank and Joe have adventures and face life-threatening situations that are generally environmental in nature.

In many ways the Hardy Boys are more like explorers than detectives. The adventures of adult detectives take place in largely urban landscapes, the dangers coming in the forms of back alley shootouts, tavern brawls, and nightclub beatings. Frank and Joe Hardy, in contrast, typically face danger from natural threats — rough surf, cave-ins, snakes, and avalanches — and accidents — car and train wrecks, sinking ships, and fouled plane engines. Not only do the out-of-the-way hideouts used by criminals lead Frank and Joe far from metropolitan settings with their adult temptations, they expose the boys to a host of environmental threats. The fact that the villains seek distant caves, islands, abandoned buildings, and remote camps for hideouts and headquarters means that much of the action occurs with the Hardys trying to locate their foes or fleeing from them. The danger lies in moving toward or away from their adversaries rather than in direct confrontations.

The Missing Chums (1928) is one of the most haunting and terrifying of the early McFarlane novels. In the opening chapter the chums are nearly killed when a "big brute of a motorboat" overtakes Biff Hooper's *Envoy* on Barmet Bay. The "strange craft" is painted a "dingy gray" and piloted by a "sneering" man who bears right down on the chums' boat. Unable to avoid the motorboat racing toward them without hitting nearby sailboats, Biff is trapped and a "hideous collision" appears inevitable (9). The chums escape with their lives, puzzled by the actions of the men in the "strange" powerboat.

A few days later Chet and Biff set off on a boat trip up the coast. Barmet Bay, always known for threatening weather, brews up a storm as a dark cloud causes "gloom to spread over the bay" (34). Soon sheets of lightning and claps of thunder announce a deluge with the wind sweeping in "with a violence that surprised them," tossing white caps in a "leaden wall of rain" (34). Frank and Joe race their boat to shore to escape one of the worst storms that had ever swept the bay when "a great wave" strikes their boat, which reels as if "struck by a giant hand" (37).

The Hardys survive the storm but worry about the fate of their chums who have disappeared. They plan to set out on a rescue trip when a ransom letter arrives at the Hardy home. Frank and Joe realize that Chet and Biff have been abducted by kidnappers in a case of mistaken identity. The search for the missing chums takes Frank and Joe to Blacksnake Island, which has "a great, swampy tract of forbidding marsh at one end" with "sinister little creeks" where "dead bushes" float about in the "black water" (105). The other end of the island ends with "desolate rocks." As Frank and Joe make their way through the "fetid marsh," they spot the "triangular black heads" of poisonous snakes in the dark water. Seeking safer ground, the boys camp out on a "barren" stretch of rocks "that no human being had ever set foot upon" (107).

The island provides constant dangers to the Hardys. They fall into a deep pool of black icy water. They are hit with "oppressive" heat. A storm lashes the island with the "livid glow" of lightning flashes followed by "peals of thunder," "moaning" wind, and "driving" rain (129). The gale "shrieks" and thunder rolls like "a battery of cannon while the rain beat down on the forest in a drumming downpour" (131).

When the Hardy Boys help Biff and Chet escape from their captors, much of the tension comes from their struggles not with the kidnappers but with the environment: "Chet crashed into the bushes. Branches whipped his face. Roots gripped his feet. He struggled on through the dense growth, blindly, in the darkness. Far ahead of him he could hear Frank making his way through the underbrush, but when he tried to go toward the sound he found that his sense of direction was confused" (153). The island supplies the elements that retard Chet's escape, not a fight with human adversaries. A "dark figure" looms up and snatches him. Frank, too, suffers the same fate. He crashes through bushes and tangled undergrowth that is "growing denser with every forward step" (155). The vegetation of the island seems almost animalistic in its hostility: "He blundered about in the deep thicket, turning vainly this way and that. Great vines trailed across his face; he brushed aside stubborn branches and soggy wet leaves; he stumbled over roots and little bushes; the deep grass rustled and hissed at his feet" (156). His heart beats "quickly," and he thinks he is free, when he suddenly finds himself "floundering in the midst of trees and trailing vines that entangled him" and a voice calls out, ordering him to surrender. Like Chet, Frank is recaptured without force, the restraining elements limited to the natural hazards of the island.

Direct confrontation between the chums and the gangsters is limited. Chet and Biff scuffle with members of the gang. Biff, a boxer, knocks his adversary to the ground, but the fight is described in terms of a boxing match rather than a life-and-death struggle. He knocks the man down with two blows. The less athletic Chet makes "use of strategy" and trips the man rushing toward him. The gangster flies forward and falls over a ledge. But like the wounded gangster, he is not killed. The ledge is only a few feet above the beach, but the fall is great enough to "knock the breath out of the gangster's body for several minutes at least" (193).

The boys make a second escape. This time there is gunplay as the gangsters fire shots as the chums flee to the shore. Bullets splash into the water and strike the *Sleuth* as Frank and Joe race out of range. Out at sea, they rendezvous with Tony, Jerry, and Phil aboard the *Napoli* and enlist their aid as the chums head to summon help. The chums return to Blacksnake Island with a party of "sturdy, tanned" revenue agents whose faces are "alight with the anticipation of battle" (205). Gunfire comes from the caves and a skilled rifleman drops one of the gangsters with a single shot. "And this," McFarlane wrote, "to the disappointment of the watchers, was the end of the fight" (206). The "rascals" prove cowardly and immediately surrender. The revenue men handcuff the criminals. The wounded man is given first aid, assuring "he would live to face trial with the rest for the abduction of Chet and Biff" (207).

Frank and Joe arrive armed on the island, having taken two "small and efficient-looking" automatics from Fenton Hardy's collection, but they never use the weapons against the gangsters. The first time a Hardy Boy fires a weapon, it is not at a felon but at a reptile. His "sixth sense" warning him of danger, Frank Hardy glances down at the grass and spots a five-foot-long snake, its body writhing and its "red tongue flickering wickedly" (109). Frank fires his automatic but misses. Joe finds a heavy stick and Frank snatches the branch and smashes the "hissing" reptile with the tongue that flickers like a flame until he crushes "the evil black head" (110). Murderous violence occurs, but it is directed at a repulsive snake not a human being.

The dangers the Hardys face in the following novel *Hunting for Hidden Gold* (1928) are also largely environmental. The opening chapter plunges the chums into danger—not in a boat on Barmet Bay—but on frozen Shallow Lake as a skating outing turns into a fight for life as a howling, blinding gale whips across the winter landscape. The storm becomes savage in its fury as the boys skate toward the shelter of a cliff: "The wind shrieked. The snow beat against them. The sharp flakes stung their faces, swept into their eyes. The hurricane seemed like a mighty wall, forcing them back. Doggedly, they skated on, into the face of the blizzard that seemed to be sapping their strength" (10). Once the chums "doggedly" fight their way to the cliff, the danger is not over. An avalanche occurs above their heads, one that is so strong that it carries a small cabin over the edge of the cliff.

Summoned west to help their father locate hidden gold, Frank and Joe travel to Montana. Blacksnake Island threatened the boys with poisonous reptiles, thick undergrowth, and swamps. The search for gold leads Frank and Joe below ground into dark, twisting tunnels and caverns. Descending into an abandoned mine, they are menaced by a broken ladder, treacherous rocks, poisonous gas, and cave-ins:

> An avalanche of stones descended into the shaft on top of the first downfall of rock. More followed, showers of earth came rushing down and a cloud of dust pervaded the cavern.
>
> Joe leaped back.
>
> Then, with a roar like thunder, the entire shaft caved in. Rocks and timbers came tumbling down with a terrific crash. The air was filled with the noise of smashing timbers and falling rock. The faint light from the shaft that had given some vague illumination to the cave, was blotted out. The mine reverberated with echoes and shook with the force of the crash.
>
> Silence reigned. It was broken by the sharp sounds of falling pebbles that descended in the wake of the avalanche. Then those noises too died away. The cavern was filled with a choking cloud of dust.
>
> Joe was almost stupefied by horror. He realized to the full the peril of the situation [108].

Frank and Joe seek escape by traveling down a tunnel that leads to a dead end, killing their hope of reaching the surface. Joe taps the rock wall with a crowbar, which seems to "sound their death knell," leading Frank to admit gravely, "'I guess this is our finish'" (119).

Recalling that they had passed a draft of air, Frank and Joe retrace their steps and discover a passage to the surface. When they emerge, they are nabbed by three gang members. They are held hostage but make their escape when Frank calls upon his Bayport High pitching skills and throws a rock, knocking the gun from their captor's hand. As the gang member struggles to find his weapon in the snow, the brothers dash to safety. Again, the conflict with an adversary is full of tension and action but no real violence.

As in *The Missing Chums* the environment provides most of the drama and conflict. Frank and Joe are hit by another blizzard, much stronger and more life-threatening than the one they encountered in Bayport: "The wind shrieked with a thousand voices. The snow came sweeping down on them as though lashed by invisible whips. The roar of the storm sounded in their ears and the fine snow almost blinded them" (162). McFarlane heightens the tension by having Frank and Joe lose sight of each other, building on separation anxiety that children can easily recognize and empathize with. Realizing he has lost contact with Frank, Joe calls out his name, "But the wind flung the words back into his teeth. A feeling of panic seized him" (163). Frank, too, struggles with the fear of isolation: "The wind shrieked down from the rocks. The snow swirled furiously about him. The blizzard raged. The roaring of the storm drummed in his ears as he stumbled and floundered about among the rocks and snow. The Hardy boys were lost, separated, in the storm" (166).

Reunited, the brothers escape the blizzard by entering a cave. Frank's flashlight picks up "strange, glowing green spots" shining in the darkness. The green spots turn out to be reflections from the eyes of a wolf pack. As in *The Missing Chums*, Frank uses deadly force against an animal opponent. He shoots a charging wolf, using the flashlight to keep the others at bay. But the wolves soon become more aggressive, placing the brothers again in deadly peril:

> The animals appeared to have overcome their fear of the flashlight. They no longer slunk into the shadows when its fierce glare was turned on them. Instead, they came forward boldly, with dripping, gleaming jaws.
> "I'm afraid we're trapped," declared Frank.
> "We'll die fighting, anyway. I wish I had a gun" [177].

McFarlane limits gory combat to conflicts with animals. As the boys back off and seek another passage from the cave, the wolves press forward, snarling viciously. A wolf leaps forward and Frank uses deadly force in self-defense: "His aim was true. Halfway in the air the animal gave a convulsive twist of its body and crashed on to the rocks. It writhed in its death agony, snarling ferociously and snapping at everything within reach, until it finally lay still" (179). The Hardys escape and locate the missing gold only to be caught "red-handed" by Black Pepper brandishing two revolvers. Frank and Joe toss sacks of gold at the villain who drops a gun and falls to the floor of the cave. Frank pounces on him, grabs the revolver and presses the barrel to his body, and Black Pepper immediately surrenders. The Hardys bring the gang leader to justice without firing a shot or inflicting more than a bruise or two. McFarlane devotes thirty-five pages to the final action sequence that carries Frank and Joe from fighting through a blizzard to exploring a mine, confronting the wolves, and finally discovering the gold. The altercation and subjugation of Black Pepper takes three pages. As in *The Missing Chums*, extensive action and adventure scenes are followed by an abbreviated interpersonal conflict in which the villain is deftly subdued in a brief struggle rather than a knock-down drag-out fight.

Cave-ins occur closer to home in *The Shore Road Mystery* published the following year. Investigating a series of car thefts, the boys purchase an expensive-looking automobile, park along Shore Road, and hide in the roomy trunk. As hoped, a thief finds the deserted car tempting and takes the wheel. The car becomes a Trojan horse as it is driven onto the beach and into a cavern. Once footsteps and voices disappear, the Hardys emerge from the trunk. As in the previous adventures, Frank and Joe are armed, but they make little use of their handguns. They cautiously move through a labyrinth of caves and tunnels, discovering stolen automobiles and stacks of merchandise taken from a hijacked truck. Then they face a threat to their lives not from an armed gangster but from a rock fall and "miniature avalanche" that seals them in the underground passage. When they attempt to dig out, the tunnel roof collapses, creating a rock pile they cannot possibly dislodge:

> Frank sat down on a rock, regarding the impassable heap.
> "Buried alive," he remarked, at last.
> "No one will ever find us here."
> The boys realized the gravity of their plight. No one knew they were in the tunnel. No one had seen them enter. If they perished here, their bodies might never be recovered [157].

Searching the rock walls, they discover an opening leading to a narrow tunnel that reconnects with the underground maze of passageways and caverns. They come upon the auto thieves and overhear the gang discuss their criminal operations. Discovered by the thieves, they dash into a tunnel, firing a warning shot to keep the gang at bay. The gang fires back and a bullet grazes Joe's sleeve. Then the gunplay stops. Frank reasons that surrender is their only option:

> "We're up against it," Frank admitted. "If we stay here they'll starve us out. If we try to rush them, we'll get shot."
> "I guess we'll have to surrender."
> "Looks as if there's nothing else for it. We'll give ourselves up and take our chances on escape. The way things are, we're liable to be shot" [172].

The thieves tie up Frank and Joe, planning to leave them to starve underground or toss them into an empty boxcar that might carry them hundreds of miles from Bayport, giving the gang time to flee. Frank manages to burn his ropes with a candle flame, weakening the strands enough for him to break free and grab the revolver the gang failed to take from Joe and turn the tables on their captors—without violence. He merely presses the revolver to the back of "the rascal." They tie the man up and flee the cavern to summon the police to capture the gang.

In addition to environmental hazards such as storms, avalanches, and swamps, McFarlane used mechanical failures to create scenes of dramatic action. In *What Happened at Midnight* (1931) Frank and Joe fly in a plane which runs into engine trouble. The scene is reminiscent of the motion pictures of the era that depicted the thrill and risk of flying, which was still seen by the public as inherently dangerous. The engine of the small plane quits, sputters, comes to life, sputters, and dies. Heavy fog makes a forced landing impossible because a "blind landing in that mist ... would be disaster, perhaps death to them all" (182). The pilot tells the boys to bail out.

McFarlane creates a powerful narrative of suspense, anticipation, and danger. Jumping out of a plane in the mist, the brothers have no idea what lies beneath them so "they might be plunging directly toward a lake or into a city street" (184). Frank jumps from the plane and plummets "toward the earth at a terrible speed" as he struggles to find the ripcord. He pulls the ring, but nothing happens. Frank continues to drop through the sky until he feels the chute open with a "sudden jerk as though a gigantic hand had grabbed him about the waist" (185). As the fog clears, Frank sees that he is falling into a freshly plowed field. Joe lands safely nearby. As they struggle to their feet, the plane whizzes through fog and plunges "wildly to the earth" with a "terrific crash" (186).

In *The Secret Warning* (1938) Frank faces life-threatening elements underwater when he attempts to rescue a trapped diver. Encased in deep-sea diving gear, he descends into the ocean McFarlane describes as being "like a vast, bottomless grotto of black liquid in a mysterious world a million miles from the one in which he had been accustomed to living" (145). This strange, surreal world turns deadly when he notices that an anchor has come loose and is swinging in a circular motion. Caught in the center of "its fateful orbit," Frank realizes that there is no escape. No matter which direction he might move, "a thousand tons of steel would smash him like a fly before he could get away" (154). Frank finds himself in a "hideous nightmare come true" (154).

When the anchor is hoisted up, removing the threat to Frank's life, he continues his underwater search for the trapped diver, only to run into another threat — a lack of oxygen:

> Frank's head was reeling. What a horrible, lonely death this was to be! he thought, peering blankly through his helmet window. Something seemed to be wrong with his searchlight. Its bright glare had suddenly become feeble. The young diver blinked his eyes, straining to see by the fading rays. No use — his light was going out — or could it be his eyes?
>
> His head spun, and his breath came in quick, short gasps.... Blackness swept upon him, and slowly he toppled over into the black void [162].

Rescued by a diver bringing extra oxygen tanks, Frank recovers and helps save the trapped victim.

As in *The Missing Chums* and *Hunting for Hidden Gold*, Frank and Joe use deadly force to kill a threatening animal. In a scene reminiscent of *Twenty Thousand Leagues Under the Sea*, the Hardy Boys are attacked by a "monstrous" octopus. Joe manages to get out his knife but the "sea beast's powerful tentacles" pin his arms, "crushing him in its terrible death grip" (187). In a desperate act to save his brother, Frank opens his inflation valve to quickly rise toward the surface to distract the octopus. The "creature" spies him, drops Joe, and lunges toward Frank:

> A second later Frank felt a heavy, squirming cord wrap itself around his waist and pull him relentlessly toward the monster's huge, hideous body. It was to be now or never. He waited a split second until the creature was hugging him close, crushing him.
>
> With his hand jammed tightly between his own body and that of the octopus, he plunged the knife to the hilt into the horrible, jelly-like mass against him. In the brief instant that followed, before the sea-devil could recover from the shock of the wound and tighten its grip around him, the lad slashed to and fro furiously [187–188].

Joe also fights with the "sea-devil," which dives to the marshy bottom, stirring up clouds of mud and seaweed. As Frank swings his searchlight, he spots a victorious Joe emerging from the cloud. Joe aims the light toward the sea floor where "Frank could discern the tangled outline of the dead monster" (189).

McFarlane established a pattern that is followed throughout the series. He has to supply readers with tension, action, excitement, suspense, and fear without violent altercations between hero and villain. What occurs is a form of indirect violence. Villains do not shoot, stab, or even punch the Hardy Boys so much as place them in a perilous situation where they have to overcome a natural or contrived threat to survive. The boys are often left alone to face death. Their dramatic struggles are against the elements, not individuals. There are no extended fights with punches, kicks, and jabs meant to kill or maim a human being. As Leslie McFarlane noted in his autobiography, "The Hardy Boys could face extinction by fire or water, they could tumble through trapdoors and they could be pushed off cliffs, they could be captured, tied up, imprisoned and knocked on the head. But blood never flowed" (178).

There is, instead of violence, heart-pounding danger. In *While the Clock Ticked* (1932) Frank and Joe are tied up by a lunatic with a time bomb ticking at their feet. Not satisfied with simply killing his prey, the madman decides to destroy all evidence of their murder by causing a fire that will consume the entire house:

He pointed to the infernal machine in the floor.

"You see that?" he shouted. "It's a bomb. A deadly bomb. Filled with high explosive. It is attached to the clock. When the hands of the clock reach the appointed hour there will be an electric contact. The bomb will explode...."

Then he regarded the bomb intently.

"Might as well make a thorough job of it," he said.

The old man vanished through the aperture in the clock and went into the secret recess beyond. He returned in a few moments with a heavy can and a small bag. He placed the bag on the floor, unscrewed the stopper of the can and went about the room, slopping liquid on the floor.

Instantly Frank and Joe became aware of the pungent odor of gasoline.

"There will be no trace of you, you see," chuckled the madman. "The bomb will explode, the gasoline will catch fire. The house will be destroyed. No one can ever charge me with murder because no one will know you that you died here."

The Hardy boys were frozen with horror. They watched as the old man picked up the bag and began scattering the contents about the floor.

The bag contained gunpowder [174-175].

The Hardys are left facing death from a WMD cocktail of high explosives, gasoline, and gunpowder. McFarlane's detailed description of the madman's piling on deadly components creates fear, apprehension, and terror — but there is no real violence. The Hardys are bound and helpless. They struggle not with a human adversary but with a ticking clock. Only the unexpected appearance of eccentric Hurd Applegate saves them from immolation.

In *The Twisted Claw* (1939) Fenton Hardy and his sons are trapped in a cabin encircled by a forest fire. In *The Secret of Wildcat Swamp* (1952), Frank and Joe are captured by outlaws and locked in the "icy dungeon" of a refrigerated rail car. In *The Ghost at Skeleton Rock* (1957) Frank is locked in the unpressurized cargo compartment of an airplane. All of these entrapments create tension, danger, and action but involve no personal violence. Instead of the thrill of violence, there is the suspense and excitement of the escape. Frank and Joe are not so much tough fighters as they are skilled escape artists capable of Houdini-like acrobatics to avoid traps set by their captors.

In defeating their adversaries, the Hardy Boys generally call upon adult authorities to bring the criminals to justice. They act as ancillary agents of the law, tracking down and locating criminals who are rounded up and on occasion shot by uniformed officers. The boys themselves remain bystanders to adult violence.

The Hardy Boys use non-lethal means to subdue villains, never using force or the threat of violence to punish, extract information, or gain revenge. In the entire series, Frank and Joe never shoot or stab a single villain. Instead, they get the drop on their captors, who surrender to the mere display of a weapon or the press of a muzzle against their backs.

Teenage wit and agility are shown overcoming the brute strength and cruelty of adult adversaries. When the drunken pilot Giles Ducroy attacks Frank in *The Great Airport Mystery* (1930), Frank counters the power of the older, larger male with choreographed moves that rely on youthful speed and limit physical contact:

> The pilot swung at him, but Frank ducked, came in, and stung Ducroy's face with an uppercut. Ducroy was bigger than Frank and considerably heavier, but he was far from being a scientific fighter, relying chiefly on bull-like rushes and ponderous swinging blows that would have done damage had they landed, but seldom did. Ducroy rushed Frank back across the pavement, his heavy fists swinging, but Frank backed away, ducking and dodging, watching for an opening.
> It soon came.
> Ducroy swung so wildly that he left himself completely unprotected. Frank's fist shot out. The blow caught Ducroy directly on the point of the jaw, and he went down in a heap [31].

The scene plausibly shows how teenage Frank can defend himself against a larger adversary, fulfilling an adolescent male fantasy of overpowering an adult. It also limits the fight to two bloodless punches, substituting skill for violence.

In *The Shattered Helmet* (1973) a villain named Spiro Vanides holds Frank and Chet at gunpoint, threatening to send them to the bottom of the ocean. A prank and some skilled karate chops allow the chums to overcome their captors without deadly force:

> At that instant the whole cave reverberated with the staccato of explosions.
> "Joe's back with the cops!" Chet shouted.
> Vanides stood dumbfounded for a second. The gun slumped momentarily. Frank knocked it from Vanides' hand with a karate chop. At the same time Chet and Evan set upon their tormentors with strength born of desperation.
> The cave was filled with groans and grunts as the battle raged evenly. The sudden appearance of Joe gave the boys the advantage. He kayoed Gerrold with a smash to the point of the chin. Chet took care of Dimitri while Frank and Evan tied up the hapless Vanides.
> Then Frank picked up the gun with his handkerchief and pocketed it as evidence. As the other two were being tied, he asked, "Where are the police with the guns, Joe?"
> His brother grinned wryly. "Guns? What guns?"
> "The explosions!"
> "Oh those were firecrackers. Thank Chet. I still had them in my windbreaker." Chet chuckled. "I had a hunch we'd need them!" [177–178].

Not only do these easy victories eliminate violence, but they also demonstrate a truism that runs throughout the Hardy series — that outlaws, criminals, and villains, no matter how vile or sadistic — are sniveling cowards. While their tormentors may sadistically contemplate their demise, Frank and Joe show restraint. In *The Secret of Skull Mountain* (1948), the Hardy brothers are held in a cavern. Their captor tells them he plans to dump them into a sluiceway. Their bodies, he notes, might reach Barmet Bay. Then he changes his mind, "thoughtfully" suggesting a new method of elimination: dynamite. He will seal them inside a cave where their remains will never be located. In making their escape, Frank and Joe start a fire to produce smoke to overcome the gang. Frank cautions Joe to bank the fire once he makes enough smoke, stating, "'We just want to feed Klenger and Stoper enough smoke to make them helpless ... not suffocate them!'" (209).

Even when confronted with a hate-filled terrorist threatening to blow up caches of dynamite all over America, the Hardy Boys are capable of mature compassion. After listening to Ivan Vilnoff's heated rant in *The Sinister Signpost* (1936), Frank tries to reason with the mad inventor, "'Why don't you come along with us now? We'll see that nothing dreadful happens to you,' he added, knowing that the place for this strange individual was an asylum" (185).

Teenage Frank and Joe never give into emotional rage and never display violence that might be construed as adolescent rebelliousness or delinquency. They remain deferential to adults, even their adversaries, who, once located, are turned over to adult authorities without harm.

Chapter 13

Bayport, USA

Don't bother to look it up. You won't find it on a map.
—Leslie McFarland

The base of operations for all fifty-eight novels in the original Hardy Boys series is Bayport. As high school students living with their parents, Frank and Joe Hardy are rooted to their hometown. Although in the later novels, the Hardy Boys travel to Iceland, Britain, Hong Kong, and North Africa, each adventure typically begins and ends in Bayport. The Hardy home is ground zero, detective central. At times a chance encounter with a stranger on a Bayport street will lead the brothers to a cross-country investigation. In other cases, people arrive in Bayport seeking help from Fenton Hardy. Letters, telegrams, phone calls, and radio messages summon the boys to help their father solve a mystery in Montana or rescue a chum in Alaska.

The nature of mythical Bayport is important because it both launches the Hardys into action and adventure and also grounds them to the commonplace world familiar to their adolescent readers. It is a key element in making the stories both believable and exciting by linking the everyday childhood world of chores and homework to the wider adult world of distant cities, exotic locations, independence, and adventure. Hardy Boys novels frequently begin with Frank and Joe engaged in typical teenage activities — running an errand for their parents, riding motorcycles, skating with friends — when an event or encounter propels them into a mystery. A man stops and asks for change, passing the boys a phony five-dollar bill, which leads them to track down counterfeiters in an abandoned flourmill. A scuffle in an automat (the fast food restaurant of the era) leads Joe to collide with a diamond thief, who fearing the Hardy boy has seen the jewels he is carrying, kidnaps him.

Leaving a movie theater, the chums spot a holdup in progress. In an instant the plot takes readers from the common predictable world of teens looking for something to do into an imaginary world of action and adventure free of parents and homework. Bayport is both a believably mundane hometown of middle-class normality and a portal to intrigue and excitement.

Stratemeyer provided his contract writers with a brief description of Bayport in the original outline for the series: "Bayport, a city of fifty thousand, located on Barmet Bay, which opens three miles down on the Atlantic Ocean. Bayport has a steamboat office and a railroad station, with trains to New York and South. Ships coal lumber and bricks, and has foundries. North, toward south opening of bay is Willow River, running back westward through farms and hills (all fictitious)."[1] The novels never mention "coal lumber and bricks" or set a mystery in a foundry; however, they capitalize on Barmet Bay and the railroad station. Barmet Bay allows the boys to race speedboats in summer and ice boats in winter. Subject to sudden storms, the bay provided writers with an endless stream of shipwrecks, collisions, and near drownings. The train station connects Bayport to New York and all places west.

Bayport is a transportation hub. In addition to the steamboat office and train station, the town has a taxi company, bus service to New York, a ferry line, and later, an airport. All these allow the Hardys to be highly mobile, making quick trips to follow up clues in Chicago or Morocco. The nearby bay and airport also give the boys quick access to their motorboat and their father's private plane. Being a seaport, Bayport can accommodate foreign ships and serves as an ideal landing spot for a host of pirates, smugglers, and foreign agents.

The geography of Bayport is uniquely designed for adventure. Like a theme park or Hollywood back lot, distinctly different venues are arranged in close proximity. Within a few miles of the safe comfort of the Hardy home are towering cliffs, caves (often used as criminal hideouts), secluded beaches, woods, a mill race, Willow River, stormy Barmet Bay, islands, farms, an amusement park, museums, mountains, a race track, palatial mansions, abandoned houses, a Chinatown, a seedy waterfront, a thriving business district, and the Atlantic Ocean. The closeness of these disparate features is vital because it allows high school students Frank and Joe to have a range of adventures and face life-threatening situations without having to skip class or risk being late for dinner.

Many of the characteristics of the region in and around Bayport were the inventions of Leslie McFarlane, who expanded upon Stratemeyer's sparse outline by drawing upon his memories of his Canadian hometown, Haileybury, Ontario, and its surrounding cliffs, lakes, and rivers. His fictional Barmet Bay, which is featured in many key scenes in the books, mirrors Lake Temiskaming, a seven-mile-wide stretch of the Ottawa River, dotted with islands and bordered by high cliffs. The lake made an indelible impression on McFarlane, who described it vividly in his autobiography:

> The lake was the enduring element that gave Haileybury its character. Not only did it convey a majestic sense of spaciousness, but it was infinite with change. Its mood would vary with the seasons, the weather, even with the time of day. On fine mornings in the summer it lay glassy and still with a shimmer on the water under a cloudless sky. When clouds gathered and there was a tossing of whitecaps, you could see the rain coming down from the north. You could watch its progress as it obscured the headlands and the islands, as it blotted out the distant Quebec shore and came sweeping southward in great sheets over the waves rolling before the wind. In winter it was a vast expanse of white snow, acres of purity in a light so clear that even the small dwellings on the other shore were sharply defined. When the snowstorms came they advanced with white banners flying in an onrush of dancing flakes that softly enclosed our world.[2]

In drafting the opening scene of *The Tower Treasure* in which a speed demon overtakes the Hardy Boys on the shore road, McFarlane decided to "arrange the topography" to heighten the drama, adding some Haileyburian touches: "I decided to conjure up a very steep cliff towering above the road on the left and balance it with a very steep declivity dropping off precipitously on the right, straight down into the waters of Barmet Bay. Without a shoulder for refuge, the situation now contained the essential elements of peril, as the pursing car and lunatic-in-charge gained rapidly on the Hardy boys."[3]

Despite these geographic details, Bayport remains something of a blank slate. Unlike the London of Sherlock Holmes or the Los Angeles of Philip Marlowe, Bayport is a kind of no place and everyplace. Aside perhaps from the tower mansion that leads visitors to ask "Who owns that magnificent house on the hill?" the town is devoid of distinctive characteristics:

> Since Franklin W. Dixon is a cardboard writer, it is, of course, understandable that Bayport remains only a formulaic backdrop, as forgettable as the settings in soap operas or 1950s television situation comedies.... It's there for characters to live in, it is secure, it throws up no real dilemmas — and Bayport is a handy place for the Hardys to be since so many criminals flock there. But it is not a spot that takes on its own life. In short, it is *not* Sherwood Anderson's Winesburg, Ohio (who would expect it to be?).... It is a frozen and fixed world where mysteries come and go, but there is no change or human complexity.[4]

Formulaic Bayport remains vague and formless throughout the series. It is both urban and rural, small town and suburban. Bayport has busy streets, stores, office buildings, cabs, mansions, and a slum (which Leslie McFarlane preferred to call "a poor quarter") like a city. *The Melted Coins* (1944), for example, details the dark underside of Bayport located along the docks: "Bayport's waterfront was a picturesque but squalid part of the city. The streets were dark and crooked, crowded with second-hand stores, cheap hotels, and shabby restaurants. There was an unpleasant odor of strong food in the air. Mahogany-tanned men in caps and pea jackets strode the streets, ambling along with the rolling gait particular to sailors" (93). This urban landscape of seedy shops and tattoo parlors is surrounded by open country, dirt roads, small villages, woodlands, and farms. Chet Morton, whom the Hardys visit often, lives on a farm. There are frequent references to orchards, fields, and barns. The Hardy property has a barn, converted to a gymnasium, in the backyard. Though Bayport is a "thriving" metropolis with several newspapers and a radio station, it is small enough to have a single high school like a suburban community.

In any given book, the chums may be walking down a busy street or driving past a hay wagon on a shady country lane. This blend of big city and small town serves two vital purposes to the success of the series. On one hand, it provides writers with ample plot devices. Frank and Joe are not stuck in the Bronx, their actions limited to tenements, stores, office buildings, alleys, and cabs, nor are they isolated on a farm or in a small town with adventures confined to natural hazards such as rock slides or blizzards. A quick spin in a roadster can carry the chums to an abandoned house on a cliff, a seedy waterfront dive, Chet's farm, Bayport High, the Tower Mansion, a Chinese laundry, or an automat. The *Sleuth* can take the chums to deserted Cabin Island in Barmet Bay, up the Willow River to an abandoned flourmill, or out to sea to rendezvous with a suspicious freighter. In addition, the urban/rural features of Bayport let readers throughout the country identify with Frank and Joe. There are enough urban references to appeal to boys living in Brooklyn and Boston and sufficient rural descriptions to make boys living on farms or in small towns feel connected to their heroes.

Bayport presents a strong contrast between good and evil. Though wholesomely middle class with its comfortable homes, impressive mansions, friendly proprietors, all–American high school, highly functional families, and clean-cut youth given to hiking and picnicking, Bayport is, as Arthur Prager notes, a nexus of crime, espionage, corruption, and fraud: "Never were so many assorted felonies committed in a simple American small town. Murder, drug peddling, race horse kidnapping, diamond smuggling, medical malpractice, big-time auto theft, and even (in the 1940s) the hijacking of strategic materials and espionage, all were conducted with Bayport as a nucleus."[5] Prager could have added counterfeiting, illegal alien smuggling, terrorism, muggings, and the machinations of mad scientists to the list.

Bayport is a microcosm of the America presented in the series. The United States is depicted in wholly positive terms. Government officials, aside from Bayport's bumbling and self-aggrandizing cops, are sincere, intelligent, fair, and dedicated. Businesses, for the most part, are honest, socially responsible, and essential to the American way of life. Parents, teachers, and, above all, federal officials are to be trusted and respected. Unlike most Hollywood scripts, corruption in the Hardy Boys series is not linked to vague, mysterious conspiracies involving secretive government agencies and faceless corporations but to individual lawbreakers or at best a cultish group of wrongdoers. Despite the appearance of thieves, racketeers, counterfeiters, terrorists, and kidnappers, Bayport maintains an image of wholesome normality. As Carol Billman notes, "Inordinate criminal activity notwithstanding, Bayport smells sweet. It is indeed a rarefied, almost fantastic place."[6] In contrast to adult detectives who solve a single crime amid an urban sea of dope dealers, gangsters, and prostitutes (who often act as witnesses or informants), Frank and Joe operate in a wholesome environment, tracking down leads from honest proprietors and shopkeepers to identify and bring to justice the lone villain. Part of the appeal of the adult detective story is its ability to offer readers or viewers a form of justified voyeurism as the investigator is obliged to follow clues through an underworld of sin and vice. Carol Billman points out that "there is a great difference between the 'mean streets' of the adult genre, where murder comes cheap and the entire world is stained by corruption, and the crime-ridden though ultimately comfortable and serene world of Bayport."[7] The message of the Hardy Boys books is that Bayport and America are essentially good and wholesome places threatened by a handful of easily identifiable evil-doers. At novel's end, with the rogues jailed, Bayport — and by extension American society — is restored to its customary peace, order, and security.

Where Is Bayport?

Stratemeyer did not place fictional Bayport in any state, though fans and readers glean through the novels trying to detect just where Frank and Joe live on the Atlantic Coast. The rocky coastline, nearby mountains, and rugged winters lead Robert L. Crawford to argue that Bayport is situated in Maine. The repeated references to snowball fights, bobsledding, ice skating, ice boats, skiing, and sleigh rides (elements of McFarlane's Canadian boyhood) all point, he suggests, to New England.[8] However, dialogue in several novels clearly suggest that Bayport could not be located in Maine. In *While the Clock Ticked* (1932) Aunt Gertrude mentions that the boys' parents are vacationing in Maine some three hundred miles away, which would place Bayport in the metropolitan New York area. In *The House on the Cliff* (1927), Fenton Hardy states that the villain Snackley had a smuggling operation "up on the New England coast," suggesting Bayport is south of New England. In 1965's *The Haunted Fort*, the chums drive north several hours to reach a spot in New England,

Features of McFarlane's Canadian hometown shaped his descriptions of Bayport.

Devil's Rock, Haileybury, Ontario. Richard Steward.

again suggesting that Bayport is in the greater New York region. In addition, a Maine location would make Boston, not New York, the nearest large city, so that connecting flights to overseas destinations would likely depart from Logan Airport rather than JFK.

Other readers suggest that coastal Bayport is set in Stratemeyer's home state of New Jersey, which is located near New York and would be a likely spot for a retired NYPD detective like Fenton Hardy to set up shop (much like Stratemeyer himself). New Jersey has bays, islands, ports, seedy waterfronts, airports, rivers, small towns, and farms. But the novels contain clear evidence that the Hardys are not residents of New Jersey. In *The Tower Treasure* Fenton Hardy tells his sons that Red Jackley "got out of the city, out into New Jersey" suggesting that Bayport would not be in the Garden State. In *The Missing Chums* (1928) Fenton Hardy tells Frank and Joe that Baldy Turk "'held up a bank in a small New Jersey town about a month ago,'" which again would suggest they live in a different state. In 1934's *The Mark on the Door* Fenton Hardy and his sons take a taxi to the airport and take a flight to a "Jersey field" where they transfer to a larger plane bound for Texas. In *The Firebird Rocket* (1978) he asks his sons to travel to Princeton. Frank's response, "'You mean Princeton University?... In New Jersey?'" (11), also indicates they live in another state.

The "Real" Bayport

There is, of course, a real town named Bayport on Long Island sixty miles east of Manhattan. Situated on Great South Bay near a river and four miles from Fire Island and connected to New York City by rail, the town bears a striking resemblance to Stratemeyer's city. In the 1920s much of Long Island was still rural with working farms and the baronial estates of New York's wealthy families. Fans who claim the Long Island town is the model for the fictional Bayport argue that Stratemeyer, who grew up in North Jersey and worked in New York, would have likely heard of Bayport and certainly be familiar with Long Island. In *The Tower Treasure* Fenton Hardy arrives in Bayport from New York City by taking a "train from the west" (116), which suggests a Long Island location.

The real Bayport, however, was hardly a thriving city of 50,000 in 1927. By 2000, the census reported a population of only 8,662. Although it has the waterways, ferry service, and train station mentioned in *The Tower Treasure*, it lacks the cliffs, mountains, and other topographical features that come into play in other novels. Still, Long Island readers make a strong case for arguing that Bayport is the model for the city that Stratemeyer and McFarlane enlarged and embellished with seedy waterfronts, palatial mansions, cliffs, coves, and caves.

It is clear that the fictional Bayport is located somewhere near New York City. It is the largest real city repeatedly named in the novels. It is from New York that Fenton Hardy and his sons make train and plane connections to head to Montana or Switzerland. Bayport's exact proximity to the Big Apple, however, remains ambiguous. Bayport seems to move back and forth, trombone-like, as it appears nearer and farther and finally closer to New York City.

In 1931's *What Happened at Midnight* the boys follow a suspect onto a train heading "northward" to New York. Later when they face hitchhiking home from Manhattan, Frank mentions they have a 200-mile walk before them. They tell a driver they are heading "down the coast," which would place Bayport somewhere near Baltimore rather than Long Island. In *The Secret of Wildcat Swamp* (1952) Fenton Hardy takes a plane to New York. In 1956's *The Clue in the Embers* a man arrives in Bayport to see the Hardys, telling them that he had taken a "sleeper" from New York, indicating an extended rail trip. Joe is surprised that someone would travel such a distance to see them, asking "incredulously" why he would "travel all the way here from New York just to see us" (37). A decade later, New York appears to be quite distant from Bayport. In *The Mystery of the Spiral Bridge* (1966) Frank and Joe fly their father's plane to New York. The trip lasts long enough for the brothers to take turns piloting. Finally, as Robert L. Crawford notes in *The Lost Hardys: A Concordance*, Frank and Joe take a day-long trip to Philadelphia in *The Secret of the Lost Tunnel* (1950).[9] Heading south to solve a Civil War mystery, the boys leave Bayport "at dawn" (35) and arrive in Philadelphia "late that afternoon" (37). Even in the era before the New Jersey Turnpike, a road trip from Long Island to Philadelphia would not take more than three hours. An eight- or nine-hour drive to Philadelphia would place Bayport much farther north of New York City, perhaps Boston or even Maine. In the final novels of the series, Bayport slides closer to New York City. In 1977's *The Jungle Pyramid*, the boys investigate a gold robbery in Wakefield that is "a hundred miles from Bayport on the way to New York City" (3) which appears to be within easy driving distance, suggesting that Bayport is no more than one hundred and fifty miles or so from Manhattan. In *The Firebird Rocket* the brothers and Chet drive to Princeton University in New Jersey. Though the novel includes no mention of mileage or travel time, the trip from Bayport to Princeton appears to take not more than a few hours, as they leave in the morning and arrive on campus with enough time to spend the rest of the day conducting an investigation. The actual distance from Bayport, New York, to Princeton, New Jersey, is 109 miles, currently estimated as a two-hour trip. In *The Sting of the Scorpion*, published a year later, Frank and Joe take a bus to New York City. They leave Bayport in the morning and arrive at the Port Authority Terminal in Manhattan "a few minutes after eleven o'clock," suggesting a trip of perhaps two hours or less. After a full day of following leads, the brothers take a bus home, arriving sometime before evening.

    The mystery of where Bayport is located is not resolved until a later series. Hardy Boys Casefiles #39 *Flesh and Blood* (1990) settles the geographical debate with its opening description of a storm-ravaged Bayport:

"This is worse than a nightmare!"
Frank Hardy brushed back his wet brown hair and scanned the area. The

scene looked more like a set for a war movie than downtown Bayport. Several buildings had been leveled, cars had been thrown about like toys, and traffic signs were twisted into pretzel shapes.

What stunned Frank even more was the fact that the destruction had been caused by a tornado.

Tornado? Frank thought with a shake of his head. He had seen pictures of tornadoes hitting places like Oklahoma but not in New York and especially not in a coastal city like Bayport. A hurricane would have been more natural [1].

The Hardy Home

Frank and Joe live with their parents Fenton and Laura (sometimes called Mildred) Hardy on the corner of High and Elm Streets in a "handsome stone residence." The corner address explains why different street addresses are given throughout the series. Evidently contract authors could not agree whether the house faced High or Elm. There are two additional buildings on the Hardy property. A two-story garage houses the family cars, including the boys' roadster. The upper floor is used variously as a crime lab, dark room, and Chet's taxidermy shop. An attached shed provides storage for the brothers' motorcycles. There is also an old barn in the back yard that has been transformed into a gymnasium that contains, according to *The Tower Treasure*, "the usual collection of old toys, footballs, broken baseball bats and such paraphernalia, to be found wherever boys store their cherished possessions" (133).

The house itself is substantially upper middle class. There is a large central hall, living room, kitchen, and dining room on the first floor and four bedrooms on the second floor. In addition to the parents' master bedroom and the boys' room, there is a guest room and one set aside for Aunt Gertrude, who is often in residence. Fenton Hardy maintains his detective headquarters in a room on the second floor variously described as a "library," "den," "office," and "study." In addition to its desk and deep leather sofa, the room contains his collection of disguises, detective equipment, reference books, a safe, and file cabinets holding his extensive collection of records and photographs of criminals. He keeps a club bag packed with essentials in case of sudden trips. The house also has a powerful short-wave radio. The radio moves from the attic in 1945's *The Short-Wave Mystery* to the basement crime lab in *The Mystery of the Chinese Junk* (1960) to Fenton Hardy's study in *The Viking Symbol Mystery* (1963). In 1927's *The Tower Treasure* the Hardy household includes servants.

As detective central, the Hardy home is a magnet for criminals, con men, spies, intruders, burglars, and vandals. Mrs. Hardy is twice victimized in her own home. In *The Secret of the Old Mill* (1927) a swindler posing as a rug merchant purchases her Turkish carpets and pays her in counterfeit money.

In 1953's *The Crisscross Shadow* a "suspicious salesman" sells her a leather key case, pockets a key, snatches a picture of Fenton Hardy off the piano, and storms out of the house before he can be stopped. An overnight guest steals documents from one of Fenton Hardy's suits in *Footprints Under the Window* (1933). Frank and Joe discover Aunt Gertrude and their Irish laundress gagged and tied to a drain pipe in the basement in *The Twisted Claw* (1939). Spies plant microphones in the living room and Fenton Hardy's second-floor den in *The Mystery of the* Flying Express (1941). Frank and Joe arrive home just in time to spot a man dropping to the roof of the kitchen porch from the second story in *The Crisscross Shadow*. Two years later in *The Clue in the Embers* a masked intruder uses gas pellets to render the Hardys unconscious but is caught after chopping into a file cabinet with a hatchet. In 1961's *The Mystery of the Desert Giant* Chet rushes from the garage darkroom and is slugged by an eavesdropper. A note attached to a heavy bolt is thrown through the window in *The Bombay Boomerang* (1970). The radio antenna near the garage is pulled down by vandals in *The Viking Symbol Mystery*. The greatest damage to the Hardy home occurs in *The Flickering Torch Mystery* (1943) when an arsonist torches the house, gutting the rear of the house. Only quick action by a passing Chet Morton saves the Hardy home from burning to the ground.

With all these intrusions, assaults, and attacks, home security is a constant challenge. In *The Mystery of the* Flying Express and *The Secret Panel* (1946), bogus workmen are caught tampering with the lock on the back door. In addition to changing locks, Frank and Joe wire them so that a radio switches on whenever a key is inserted to alert them to possible intruders. Chet crouches in the bushes with an infrared camera to photograph suspects approaching the Hardy front door in *The Mystery of the Desert Giant*. In *The Mystery of the Chinese Junk*, the Hardy home is equipped with a state-of-the-art security system. Aunt Gertrude reports that a prowler was thwarted when the alarm bell sounded and floodlights illuminated the lawn. However, when a medicated Aunt Gertrude carelessly leaves a door open, the alarm system fails to detect agents of the Chameleon gang entering the house and stealing evidence from Fenton Hardy's safe.

But like Bayport, the Hardy home is always purged of danger by novel's end. The Hardy home, like the rest of Bayport and the country it represents, endures as a symbol of comfort and safety.

Bayport Village

The special allure of the fictional Bayport was not lost on real estate developers in Haileybury, Ontario, Leslie McFarlane's hometown. In 2003 twenty-five upscale town homes were constructed along Lake Temiskaming in a subdivision called Bayport Village. Located near the marina, the homes offer residents a number of amenities. They can, like the Hardy Boys, have easy access to boats and explore the islands and rocky cliffs that inspired the topography of Barmet Bay in the opening pages of *The Tower Treasure*. They can also drive past stately homes on a shore road or turn inland a few blocks to the house at 580 Brewster Street where eleven of the original Hardy Boys books were written.[10]

CHAPTER 14

The Hardy Boys on Stage, on Screen, and in Parody

> "Oh, no!" Joe shrieked as they raced into the informal cozy living room of the Hardly home. "The overstuffed flower-patterned chintz chairs which blend happily with the ice-green walls have been turned over and their cushions tossed about in a disorderly fashion!"
> — Mabel Maney, *A Ghost in the Closet*

The popularity and longevity of the Hardy Boys series made Frank and Joe natural subjects for other media. According to Leslie McFarlane, Enda Mae Oliver, best known for playing "outspoken aunts" in a variety of films, was slated to star in a radio program based on the Hardy Boys to be called *Aunt Gertrude and the Boys*. Oliver died unexpectedly in 1942 at the age of fifty-nine, and the program never materialized. Bonita Granville played Nancy Drew in a short-lived series of hour-long films released by Warners and First National beginning in 1938. However, no Hardy Boys films were produced by Hollywood studios in the Thirties or Forties. Studio executives may have had reservations about bringing Frank and Joe Hardy to the screen because of possible confusion with the popular Andy Hardy juvenile series featuring Mickey Rooney.

The Mickey Mouse Club

Near the end of the Second World War, Walt Disney, who had produced cartoons and award-winning films such as *Snow White and the Seven Dwarfs*,

Fantasia, and *Cinderella*, wanted a presence on the new medium of television. After studying the financial risks and potential rewards in the quickly growing broadcasting market, the Disney studios produced an hour-long holiday special that aired on Christmas Day in 1950. The program's success with critics and viewers led Disney to explore the possibility of creating a television series.[1]

Walt Disney's *The Mickey Mouse Club* premiered on the afternoon of October 3, 1955, on ABC and became an immediate hit and a landmark feature of Baby Boom popular culture. Nearly 45 percent of the television sets in the United States tuned into the first broadcast. Later in the season, a ratings survey revealed the Disney program was being watched by 14 million viewers, a third of them adults.[2]

The Mickey Mouse Club was a carefully crafted and well-executed children's variety show that took advantage of the talent and resources Disney had acquired over twenty years of producing motion pictures. Features of the sixty-minute daily program were specially selected to engage a young audience and generate a loyal fan-base. For instance, each show opened with a cartoon of Donald Duck hitting a gong. Instead of using the standard set introduction, Disney created a novel attention-getter by presenting a dozen variations. One day the gong would splatter like a pie, on another it would shatter to pieces, and yet on another a nephew would rush in and beat Donald to the punch. Each weekday had a special designation — Monday was "Fun With Music Day" and Wednesday was "Anything Can Happen Day." Children came to believe that the show was not just a program but a real club with activities. They could buy Mickey Mouse Club regalia and even obtain a Mickey Mouse Club membership card. The adult hosts looked into the camera and addressed children directly, encouraging the sense they were not just watching but participating with other children. *The Mickey Mouse Club* featured the Mouseketeers wearing club T shirts and the trademark mouse ears (who ended each show mournfully singing the famous "M–I–C–K–E–Y— *Why? Because we like you*" song), cartoons from the Disney vault, travelogues, newsreels with child reporters, sermonettes by Jimmie Dodd ("Words to Grow By"), promos for Disney films, guest stars, and series. Modeled after the movie serials of the Thirties and a precursor to the adult television mini-series of the 1970s, the specially produced adventure series became some of the most popular segments of *The Mickey Mouse Club*.[3]

The second season of *The Mickey Mouse Club* (1956–1957) included the series *The Mystery of the Applegate Treasure*. Written by Jackson Gillis, the script was based on the first Hardy Boys novel *The Tower Treasure*. Presented in nineteen fifteen- minute episodes, the series starred Tim Considine as Frank, Tommy Kirk as Joe, Russ Conway as Fenton Hardy, Sarah Shelby as Aunt Gertrude, and Carole Ann Campbell as Iola Morton. Aunt Gertrude, who

14. The Hardy Boys on Stage, on Screen, and in Parody

Tim Considine and Tommy Kirk as Frank and Joe Hardy in the Disney series, 1955–1957. Photofest.

did not appear in *The Tower Treasure*, was highlighted in the series, no doubt because she had become a favorite Hardy Boys character with readers. The story line did not mention Laura Hardy, leading many viewers to assume the boys were motherless. Tim Considine and Tommy Kirk were fifteen and fourteen when the series was filmed, making them younger than the eighteen-year-old and seventeen-year-old Hardy brothers appearing in the books published in the Fifties and making them a bit younger than the characters in the original books. The boys were cast younger to appeal to the show's after-school audience. Frank and Joe's dress, demeanor, and interactions with Aunt Gertrude made them appear more like eleven- and twelve-year-olds than teenagers.[4]

In the Jackson Gillis series Frank and Joe want to become detectives like their father. Fenton Hardy, however, dissuades them, arguing they are too young. As in the McFarlane novels, a minor incident leads the Hardys into a mystery involving "Silas" Applegate, the owner of a decrepit mansion; Perry Robinson; a criminal named Jackley; a stolen treasure; and an old railroad water tower.

A mysterious stranger steals Iola Morton's purse, leading Frank and Joe to the grounds of the Applegate estate. When the boys discover tools taken from their home, Applegate blames Perry Robinson and discharges him but not before the young gardener gives Joe a gold doubloon to hold for him. The boys learn that the coin may be part of the legendary Applegate treasure that was stolen ten years before. Because most people in Bayport have dismissed Applegate's claims about his family's lost gold, the old man is pleased that Frank and Joe believe his story.[5]

Applegate is angered, however, when treasure hunters pepper his lawn with holes and blames Frank and Joe for the damage. A subsequent search of the mansion's old tower reveals that it has been ripped apart, evidently by an intruder conducting an illicit search. The boys obtain a clue, a note referring to the "old tower." As in the McFarlane novel, a search of the mansion's old tower proves fruitless. The boys guess the note might refer to another old tower. When Frank discovers a crumbling railroad water tower, the brothers climb up to investigate. They are spotted by Jackley, Applegate's plumber. He follows and pretends to help Frank and Joe, then tries to seize the treasure for himself. Patrolmen come to the aid of the Hardy Boys and subdue Jackley. The treasure of gold doubloons is returned to an appreciative Silas Applegate.[6] Although the title and plot were altered, the televised dramatization bore enough resemblance to *The Tower Treasure* to attract attention to the first Hardy Boy novel.

A year later Frank and Joe reappeared in a new series *The Mystery of Ghost Farm*. Though based on Stratemeyer's characters, the fifteen-episode drama is not linked to any Hardy Boys book. In Jackson Gillis' original script Joe runs an errand in the country and discovers a "ghost farm." Like a Wild West ghost town, the place seems deserted, except for a number of aging farm animals, including a belligerent billy goat. Although there is no evidence that anyone lives on the farm, the animals are fed and cared for, apparently by a ghost. Investigating the farm, Frank and Joe encounter the "ghost" — an old man who says he was a friend of Lacey, the deceased owner. He tells the young detectives that he taking care of the orphaned animals. Eventually, the old man admits he is Lacey and explains that he faked his death to obtain insurance money to keep his farm going. Lacey, however, is unable to save the property from foreclosure or the animals from being sold to a slaughterhouse. Frank and Joe disprove a false will, discover Lacey's long-forgotten government bonds, and rescue the animals from destruction.[7]

In addition to being a highly popular television program, *The Mickey Mouse Club* was a merchandising machine for the Disney enterprises. In 1957 *Walt Disney's Mickey Mouse Club Magazine*, a companion publication to the hit show, carried condensed revisions of two novels: *The Shore Road Mystery* and *The House on the Cliff*. Disney produced or licensed a line of ancillary products related to the series. Beginning in 1956 Dell released four Hardy Boys comic books with Tim Considine and Tommy Kirk on their covers, two based on the *Mickey Mouse Club* series and two based on original McFarlane novels: *The Secret of the Old Mill* and *The Mystery of the Caves*. Whitman Publishing printed a Hardy Boys coloring book in 1957. That same year Parker Brothers produced a board game, The Hardy Boys Treasure Game, based on *The Tower Treasure* with the Disney stars on the box.[8] Grosset & Dunlap and bookstores capitalized on the popular TV show by promoting the thirty-year-old novels. *The House on the Cliff* was offered free with the purchase of *The Tower Treasure*. Hardy Boys titles were sold in supermarkets in special displays, bringing Frank and Joe into easy reach of mothers eager to encourage their children to read in the era of TV. Bookstore notices and print ads linked the television show to the hardcover books. Grosset & Dunlap packaged Hardy Boys books in special wrappers picturing Tim Considine and Tommy Kirk alongside a mention of *The Mickey Mouse Club* on ABC.

The television program not only popularized Frank and Joe Hardy, but it also helped remove the syndicate stigma that kept their books off library shelves. Teachers and school librarians, who decades before considered the series book juvenile rubbish, now saw the Hardy Boys as a valuable bridge from television viewing to reading, particularly for boys. Though Hardy Boys books might not be assigned in class or even included on library shelves, few teachers or parents would discourage a fifth grader from reading *The Tower Treasure*. In the video age, concerned adults were glad to see children reading books that, if not great literature, would foster the reading habit and perhaps lead them to consider more serious books when they outgrew their fascination with Frank and Joe Hardy's repetitive adventures.

The sale of these freshly printed copies of books written in the 1920s and 1930s gave new life to the syndicate heroes, introducing a new and more affluent generation of readers to the Hardy Boys series. It also led the syndicate to start the Great Purge of the Fifties to eliminate the ethnic slurs that troubled parents and modernize, simplify, and streamline the novels to appeal to a younger audience in the TV age.

The Mystery of the Chinese Junk

In 1967 Frank and Joe appeared in the television show *The Mystery of the Chinese Junk*, based on the 1960 novel of the same title. Designed as a pilot for a never-produced television series, the story followed the basic plot of the book and character list, including not only Fenton Hardy, Chet Morton, Biff, Tony Prito, and Aunt Gertrude but also novel-specific characters like Clams Daggett and Jimmy Foy. Richard Gates played Frank Hardy and Tim Matheson (then spelled Mathieson) played Joe Hardy. Both twenty at the time of production, Gates and Matheson portrayed the Hardys as young adults rather than children as in *The Mickey Mouse Club*. Teri Garr appeared in the film as did Jan Michael Vincent, who made his film debut playing Tony Prito.[9]

Written and produced by Richard Murphy, the hour-long film was directed by Larry Peerce, son of opera tenor Jan Peerce. Two years later Larry Peerce would receive an Academy Award nomination for directing the 1969 hit *Goodbye Columbus* starring Ali McGraw and Richard Benjamin.

"The Grooviest Cartoon Show in History"

Animated Hardy Boys in "the grooviest cartoon show in history," 1969. Photofest.

Richard Gates and Tim Matheson as Frank and Joe Hardy in *The Mystery of the Chinese Junk*, 1967. Photofest.

In 1969 the Hardy Boys appeared in a thirty-four-episode animated cartoon series that blended their sleuthing skills with rock music. In this improbable plot line, Frank and Joe are mystery-solving rock singers. Produced by Norm Prescott and Lou Scheimer, the program included Fenton Hardy, Aunt Gertrude, "Chubby" Morton, and a character named Wanda Kay

Breckenridge. The series about an Archies-like pair of singing detectives dancing in platform shoes and driving around in a mod Rolls Royce against psychedelic backdrops lasted one season. The brief series was notable for being the first cartoon show to include a black character. Although aimed at young children, some of the stories dealt with illegal drugs, an unlikely topic for a cartoon. Animated Frank and Joe also made history by including public service announcements about smoking and wearing seatbelts.[10]

As with *The Mickey Mouse Club* a decade before, the animated cartoon produced a stream of merchandise, including four comic books, Halloween costumes, Viewmaster slides, sheet music, LPs, a Milton Bradley board game, and a miniature version of the Hardy band's Rolls Royce.

The Hardy Boys Meet Nancy Drew

Frank and Joe Hardy returned to the screen a decade later in 1977 in an hour-long series called *The Hardy Boys/Nancy Drew Mysteries*. Parker Stevenson and Shaun Cassidy starred as Frank and Joe Hardy with Pamela Sue Martin playing Nancy Drew. The separate detective series alternated weeks with

Shaun Cassidy and Parker Stevenson as Joe and Frank Hardy in *The Hardy Boys Mysteries*, 1979. Photofest.

independent plots. Placing the Hardy Boys alongside but apart from Nancy Drew followed Stratemeyer's original policy of segregating boys and girls into parallel series.

At twenty-four and eighteen during the original filming, Stevenson and Cassidy were cast as young adults rather than children to appeal to an older, primetime television audience. Some of the episodes were based, albeit loosely, on existing Hardy Boys novels. "The Disappearing Floor" and "The Flickering Torch Mystery" both aired in 1977. The series, which received an Emmy nomination, retained the basic cast of characters from the original novels — Fenton Hardy, Aunt Gertrude, Chet Morton, Callie Shaw (played by Lisa Eilbacher), and Chief Collig. Guest stars included Kim Cattrall, Ray Milland, Linda Dano, Howard Duff, Vic Damone, Troy Donahue, and Ricky Nelson.

This show launched the largest merchandising of Hardy Boys products since *The Mickey Mouse Club* aired twenty years before. Items included lunch boxes, comic books, greeting card sets, Halloween costumes, a jigsaw puzzle, model cars, a Parker Brothers board game, stickers, T shirts, and coloring books. Posters featuring Shaun Cassidy, whose brother was teen idol David Cassidy, were popular, especially with teenage girls.

The children's magazines *Jack and Jill* and *Scholastics* ran articles about the Hardy Boys, connecting the television characters with young readers.

New Line Hardy Boys

Eighteen years later, Frank and Joe Hardy returned to television in a syndicated Canadian series developed by New Line Television, a division of New Line Cinema. In this series an older Frank Hardy (played by Colin Gray) worked for a newspaper while Joe Hardy (played by Paul Popowich) attended college. The thirteen-episode series aired in the fall of 1995. Dubbed into French, the programs were also broadcast in Quebec and France. Failing to attract an audience, the show was discontinued. Photos of Gray and Popowich appeared on covers of sixteen books in the Hardy Boys Casefile series.[11]

The television versions of the Hardy Boys ranged forty years, keeping the names Frank and Joe Hardy fresh in the minds of aging Baby Boomers and introducing the characters to their children and grandchildren. These television productions, no matter how loosely associated with the Stratemeyer novels, ensured that Frank and Joe Hardy would become icons of popular culture long after the Rover Boys, Bomba the Jungle Boy, Ted Scott, and the Bobbsey Twins would fade from public memory.

The Hardy Boys on Stage

The iconic status of the Hardy Boys made them perfect subjects for playwrights as well as television producers. In 1993, Joe Klein, an off-Broadway playwright and later a playwright in residence at American Repertory Theatre in Cambridge, Massachusetts, adapted *The House on the Cliff* into a children's play called *The Hardy Boys in the Mystery of the Haunted House* for Seattle Children's Theater. In Klein's play Frank and Joe investigate an eerie mansion above Barmet Bay. The play, staged in the 1993–1994 season, was later produced by The Austin Theatre for Youth. The popularity of this play led Seattle Children's Theatre to commission a second Hardy Boys drama. Klein created an original story, *The Hardy Boys in the Secret of Skullbone Mountain*, in which Frank and Joe solve a mystery involving the ghost of Redbeard, a pirate, who reappears to threaten Bayport after a ship carrying a gold Pharaoh's bust sinks in Barmet Bay. Children and parents (who buy the tickets) can instantly grasp the nature of a play with established characters or titles. A new play with the Hardy Boys in the title is bound to connect with children interested in mysteries and assure parents about the wholesome nature of the production.

The fact that the Hardy Boys could conjure immediate associations made them appealing figures for satire. With their well-established image of all–American wholesome and youthful naiveté, Frank and Joe were perfect figures for parody and satire.

Christopher Durang, best known for his satiric plays *Sister Mary Ignatius Explains It All For You*, *Beyond Therapy*, and *Betty's Summer Vacation*, wrote a one-act parody, *The Hardy Boys and the Mystery of Where Babies Come From*. Frank and Joe's innocence is highlighted as the sexually clueless detectives, who are always changing their sweaters, try to unravel a new mystery:

> JOE: Now what's the mystery?
> FRANK: Well, I heard someone at school say that Nancy Drew may have to get married because "She has a bun in the oven."
> [*They both look baffled.*]
> JOE: Gosh, Frank, that doesn't make any sense at all. Our housekeeper Mrs. Danvers has had whole cakes in the oven, and she's never had to get married.[12]

Hoping to get to the bottom of the mystery, Frank and Joe decide to sound out the school nurse who had mentioned the mystifying "bun in the oven" remark about Nancy Drew. Trying to be subtle, the boys decide to feign strep throats to engage Nurse Ratched in conversation. The sexually aggressive nurse finds the boys delightfully appealing and orders them to undress for an examination. In the next scene Frank and Joe, stripped to their underwear, are tied up back-to-back, still no closer to solving the mystery:

FRANK: I didn't know they had to tie you up to check for strep throat.
JOE: Neither did I.
FRANK: Okay, let's add up the facts we know so far about the mystery.
JOE: Well, Nurse Ratched says we don't have hernias because she gave us that coughing test for two hours.
FRANK: Alright, that's fact number one. What else?
JOE: Well, she thinks we're cute.
FRANK: I think we're cute too, but we need more clues than that to solve this mystery. Nancy may be in trouble![13]

Fenton Hardy appears and tells his sons Nancy is pregnant. The boys are astonished and still clueless, not knowing what the word pregnant means. Fenton Hardy, who wanted to wait until the boys were thirty-five before explaining the facts of life, starts to tell the boys where babies come from. His speech about bees, pollen, and eggs is cut short when Nurse Ratched silences the detective with a chloroformed cloth. Frank and Joe are left trying to decipher the meaning of their father's clues:

FRANK: ....He said something about eggs, and you make eggs on *top* of the oven, while you make buns *inside* the oven. Maybe there's some clue about being on top, and being inside.
JOE: It doesn't ring any bells with me, Frank...[14]

Durang's play, which *The Milwaukee Journal Sentinel* compared to a *Saturday Night Live* sketch, has been performed in college and repertory theatres in Idaho and Wisconsin, often as part of an evening of Durang one-acts.

Running with Scissors, a theatre group founded in New Orleans in 2000 by Richard Read and Flynn DeMarco, is known for blending pop culture parodies into campy satires. Productions have included *The Titanic Adventures of the Love Boat Poseidon, The Scooby Witch Project,* and *Gilligan's Island Survivor.* In 2005 the theater group staged *Nancy Drew & the Hardy Boys: The Wax Museum Mystery* at the One Eyed Jacks Theatre in the French Quarter. In Flynn DeMarco's original play Nancy Drew, Frank and Joe Hardy, and their chums Chet and Bess go on a "globetrotting voyage to London, Morocco, and beyond" to return a collection of costumes they discovered in an old trunk. In London they encounter a spooky proprietor of a wax museum. A review captured the tone of the play by echoing the cliffhanging questions posed at the end of Thirties matinee serials: "Will our young sleuths survive a night in Professor Jared's waxworks? Will they recover the Countess de Lave's precious family jewels? Will Bess escape her bumbling kidnappers before she's sold into slavery? Will Chet ever stop eating?"[15]

In an interview with Austin Johnson, Flynn DeMarco explained his inspiration for building a satire on the Hardy Boys: "Oh, I've been a big fan since I was a little boy. I had all the books and watched the TV show. The idea for this play had been around since the start of our company a few years so, but the right time—and right cast—wasn't found until now."[16] In creating an original play, DeMarco tried to maintain elements from the original books playgoers would identify:

> We branched out a little, but we tried basically to touch on the major themes in both series. We tried to make sure we included stuff the audience could recognize—Chet eating all the time, Bess worried about everything. Someone got knocked out, there was a secret passage, you know the stuff. We went through and culled out the major ideas in the books. Jet-setting with an endless amount of cash came about when the group had the idea to go to London—"I'm sure Dad can arrange it for us!" ... we combined not just the Hardys and Drew, but some other things. I love wax museums and gothic horror films. We pulled out all the stops and had the ghost behind the mirror trick, a falling chandelier—everything![17]

The most outrageous and over-the-top parody is Timothy Cope and Paul Boesing's *The Secret of the Old Queen—A Hardy Boys Musical*. First produced in 2000 at the New Conservatory Theater Center in San Francisco, the satire plays on a gay theme: "There are queer goings-on in Bayport and can the Hardy Boys sort out what is happening?" The Madison Theatre Guild described the play as "a delightful musical romp in which the only mystery the Hardy Boys can't seem to solve is that of their own sexual identity."[18]

Frank and Joe as Icons of Satire in the Running With Scissors production of Richard Read and Flynn De Marco's *Nancy Drew & The Hardy Boys: The Wax Museum Mystery*, New Orleans, 2005. Courtesy of Running With Scissors.

Musical numbers include "The Skies Are Always Blue in Bayport," "Boys Are Made for Danger," "Chums," "I Haven't Got a Clue," and "You Need to Tell a Woman From a Man." Set in all–American Bayport, the parody includes not only Frank and Joe but also a voracious Chet, Iola, Callie, Chief Collig, and Fenton Hardy. In the play, the sexually clueless and confused Hardy siblings are hired by a cross-dressing art collector named Cornelius Digby to guard his latest acquisition at a museum gala. The combination of Cope's "funny, lightly subversive script"[19] and Boesing's "tuneful and peppy" score[20] made the play a hit with local critics and audiences, though one playgoer registered a complaint — "not enough Aunt Gertrude!"[21]

"Hardly Boys" and Hardy Men

Mabel Maney's 1995 novel *A Ghost in the Closet* is a gay parody of series protagonists Nancy Drew and the Hardy Boys. In this mystery, Nancy "Clue" and Frank and Joe "Hardly" unravel a mystery involving mad scientists, caves, and secret agents. As in the stage parodies, Frank and Joe are presented as sexually clueless:

> "Oh my," Frank fluttered, "dear me." He and his brother were clearly out of their realm of expertise. Girls' love lives always seemed so very complicated, especially to two fresh-faced lads whose devotion to their family — not to mention their exciting careers as famous detectives known far and wide for their keen sleuthing abilities — left them little time for romance![22]

Mabel Maney's gay satire *A Ghost in the Closet*, 1995.

As in a *National Lampoon* sketch, Frank and Joe are placed in situations described in overtly sexual terms:

> "Stand back, Joe," Willy ordered as he picked up the crowbar and jammed the tool into the wall. Sweat glistened on Willy's thick corded neck as he pressed his broad powerful shoulder against the rod. He rocked back and forth until he had created a deep vertical groove....
>
> He thrust his sturdy tool into the pliant wood over and over again. The panel groaned and creaked with each powerful probe, bringing it closer and closer to bursting wide open. "Just a little more," Willy cried. "This one ought to do it." Harder and harder he slammed the bar into the wall, each time coming closer to whatever lay beyond its barrier.
>
> Joe was so excited he could hardly breathe! He clutched the shirt to his chest and watched with bated breath as the muscular man worked. How long could Willy keep it up? Finally there was a shudder and a heave, and the crowbar found its mark. The entire wall, molding, floorboards and all, seemed to explode and fell in splinters around Willy's boots.
>
> "Look, Frank! A door!" Joe cried. Joe gasped as Willy flung open the warped wooden door only to reveal ... *an empty closet!*[23]

Like Cope's musical, Maney's novel plays on the gay theme using the word "queer" that McFarlane used so liberally in the Twenties and Thirties. At the end of the mystery, Mrs. Hardly tells Frank and Joe that they are adopted. While investigating a corrupt orphanage in Chicago run by the villainous Newton Gangrene, Fennel Hardly came across two abused boys—"one fair-haired with a serious expression in his hazel eyes, the other with curly brown locks and a sunny smile."[24] Fennell, she explains, lived in fear the boys would discover their father's secret and would not understand. Frank, however, accepted the truth without regret: "We'll always be proud to be the Hardly boys," Frank cried out, "only now we're men, too. Father, we're just sorry you had to carry the burden of these secrets for so long." "People can be awfully queer about the truth," Nancy piped up.[25]

In 2007 *Variety* and the *Hollywood Reporter* announced that Twentieth Century–Fox was developing a film about the Hardy Boys to be called *Hardy Men*. Slated to star Ben Stiller and Tom Cruise, the film planned to portray Frank and Joe as adults, coming together after a long estrangement to solve a crime.

Eighty years after they first roared out of the pages of *The Tower Treasure*, Frank and Joe Hardy are still fixtures in popular culture, still valuable commodities for commercial exploitation.

CHAPTER 15

Book Wars: The Series Book Under Fire

> I wish I could label each one of these books: "Explosives! Guaranteed to Blow Your Boy's Brains Out."
> — Franklin K. Mathiews, 1914

Non-smoking, non-drinking, church-going, and parent-loving Frank and Joe Hardy scarcely appear to be subversive influences, but like their virginal sister sleuth Nancy Drew and gadget-minded Tom Swift, they have been the subjects of ongoing controversies for generations. Stratemeyer's creations have been pulled from public library bookshelves, excluded from classrooms, withdrawn from recommended reading lists, and condemned as being as dangerous to minors as alcohol and narcotics.

Even before Frank and Joe took to the Shore Road on their motorcycles, the series book was under fire.

"Blowing Out the Boy's Brains"

The lead article in the November 18, 1914, issue of the popular magazine *The Outlook* reported on the expanding war in Europe. The same issue contained a warning about another threat looming at home. Franklin K. Mathiews, Chief Scout Librarian of the Boy Scouts of America, informed the public of the dangers of what he called the "underground library" of "cheap" and "pernicious" juvenile fiction. His article, ominously titled "Blowing Out the Boy's Brains," alerted the nation about a new menace to America's youth

Children's Book Week Poster, 1921.

that would "debauch and vitiate" a young man's imagination just as "brain and body are debauched and destroyed by strong drink."[1]

Mathiews' article celebrated the death of the dime novel, which had been brought about by the "good influences of the public libraries and schools and the successful competition of the 'movies.'"[2] He pointed out, however, that dangerous literary products were still being marketed, their deleterious sensationalism camouflaged in a new form: "But alas! the modern 'penny dreadful' has not been banished quite so completely as at first appears. Its latest appearance is in the disguise of the bound book, and sometimes so attractively bound that it takes its place on the retail book-store shelf alongside the best juvenile fiction."[3] Arguing that the "motives and methods" of the producers of the bound novel were no less avaricious than those of the dime novel publishers, he believed people would be interested to know that these novels were "not written, but manufactured." Although he never mentioned Edward Stratemeyer by name, Mathiews accurately described the operations of his literary "syndicate":

> There is usually one man who is resourceful as a Balzac so far as ideas and plots for stories are concerned. He cannot, though, develop them all, so he employs a number of men who write for him. I know of one man who has a contract to furnish his publisher each year with twenty-five books manufactured in this way. Another author manufactured last year more than fifty. By such methods from year to year the popular-priced series are kept going, the manager of the writing syndicate being able to furnish the publisher upon demand any kind of a story that may be needed.[4]

Discovering that a single business venture was "manufacturing" 80 percent of the books read by American juveniles, Mathiews sensed that a conspiratorial monopoly was at work, hiding behind a screen of pseudonyms. He condemned the syndicate for its aggressive and, in his view, devious marketing operation. He was troubled by the use of traveling salesmen who made sure series books were placed in every possible newsstand, pharmacy, and grocery store in the country; direct mail campaigns targeted to children; and syndicate-concocted recommended reading lists purportedly compiled by independent organizations circulated to parents and teachers. If the mass production and slick marketing of fifty-centers seemed suspicious, the content of these books, in Mathiews' judgment, was dangerous and debilitating:

> In almost all of this "mile-a-minute fiction" some inflammable tale of improbable adventure is told. Boys move about in aeroplanes as easily as though on bicycles; criminals are captured by them with a facility that matches the ability of Sherlock Holmes; and when it comes to getting on in the world, the cleverness of these hustling boys in comparable only to those captains of industry and Napoleons of finance who have made millions in a minute.

For Mathiews, all this hyperactivity and emphasis on immediate gratification damaged what he considered a boy's most valuable asset: his imagination. Good literature, he asserted, can "stimulate and conserve this noble faculty, while those of the viler and cheaper sort" overstimulate and weaken a boy's imagination. The difference between a good adventure book like *Treasure Island* and a syndicate novel, he argued, "is not a difference in the elements so much as the use each author makes of them."[6] Robert Louis Stevenson used what Mathiews called "combustibles"—adventure, action, danger, and thrills—with "care and caution" while in the "modern 'thriller' the author works with the same materials, but with no moral purpose, with no real intelligence."[7] Because these writers fail to control the explosive nature of these combustible elements, they create books that pose a serious threat to young minds. The boys who read these dangerous novels risk having their imaginations "literally 'blown out,' as they go into life as terribly crippled as though by some material explosion they had lost a hand or foot."[8]

Mathiews was distressed that the danger these books posed was not appreciated by parents and educators. The fact that these explosive volumes were given to children as Christmas gifts and Sunday school prizes indicated to Mathiews that unsuspecting adults were largely responsible for spreading their insidious influence.

In addressing the role adults had in the distribution of "pernicious books," Mathiews focused on the impact of economics, attacking the appeal of the "fifty-center" to budget-minded parents:

> The "weakness" is not with the boy's taste, but with the parent's pocketbook; the fault lies not so much behind the counter as in front of it. But help is near to meet this weakness and correct this fault. Many of the reputable publishers are placing in competition with the trashy books reprint editions of some of their very best juveniles, all of them written by those modern authors whose books are so popular with all boys. These retail for fifty cents.[9]

Mathiews closed his article with a tale of personal tragedy that demonstrated the need for literary reform. A boy named Guy Arthur Phinisey, he noted, had run away from home that September. Having a good home and "quiet and thrifty" parents, the boy appeared to have no reason to run off. The youth's scoutmaster wrote Mathiews that the only "possible clue" for Guy's inexplicable behavior was "'cheap reading.'"[10]

The Mathiews article was widely reprinted as a tract and circulated among librarians, teachers, and parents' organizations for decades. Mathiews personally lobbied publishers with lists of "good books" and championed his own scouting series based, he claimed, on true stories about Boy Scouts. According to a *Fortune* article published twenty years later, Mathiews's call to arms led to action. Mothers protested at bookstores, demanding that series books be pulled from the shelves, leading booksellers to pack up stacks of Tom Swift novels and return them to the publisher.[11]

As Chief Scout Librarian of the nation's leading organization for boys, Mathiews had great influence. His attack on syndicate-produced books, however, may have been motivated more by their commercial success than by their volatile content. The Boy Scouts of America produced its own books, and Mathiews loathed the popularity of the rival fifty-centers. Stratemeyer had capitalized on the creation of the Boy Scouts by launching a scouting series, which competed with the organization's own books. Mathiews' resentment was shared by children's authors (real authors who wrote books under their own names), publishers, and librarians seeking to support genuine children's literature. The fifty-center was pernicious largely because of its price. In the world of children's literature, the Stratemeyer Syndicate was a Wal-Mart, tasteless and unstoppable. The American Library Association's Winnetka survey of 40,000 schoolchildren in thirty-four cities revealed that 98 percent of the students queried read series books.[12] Other surveys showed that after the Bible the most popular books for boys were Tom Swift titles; for girls, Nancy Drew.

Mathiews was not the first critic of popular children's books. E. W. Mumford delivered a paper called "Juvenile Readers as an Asset" at the American Booksellers Association Convention in 1912. Summarized in the *New York Times*, his remarks caught the attention of the director of the Boy Scouts of America, who brought the issue to the organization's new librarian, Franklin K. Mathiews. Mathiews appeared at the booksellers' convention in 1915, where he delivered an impassioned address called "Books as Merchandise and Something More." Mathiews toured the country for two years, promoting better books for children, and became something of a national figure. Mathiews' efforts attracted support from Frederic G. Melcher, editor of *Publishers' Weekly*, and Anne Carroll Moore, the Superintendent of Children's Works at the New York Public Library. In 1916 the Boy Scouts of America, with help from the American Booksellers Association and the American Library Association, sponsored a Good Book Week. The First World War suspended this venture, but soon after the Armistice, the movement to improve children's books resumed. Good Book Week was transformed into Children's Book Week in 1919, which encouraged booksellers to promote high-quality literature for young people. Series books were categorically excluded from consideration.[13]

In April 1934 *Fortune* contained an attack on the fifty-center titled "For It Was Indeed He" which claimed that "like so many Guy Fawkes' heaping gunpowder in the cellars of Parliament, three publishing firms annually unload well over 5,000,000 explosive fifty-centers on the American adolescents, the foundation stones of human society."[14] The article described the fifty-center in wholly unflattering terms:

The fifty-cent juvenile is, precisely, a book for boys and girls between the ages of ten and sixteen. It has few literary pretensions; it is a flat-footed account of the superhuman exploits of adolescent Ubermenschen — and if it is successful it may have sequels that ramble on for as many as thirty-six novels. It is a fortuitous cross between compound interest and perpetual motion.[15]

Critics of series books sensed that a conspiratorial fraud was being perpetrated on children. All over the country boys and girls were writing fan letters to non-existent authors. The idea that the Nancy Drew books were written not by a woman named Carolyn Keene but more likely by a chain-smoking, hard-drinking male reporter struck many as unseemly.

Children's authors, publishers, book clubs, critics, and teachers regarded the syndicate the way independent filmmakers viewed Hollywood studios, blaming the successful commercial merchants for catering to the lowest common denominator to turn a profit and stifling competition from genuine artists. Not only was the mass-produced fifty center priced lower than other children's books, new titles had established readers, many of whom wrote fan letters asking for new stories. The "throw ahead" at the end of one book whetted readers' appetites for the next volume.

Publishers attempting to introduce a single, free-standing children's book faced a double challenge. Their books had to retail for twice the price of a series book. In addition, the author, characters, and plots were unfamiliar. Adults buying books as gifts for children were more likely to choose a cheaper, well-known, reliable book than an unknown title. The series book had cross-generational appeal. Boys and girls who read the Hardy Boys or Nancy Drew within a decade or two were likely to buy them as presents for their children. A generation later, they would buy the same books for grandchildren. Children given a few free copies from an older family member would want to read more or complete a set started and abandoned by a brother or sister who had outgrown series fiction.

As guardians of better literature, teachers and librarians would take a stand against the series book for decades, waging the good fight, much like nutritionists urging children to give up candy for vegetables. They declined to include series fiction in their collections, arguing that limited school and library funds should not be spent on books lacking educational content. Nancy Drew and the Hardy Boys were rarely found in America's classrooms unless carried in by a pupil or mistakenly donated by an uninformed parent.

If critics in later years no longer viewed syndicate products as "pernicious" or "explosive," they did attack the books for their formulaic and redundant plots, colorless syntax, and lack of character development. Frank and Joe remain fixed in an unchanging world, never expressing emotion, never questioning authority, never evolving, never really learning from their experiences. The books blunt any sense of social awareness. Bland, white, middle-class Bayport is presented as the American norm. Anyone threatening it or even questioning its values is immediately suspect. Crime is never related to poverty, discrimination, or injustice. It is just bad behavior by bad people who must be caught and punished. As agents of the older generation, Frank and Joe seem determined to stunt any rebellion by their young peers. To progressive adults, the Hardy Boys were sirens of obedient conformity.

But it was these same elements that made the formulaic books so popular with children. Analyzing the experience of reading fiction from childhood to adulthood in an *American Journal of Psychology* article in 1993, Thomas Trabasso argued that the simple plots of series books "meet the needs and expectations of preadolescents for an ordered, stable, structured, repetitive, reliable, and assuring world in which one can learn and discover."[16] The characters, though flat by adult standards, "represent what children of this age want to be: fantasized, idealized embodiments blessed with unambiguous virtue, skill, popularity, and adult approval."[17] These characters provide "wish fulfillment" in which the child reader can imagine being independent within a secure environment.

Stratemeyer's creations lasted long enough to disprove their early detractors' vitriolic claims. Generations of children devoured tens of millions of fifty-centers and went on to become the Greatest Generation. Many of them also went on to become teachers, librarians, professors, and writers themselves. Jim Trelease's survey of 2,887 teachers found Nancy Drew books topping the list of their childhood favorites.[18] Millions became parents and enjoyed reliving their own childhoods by sharing the Hardy Boys and Nancy Drew with their sons and daughters.

"Read Anything"

Television, which threatened so many forms of popular literature, rescued the Hardy Boys in two key ways. *The Mickey Mouse Club* introduced Frank and Joe to the Baby Boom generation, and teachers and parents who were concerned about the impact television had on children were glad to see children reading anything. In contrast to television cartoons and *Superman*, series books seemed benign, if not outright educational. Hardy Boys novels might be simplistic, flat, repetitive, and predictable — but they were *books*. If Mathiews condemned the series book because it prevented children from appreciating real books like *Treasure Island* in 1914, a half-century later, teachers and parents were happy to see children reading *The Tower Treasure* instead of watching cartoons. Rejecting proposals to reform children's television, Raymond A. Schroth argued that television could not educate but only entertain. "Forget the 'three hours' of 'good' television and think of better things a 10-year-old could do in that time," Schroth urged parents. "For example: Read Sherlock Holmes, read the Hardy Boys, read anything."[19]

Marie Winn's best-selling book *The Plug-In Drug* documented the debilitating effects television had on children. Her thesis was that the striking difference between viewing and reading was the medium not the content. "It is not enough to compare television watching and reading from the viewpoint of quality," she argued. Although there are "junky books" and "fine, thoughtful television shows," she pointed out, it is important to realize that "the nature of each experience is different."[20] Reading requires a set of complex intellectual actions that transforms words on the page into something real in the mind. Unlike the visual image presented on the screen that is instantly recognized, the word on the page requires the brain to "carry out all the steps of decoding and investing with meaning."[21] The linguistic image engages the imagination in ways the visual image cannot: "The great difference between the 'reading images' and images we take in when viewing television is this: We create our own images when reading, based on our own experiences and reflecting our own individual needs. When we read, in fact, it is almost as if we were creating our own, small, inner television program. The result is a nourishing experience for the imagination."[22]

In addition, Winn pointed out, a reader controls the experience in a way a viewer cannot. A child can read at his or her own pace, skimming and slowing down as needed to comprehend the message. Difficult passages can be reread or reviewed. In watching television, the message proceeds at a pace beyond a viewer's control. Reading not only fuels the imagination, but it also gives children a greater sense of independence. They interact with a book in a way that does not occur with a television program.

Writing in *Booklist* in 2005, Michael O. Tunnell and James S. Jacobs argued that series books helped develop literacy precisely because of their conventional and repetitious format:

> Series books are important to literacy development because they attract readers and because they provide reading practice that develops a wide range of skills.
>
> First, series books are comfortable because they are familiar and predictable. After the first book, characters become friends, and readers are able to make successful guesses about what is going to happen in a story. Second, readers know that they are getting a comprehensible story with a clear problem and a satisfying solution.[23]

Adults might find the manufactured novel as tasteless as a fast food sandwich, but reading specialists have noted that the series book helps children overcome the frustration of getting involved in a new book because it is unfamiliar and taxing to understand.

Tunnell and Jacobs pointed out the importance of making reading enjoyable. Even the Hardy Boys and Nancy Drew, for all their literary flaws, can help children develop higher skills: "Once children find joy in reading, they read more, and the more words they read, the better readers they become. By engaging in the act of reading, children automatically develop and improve a wealth of specific reading skills."[24] Most importantly, Tunnell and Jacobs insisted that children "move on" when they outgrow the series book. "Time spent reading series books doesn't seem to stunt intellectual growth," they argued, noting that literary figures like Jacques Barzun and Louis Auchincloss read them as children.[25] If they did not have merit, at least the books produced no harm in their consumers. As Jennifer Lyn Sczerbinski observed, "No adult is still addicted to *Nancy Drew* books, however avidly he or she read them as a child."[26]

Teachers view series books as key transitions from picture and story books. For many children, series books are the first multi-chapter books they read. Like Tunnell and Jacobs, Dana Truby saw the patterned predictability of the series book as an asset: "Series books, with their consistency of characters and highly patterned plots, provide young readers with some reassurance of familiarity."[27] The easy predictability aids poor readers by enticing them to practice by simply reading more books. "Children," Sczerbinski noted, "have a much greater tendency to pick up another book if they have already read and enjoyed one with the same group of characters."[28] Laurie Pastore, a New York elementary teacher, observed that children "stay with the series book after book, until they are ready to make the leap to harder texts."[29]

Michael Cart saw other values in series fiction, noting that a "favorite series can serve a serious purpose, too; in times of stress and distress, of isolation and loneliness, of fear and anxiety, they can provide the comforting familiarity of recurring settings and characters who have become both faithful friends and family, living in a reliably unchanging alternative world, a place of sometimes necessary refuge and sanctuary."[30]

Nearly a century after Franklin Mathiews attacked Stratemeyer's manufactured novels, teachers place Hardy Boys novels on summer reading lists. The Old York Library's 2007 summer reading list for students entering fourth grade included books by Judy Blume, Roald Dahl, and Franklin W. Dixon.[31] The Loganville Christian Academy Lower School Reading Program lists the Hardy Boys series in its recommendations. In addressing parents, the school stresses the importance of reading: "Reading opens to us worlds of winsome wonder and delight. Reading gives us insight into ourselves and others; it creates opportunities for reflection and consideration; it conveys experiences and sensations that can be found nowhere else."[32] Among the books opening "worlds of winsome wonder and delight" is *The Secret Agent on Flight 101* by Franklin W. Dixon. The Parents' Choice Foundation lists the Hardy Boys in his recommended reading list, calling the books "oldies, but still goodies."[33]

Defense of the Hardy Boys is international. At the RELC Conference in Singapore in 2004, Stephen Krashen presented a paper on recreational reading, arguing that research demonstrated that "voluntary reading"—or reading for enjoyment—improved children's "reading, writing, grammar and vocabulary" in both primary and secondary languages.[34]

In particular, Krashen highlighted the importance of "narrow reading" in acquiring a second language. By concentrating on the works of a single author or genre, students restrict their leisure reading to "what the reader really wants to read." This deep reading, Krashen noted, includes series books:

> Adult second language acquirers made obvious and impressive progress in English as a second language simply by reading books from the Sweet Valley series, novels written for young girls (Sweet Valley Kids, Sweet Valley Twins) and teen-age girls (Sweet Valley High). Subjects did not attend ESL classes; their main source of English was the novels. "Maturation" and time in the US is also an unlikely factor here: All subjects had lived in the US for a considerable amount of time before starting their reading program, and had made little progress in English.[35]

Series books were also found to be beneficial for native English speakers and Krashen assumed that many of his audience had grown up reading Stratemeyer titles:

> There is some evidence supporting the narrow reading idea.... Good readers in English as a first language tended to read more books by a single author and books from a series, a result that many readers of this paper can identify with, former devotees of Nancy Drew, the Hardy Boys and Bobsey [sic] Twins. In addition, the Sweet Valley studies mentioned above are also an example of the efficacy of narrow reading. Of great interest is the fact that Sweet Valley readers eventually went on to read other authors.[36]

Mathiews launched Children's Book Week to replace the series book with "good literature." In 1945 the Children's Book Council assumed control of Children's Book Week. In 2006 the Children's Book Council website presented its "Summer Reading Extravaganza," listing "summer-themed titles, beach reads, and other books for vacation reading" from its member publishers. Among the books given the CBC imprimatur were several Hardy Boys graphic novels. The chief librarian of the Boy Scouts of America would no doubt be more perplexed and chagrined by a 1999 article in *Scouting*, the organization's official magazine, that endorsed the Hardy Boys.

Dirty Little Secrets

While critics, educators, editors, teachers, and other adults debated the merits of series books, children often had their own, deeply intimate, reasons for devouring formula fiction. "The dirty little secret of Nancy Drew and the Hardy Boys," Michael Bronski asserted, "is that they're all about sex. Sure, it's often sublimated sex aimed at an audience between the age of nine and 15 — but they are, indeed, smoldering with unmistakable eroticism."[37] For Bronski, the "explosive elements" of series fiction had little to do with the combustibles that troubled Franklin K. Mathiews. Bronski observed "there seems to be more bondage in the Nancy Drew and Hardy Boys novels than in all the writings of the Marquis de Sade.... For young people who live in nice, wholesome neighborhoods, Nancy, Frank, and Joe seem to get tied up a lot."[38] The image of youngsters being trapped, rendered helpless, and tied up by menacing adults probably stirred new and strange emotions in young readers who found a secret, compelling reason to follow the adventures of their teenage heroes. For young adolescents the freedom of Frank, Joe, and Nancy to travel and enjoy thrilling adventures away from home implies a sexual freedom as well. The characters venture into large cities and exotic locales. They fly planes and stay in hotels. They operate in adult settings, which for adolescents have clear sexual overtones. When Frank and Joe visit New York, their parents are nowhere in sight. Aside from going to a restaurant serving bootleg liquor, the boys never pass anything overtly sexual, but children, reading between the lines, can easily imagine what unsupervised teenagers could explore in Manhattan. For Bronski the books "were my first pornography, and they taught me that I could have a mysterious, adventuresome, erotic imagination of my own."[39]

Bronski was not alone in finding sexual messages in the series books. In a 1997 *Women's Studies* article, Sherrie A. Inness examined the lesbian fascination with Nancy Drew, who, like the Hardy Boys, inspired a number of adult parodies. Mable Maney, who created the effeminate Hardly Boys, wrote a lesbian novel *The Case of the Not-So-Nice Nurse* starring teenage girl detective Nancy Clue. The fact that so many lesbians were attracted to Nancy Drew as girls, in Inness' view, was based on the repetitive nature of a mystery series featuring an independent teenage girl. Nancy had "subversive potential" because she "leads a life that any lesbian would envy."[40] Like Bronski, Inness saw the repetitive odyssey of the teenage hero as a metaphor for sexual growth and awareness:

> One of the reasons for the appeal of the Drew books to lesbian readers is that their formulaic plots suggest a path through a lesbian's life. The young lesbian who has yet to discover her sexual identification has a secret in her life (her lesbianism) that she must search to discover, although she will be hindered at every step of the way by individuals who would prefer that she did not solve this mystery. At one point, the lesbian, although she most likely does not find herself trapped in a dark basement, does find herself trapped by society's conventions. Only when she discovers the secret of her lesbianism is the lesbian finally rewarded. On a mythical level, the books reassure lesbian readers that

there is a path to lesbianism that can be negotiated, despite how dangerous it might appear at first.[41]

For young adolescents Frank, Joe, and Nancy, though never in sexual situations themselves, represent the freedom, energy, and confidence their readers cannot help but unconsciously infuse with their own secrets and mysteries.

The Library Wars

The series book has sparked debate and controversy in school and public libraries for more than a century. In 1901 librarians in Newark removed syndicate books from circulation. Stratemeyer was unfazed, claiming in a letter to the head of the library's book committee that "it does not matter much to me whether or not my books are now put back on the shelves.... Taking them out of the Library has more than tripled sales in Newark."[42] Children wanted his books. If they could not find them at the public library, they would buy their own copies.

Mathiew's widely circulated 1914 article influenced librarian attitudes for decades. In 1929 the *Wilson Bulletin* published lists of series books "not circulated by standardized libraries."[43] Library journals specified Stratemeyer titles as books considered unworthy of library acquisition. Jennifer Lyn Sczerbinski observed, "For critics, Stratemeyer embodied all that was evil in the realm of popular series fiction, by being the inventor of cheaply produced, rapidly written adventure and mystery stories that many children could not put down."[44] Hope White called Stratemeyer an "archfiend" in a 1934 article in *Illinois Libraries*, which urged librarians to "battle the fifty-cent thriller until they are completely routed."[45] Scholars of children's literature and librarians saw themselves as guardians and monitors who should reject the popular series book for works of greater merit. Lillian Smith's 1953 book *The Unreluctant Years: A Critical Approach to Children's Literature* argued that adults had a moral duty to guide children to better reading:

> We should instinctively reject the mediocre, the unrewarding. We should put into their hands only the books worthy of them, the books of honesty, integrity, and vision — the books on which they can grow. For it is in the very nature of children to grow. They cannot stand still. They must have change and activity of both mind and body. Reading which does not stir their imaginations, which does not stretch their minds, not only wastes their time but will not hold children permanently. If they find no satisfaction in one medium they will immediately turn to another.[46]

The early Seventies saw a change in attitude. A second generation of children was growing up with television. Teachers were concerned about reading skills, and public libraries saw a steady decline in the number of children who checked out books. In 1970 Ervin Gaines, director of the Minneapolis Public Library, wrote an editorial in the *Library Journal* that argued that opposition to the series book was short-sighted and served only to dampen children's interest in reading. The series book, he suggested, could be used to lure children back to the library.[47] The Madison Public Library did not contain Hardy Boys or Nancy Drew books until 1971. For the previous forty years librarians in Wisconsin's state capital did not purchase series fiction "on the general grounds that the library's responsibility to children was to provide only the best books available."[48] Series books in their view "featured one-dimensional characters, poor literary style, lack of realism, and unvarying plot lines."[49] In short, they were bad books not worth buying, despite their popularity. In addition to their poor literary quality, librarians argued that because of their low price, series books were readily available to children and did not deserve public funding.

However, by the summer of 1971, patron demands for Nancy Drew and the Hardy Boys forced the library to revisit the issue. Library staff requested that the policy against series books be reconsidered. Bernard Schwab, the Library Director, asked that a new book selection policy cover Nancy Drew and the Hardy Boys. A five-page report was prepared that documented the history of the library's series book debate. The Book Selection Policy and Guidelines were examined, and the library concluded that nothing specifically excluded series books from consideration. Although the report noted the poor literary quality of series fiction, it concluded "it is insupportable for a public library to refuse to provide books in such great demand when there is nothing harmful in reading them; the literary quality is not that much worse than other titles currently purchased for popular reading by children's librarians.... Series books fill recreational needs, one of the objectives in selecting books for children."[50] On August 8, 1971, the Library Board passed the motion recommending the purchase of Hardy Boys and Nancy Drew books.

Four years later the New York Public Library would follow suit, breaking its decades-old taboo against the Hardy Boys.[51] Nancy Drew and the Hardy Boys were making inroads, winning over the guardians of children's literature who once shunned them. In an effort to win respectability and greater visibility for its lead characters, the syndicate lent out the Hardy Boys and Nancy Drew to introduce the classics to children. Frank and Joe Hardy endorsed *The Adventures of Huckleberry Finn* and *Treasure Island* for boys, and Nancy Drew introduced her own line of illustrated classic editions of *Black Beauty* and *Heidi* to girls.[52]

Stratemeyer's books remain the subject of debate and controversy. In 1999 librarians in Essex County, Ontario (McFarlane's home province), removed Hardy Boys and Nancy Drew books from the system's sixteen branch libraries. When newspaper stories about their decision sparked a flurry of protest, the books were replaced on the shelves. Despite their growing acceptance, the Hardys have not escaped outside calls for their removal from circulation. In 2004, a Connecticut church leader demanded the Milford School District examine its libraries for books containing sexual and occult themes. Among the offending titles he listed was Franklin W. Dixon's *The Witchmaster's Key*.[53] Frank and Joe Hardy found themselves joining Holden Caulfield, Harry Potter, and Huckleberry Finn as objectionable literary role models.

Much of the debate about series fiction still stemmed from the diatribes made by Mathiews in 1914 and resentment by "real" children's authors and rival publishers. The popular ghostwritten stories were seen as manufactured products rather than books of any merit. Younger librarians who read the books as children could review them with unbiased eyes and noticed that for the formulaic plots and stock characters, the books did have educational value.

In following the predictable adventures of Frank and Joe, readers are introduced to deep sea diving, Native American culture, short-wave radios, airplanes, and paleontology. *The Melted Coins* (1944), for instance, includes Fenton Hardy's brief lecture on the history of coins: "'The experts say the first ones appeared in Asia Minor, away back about 750 B.C. The Chinese, too, had metal money, long, long ago. They were clever at testing it to keep from being cheated. They could tell if a coin was genuine by holding it between the thumb and first finger" (42). After readers are taught the definition of a "numismatist," Frank and Joe receive another informative lecture from a coin collector: "'The study of coins gives one a good knowledge of history, geography, and the customs of people. Some of the ancient rulers used to commemorate nearly everything they did by setting it forth on a new piece of money. One old Roman Emperor had ten thousand varieties issued!'" (57).

Searching for a fossil in *The Secret of Wildcat Swamp* (1952), Frank and Joe receive lessons in paleontology, evolution, and scientific investigation:

> "Another interesting fact fossil hunting teaches us," Cap went on, "is that the farther back you go in history the larger the animals were. Right here in the United States there once roamed the largest animals in the world — dinosaurs, and flying reptiles with a wingspread of twenty-five feet."
>
> "Man didn't have much of a chance," Frank observed.
>
> Cap smiled. "It wasn't too long ago that certain scientists thought they had figured out how tall prehistoric men must have been."
>
> "You mean by comparing them with the animals?" Joe asked. When Cap nodded, he said, "How tall were Adam and Eve?"
>
> "Adam was one hundred twenty-three feet, nine inches tall. Eve was a comparative midget. Only one hundred eighteen feet, nine inches."
>
> "Wow!"
>
> Bailey grinned. "It's a good thing other scientists found bones of prehistoric men to *disprove* it" [31–32].

When the boys unearth the skeleton of an ancient horse, Cap provides a lecture on the animal's mysterious extinction in North America: "'No one has figured out why the horse — a much smaller one than the kind we know today — lived here from prehistoric times until the Pleistocene period, then became extinct. The horse as we know it today was imported.'" (69). Realizing that scientists are active investigators solving mysteries much like detectives, Joe states that he will no longer dismiss them as "old, stoop-shouldered characters with beards — the way they always look in the comics" (72). In other novels readers are exposed to the history of Mexico, the Pennsylvania Dutch (whom Joe explains are really from Germany), airships, and the history of Alaska.

Even the streamlined and simplified Hardy Boys books of the 1970s introduced young readers to sophisticated vocabulary. *The Bombay Boomerang* (1970), for instance, includes words such as "insufferable," "sustenance," "nonplussed," and "ensconced."

But even more important to today's librarians is the simple fact that children love the Hardy Boys. McFarlane's original formula, though eviscerated in the Great Purge, created a pattern that subsequent writers followed. Frank and Joe are flat and never develop, the plots are predictable and contrived, the approach to crime simplistic, but somehow the magic remains. In 2007 a North Carolina fifth grader posted a book review of *The Tower Treasure* on the Scholastic "Share What You're Reading!" website. "I personally love the Hardy Boys," he wrote, "and every time I think I've read them all, I find a new one!"[59]

Today *The Tower Treasure* can be found in the online catalogs of public libraries in New York, Boston, Atlanta, Chicago, Seattle, Miami, Cleveland, San Francisco, Los Angeles, New Orleans, Toronto, and Philadelphia. Libraries that once shunned Frank and Joe Hardy now feature them on summer reading lists.

Critics once declared Stratemeyer's products to be addictive. Ninety years later, librarians appear to agree, now hoping the books will hook yet another generation and eventually lead them onto harder literature.

Chronology

1862	Edward Stratemeyer born in Elizabeth, New Jersey.
1889	Stratemeyer sells first major story, "Victor Horton's Idea"; becomes dime novel author.
1892	Harriet Stratemeyer born.
1899	Stratemeyer publishes The Rover Boys trilogy, the first "breeder set," launching thirty-volume series.
1902	Leslie McFarlane born in Ontario, Canada.
1905	Stratemeyer organizes Stratemeyer Syndicate in East Orange, New Jersey; persuades publishers to halve book prices, creating the "fifty-center."
1905–1925	Stratemeyer Syndicate publishes dozens of series, including the Bobbsey Twins, Tom Swift, Ruth Fielding, the Motor Chums, Bomba the Jungle Boy, and The Motion Picture Comrades.
1926	Stratemeyer writes outline for The Hardy Boys series; hires Leslie McFarlane as contract writer.
1927	Leslie McFarlane's first three Hardy Boys novels—*The Tower Treasure*, *The House on the Cliff*, and *The Secret of the Old Mill*—released as breeder set.
1930	Nancy Drew series launched; Edward Stratemeyer dies, Harriet Stratemeyer Adams assumes control of syndicate.
1938–1943	"The Weird Period." Five novels written by John Button while Leslie McFarlane is on hiatus introduce surreal and futuristic themes.

1947	Leslie McFarlane completes his last Hardy Boys title, *The Phantom Freighter*.
1956–57	*The Mickey Mouse Club* airs two Hardy Boys serials; Grosset & Dunlap capitalizes on program's popularity to publicize series.
1959	"The Great Purge" begins. Harriet Stratemeyer Adams and Andrew Svenson start twenty-year program to modernize, shorten, and eliminate racial stereotypes from previously published titles.
1967	*The Mystery of the Chinese Junk* airs on ABC.
1976	Leslie McFarlane publishes autobiography, *Ghost of the Hardy Boys*.
1977	Leslie McFarlane dies.
1977–1979	ABC's *Hardy Boys/Nancy Drew Mysteries* airs, stimulating increased sales of both series.
1979	Last title of the Hardy Boys canon, *The Sting of the Scorpion*, published. Harriet Stratemeyer Adams accepts offer from Simon & Schuster to publish the Hardy Boys and Nancy Drew titles.
1980	Grosset & Dunlap sues the Stratemeyer Syndicate and Simon & Schuster. Court decision grants Grossett & Dunlap the right to publish the first fifty-eight Hardy Boys titles (1927–1979) in hard cover and Simon & Schuster the right to publish subsequent titles in paperback.
1982	Harriet Stratemeyer Adams dies.
1984	Stratemeyer Syndicate sold to Simon & Schuster.

The Hardy Boys Canon

Grosset & Dunlap published fifty-eight Hardy Boys books for the Stratemeyer to Syndicate from 1927 to 1979. Many of the first twenty-four novels were revised after 1959. Some were streamlined and edited for offensive language and outdated references; others were reissued under the same title with new plots and characters.

1. *The Tower Treasure*, 1927
In the first of twenty Leslie McFarlane titles, Frank and Joe Hardy outwit Bayport's bumbling police force to recover forty thousand dollars in securities and jewels stolen from Hurd Applegate's Tower Mansion.

2. *The House on the Cliff*, 1927
Frank and Joe Hardy round up the dope smugglers Ganny Snackley and Li Chang operating out of a deserted mansion; Stratemeyer objects to amount of gunplay in the final scenes.

3. *The Secret of the Old Mill*, 1927
A commuter passes Frank and Joe a phony five-dollar bill, leading the brothers to uncover a counterfeiting operation in an abandoned flourmill.

4. *The Missing Chums*, 1928
Frank and Joe travel to treacherous Blacksnake Island to rescue Chet Morton and Biff Hooper from kidnappers; Aunt Gertrude makes her initial appearance.

5. *Hunting for Hidden Gold*, 1928
Frank and Joe head to Montana to help their father locate hidden gold and capture the Black Pepper gang.

6. *The Shore Road Mystery*, 1928
Frank and Joe round up a gang of Bayport car thieves operating in caves along Barmet Bay.

7. *The Secret of the Caves*, 1929
On a trip with chums Frank and Joe find a missing professor suffering from amnesia living in a cave.

8. *The Mystery of Cabin Island*, 1929
Vacationing in a rich eccentric's island cabin, the chums recover the owner's stolen stamp collection.

9. *The Great Airport Mystery*, 1930
Frank and Joe travel by plane to break up Giles Ducroy's air-mail theft ring.

10. *What Happened at Midnight*, 1931
Chasing diamond smugglers, Frank and Joe visit New York City for the first time, sleep in Central Park after a thief reduces their funds to fifty cents, and parachute from a disabled plane.

11. *While the Clock Ticked*, 1932
Frank and Joe escape a mad inventor's clock-driven bomb and recover Hurd Applegate's stolen stamps.

12. *Footprints Under the Window*, 1933
Frank and Joe break up a coolie smuggling operation run by the evil Chinaman Louie Fong; revised during the Great Purge, the new novel of the same title takes Frank and Joe to Latin America to fight spies trying to steal secrets from the U.S. space program.

13. *The Mark on the Door*, 1934
The Hardys travel to Mexico in search of a missing witness in an oil scandal, calling upon the Mexican army to round up a bandit leader.

14. *The Hidden Harbor Mystery*, 1935
Frank and Joe unearth the cause of a long-standing feud between two Southern families and discover a disreputable servant provoking incidents to fuel the conflict; the novel was substantially revised in 1961 to delete overtly racist passages.

15. *The Sinister Signpost*, 1936
The search for a missing racehorse leads Frank and Joe to discover a crazed foreigner's cache of munitions designed to blow up Bayport and terrorize America.

16. *A Figure in Hiding*, 1937
Frank and Joe break up the "eye syndicate" run by a quack doctor defrauding elderly patients; McFarlane leaves the series to pursue other ventures.

17. *The Secret Warning*, 1938
The "Weird Period" begins; in John Button's first novel, Frank and Joe take up deep-sea diving to locate sunken treasure.

18. *The Twisted Claw*, 1939
Posing as seamen, Frank and Joe board the pirate ship *The Black Parrot*, which takes them to an island kingdom built on international smuggling.

19. *The Disappearing Floor*, 1940
Frank and Joe tackle Duke Beeson's gang of bank robbers, confront escaped tigers, encounter a tribe of sun-worshipping Ozonites, are frozen by a mad scientist's invention, and escape a mansion full of futuristic electronic gadgets.

20. *The Mystery of the* Flying Express, 1941
The Hardys track guttural speaking foreigners cross-county and locate a thousand-man spy camp.

21. *The Clue of the Broken Blade*, 1942
In the final John Button novel, Frank and Joe break up a truck hijacking operation.

22. *The Flickering Torch Mystery*, 1943
Frank and Joe break up a black-robed gang stealing government construction material; Leslie McFarlane returns to the series.

23. *The Melted Coins*, 1944
The Hardys and chums uncover a ring of coin thieves and counterfeiters.

24. *The Short-Wave Mystery*, 1945
A mysterious radio call of "Help Hudson!" leads Frank and Joe to Canada to solve the theft of valuable radio parts and locate a missing professor.

25. *The Secret Panel*, 1946
Frank and Joe solve a kidnapping in a strange mansion built without visible locks, hinges, or door knobs.

26. *The Phantom Freighter*, 1947
In Leslie McFarlane's last novel, Frank and Joe break up a smuggling operation.

27. *The Secret of Skull Mountain*, 1948
Frank and Joe solve the mysterious disappearance of water from a reservoir supplying Bayport.

28. *The Sign of the Crooked Arrow*, 1949
Frank and Joe travel to a cousin's New Mexico ranch to break up a gang of thieves using fake cigarettes that emit gas to render their victims unconscious.

29. *The Secret of the Lost Tunnel*, 1950
Frank and Joe travel to the South to unravel a Civil War mystery.

30. *The Wailing Siren Mystery,* 1951
A wallet falling from the sky leads the Hardys to the North Woods and the capture of a gang planning to start uprisings in Central America.

31. *The Secret of Wildcat Swamp,* 1952
A paleontology excursion with a teacher from Bayport High leads Frank and Joe to battle a gang of freight train thieves.

32. *The Crisscross Shadow,* 1953
Frank and Joe solve the riddle of a missing deed and prevent an Indian tribe from losing its land to a gang of saboteurs.

33. *The Yellow Feather Mystery,* 1954
Frank and Joe solve the mystery of a missing will at a private academy.

34. *The Hooded Hawk Mystery,* 1955
Frank and Joe break up a gang smuggling aliens from India and rescue a kidnapped Indian prince.

35. *The Clue in the Embers,* 1956
Tony Prito inherits a number of curios containing clues that lead Frank and Joe to unearth buried treasure in Guatemala.

36. *The Secret of Pirates' Hill,* 1957
The search for an ancient cannon leads Frank and Joe to discover a sunken ship laden with gold treasure.

37. *The Ghost at Skeleton Rock,* 1958
Frank and Joe thwart a plot by rebels to obtain a nuclear weapon and topple the Cuban government.

38. *The Mystery at Devil's Paw,* 1959
Answering a call for help from Tony Prito, the Hardys travel north to Alaska and prevent foreign agents from locating a missing American rocket.

39. *The Mystery of the Chinese Junk,* 1960
With help from Chinese chum Jimmy Foy, Frank and Joe buy a junk to run a ferry service on Barmet Bay and find a missing treasure.

40. *The Mystery of the Desert Giant,* 1961
The Hardys travel to the California desert to locate a missing industrialist.

41. *The Clue of the Screeching Owl,* 1962
On a trip to the Poconos the Hardy Boys and Chet discover a secret cabin and break up a hijacking gang.

42. *The Viking Symbol Mystery,* 1963
A radio threat and a book stolen from the Bayport library lead Frank and Joe to Canada where they discover a Viking treasure.

43. *The Mystery of the Aztec Warrior*, 1964
A mysterious will leads Frank and Joe to Mexico to solve the riddle of a long-lost Aztec relic.

44. *The Haunted Fort*, 1965
Summoned by Chet, the Hardys go to an art school and solve the mystery of missing paintings that hold clues to a long-lost treasure.

45. *The Mystery of the Spiral Bridge*, 1966
Frank and Joe head to Kentucky to break up a gang responsible for sabotaging a Prito construction project and kidnapping Fenton Hardy.

46. *The Secret Agent on Flight 101*, 1967
The Hardys travel to Scotland to break up an international spy ring.

47. *The Mystery of the Whale Tattoo*, 1968
Frank and Joe follow clues leading to a band of tattooed robbers.

48. *The Arctic Patrol Mystery*, 1969
The Hardys travel to Iceland to disrupt a plot against a NASA moon mission.

49. *The Bombay Boomerang*, 1970
An investigation of stolen mercury shipments leads Frank and Joe to foil a terrorist plot to fire a stolen missile into an army nerve gas depot to inflict mass casualties and cause social unrest.

50. *Danger on Vampire Trail*, 1971
The Hardys and chums travel to Colorado to take down a gang counterfeiting credit cards.

51. *The Masked Monkey*, 1972
Frank and Joe travel to Brazil in search of an industrialist's missing son.

52. *The Shattered Helmet*, 1973
While attending film school, Frank and Joe find clues that lead them to Greece in search of an ancient helmet.

53. *The Clue of the Hissing Serpent*, 1974
A mysterious serpent balloon and a missing chess trophy lead Frank and Joe to Hong Kong where they smash an international criminal organization.

54. *The Mysterious Caravan*, 1975
The discovery of an ancient death mask on a Jamaican beach leads Frank and Joe to North Africa to unearth gold treasure and break up a ring of airline ticket thieves.

55. *The Witchmaster's Key*, 1976
Frank and Joe rendezvous with Chet and Phil Cohen in Britain to solve a mystery involving witches and a museum robbery; in Dublin Frank researches the Hardy family's Irish roots.

56. *The Jungle Pyramid,* 1977
Frank and Joe follow leads to Switzerland and finally to the Yucatan to locate missing gold bullion.

57. *The Firebird Rocket,* 1978
The search for a missing rocket scientist takes the Hardys to the Australian Outback.

58. *The Sting of the Scorpion,* 1979
Frank and Joe thwart a terrorist cell sabotaging an entrepreneur's dirigible company.

Twenty Opening Lines

"After the help we gave dad on that forgery case I guess he'll begin to think we *could* be detectives when we grow up."
The Tower Treasure

"A fortune in hidden gold! That certainly sounds mighty interesting."
Hunting for Hidden Gold

"Well, the stealing of autos in this neighborhood has come to an end, Frank. Wonder if anybody will ever take to stealing motorboats."
The Secret of the Caves

"This is going to be a terrible night on the open sea," said Joe Hardy.
The Hidden Harbor Mystery

When Frank and Joe Hardy returned from a hike down the Shore Road one afternoon and found in the mail-box a notice to the effect that a message was awaiting them at the local telegraph office, they were immediately very much excited.
Footprints Under the Window

"Better head for shore, Frank! It's blowing up a gale!"
The Mark on the Door

When Frank Hardy answered the doorbell that morning, he had no idea that its shrill ringing was a summons to excitement, adventure and peril.
The Flickering Torch Mystery

"What a strange letter!" exclaimed Frank Hardy.
The Phantom Freighter

"Don't forget, Frank, any treasure we find will be divided fifty-fifty."
The Secret of Pirates' Hill

The telephone in the Hardy home gave a long, urgent ring, as the clock struck four.
The Secret of the Lost Tunnel

The *Sleuth* roared toward Barmet Bay as fast as its propeller could churn the sullen sea.
The Wailing Siren Mystery

"Joe, look out! That launch will hit you!" shouted Frank Hardy from the beach.
The Mystery of the Chinese Junk

"Do you boys feel up to tackling a counterfeit case?" Detective Fenton Hardy asked his sons.
Danger on Vampire Trail

"Chet Morton inviting us to a mystery — I don't believe it!"
The Haunted Fort

"How would you boys like to fly to Iceland?" Mr. Hardy asked his sons.
The Arctic Patrol Mystery

"Can you tell a Greek by looking at him?" asked Joe Hardy.
The Shattered Helmet

Hardyisms

Frank and Joe, their hearts too full for utterance, withdrew softly from the room.
The Tower Treasure

Joe raised a sandwich to his lips absently, essayed a bite and missed the sandwich altogether.
The Tower Treasure

Biff Hooper did not care to seem guilty of cowardice by staying behind while his companions returned to the house, and he was on the point of a reluctant consent when the matter was suddenly solved for them all by a downpour of rain.
The House on the Cliff

Although two or three of the boys backed out when they learned that the destination was to be the haunted house, the majority were willing enough, and by nightfall all was in readiness for the journey on the morrow.
The House on the Cliff

As though to emphasize his commands, the man in the black hat reached suddenly into his pocket and whipped out a wicked-looking revolver.
The House on the Cliff

"Sign this paper, Hardy, or you'll starve — as sure as my name is Snackley!"
The House on the Cliff

Utter confusion prevailed. The place was in absolute darkness and out in the yard shots, shouts, and hoarse imprecations mingled in an indescribable uproar.
The House on the Cliff

Because of the pride they took in their achievements as amateur detectives, the Hardy boys felt very keenly the ignominy of being so easily fooled by the stranger who had passed the counterfeit money upon them.
The Secret of the Old Mill

The lad toppled backward, striking his head on the rock, but Joe made a frantic grab for him, at imminent risk of precipitating himself into the water again.
The Secret of the Old Mill

The Hardy boys had no particular object in going to Barmet, beyond the fact that the village served as a destination and gave their boating trip more of a purpose than there would have been had they merely cruised aimlessly around.
The Secret of the Old Mill

"I'll just bet dollars to doughnuts that there is counterfeit money in that package instead of breakfast food."
The Secret of the Old Mill

Tony Prito was afire with enthusiasm when they broached the subject to him.
The Missing Chums

"Sweet spirits of nitre! Aunt Gertrude herself!"
The Missing Chums

Again the revolver crashed out and again the tongue of crimson flame licked its way through the blackness.
The Missing Chums

Profound darkness enveloped the Hardy boys.
The Missing Chums

Then the Hardy Boys were called on to explain how they had encountered the revenue cutter and how they had told their story and prevailed upon the revenue men to come with them to Blacksnake Island to effect the rescue of their chums.
The Missing Chums

But as if the forces of Nature as well as men were conspiring against the Hardys, a flash of lightning streaked the sky, followed by a deep roll of thunder.
The Secret of the Lost Tunnel

Chapter Notes

Introduction

1. McFarlane, *Ghost of the Hardy Boys*, i.
2. Freireich, "Travel Advisory."
3. Prager, *Rascals at Large*, 122.
4. Billman, *Secret of the Stratemeyer Syndicate*, 94.
5. Ibid.
6. Frye, *Educated Imagination*, 102.
7. *Ibid.*
8. Billman, *Secret of the Stratemeyer Syndicate*, 96.
9. *Ibid.*
10. Kismaric and Heiferman, *Mysterious Case of Nancy Drew & the Hardy Boys*, 32.
11. "Kyoto Sangyo University Extensive Reading Program."
12. Barnicle, "Made in Vietnam."
13. Praveen. "Ruminations of a Meandering Mind."
14. Dhindsa, "Brown Man's Burden."
15. Thakur, "Harry Potter and the Indian Writers."
16. Ramnarayan, "Great Children's Books ... Alas, Still a Fairytale."
17. Padayatty, "Catch 22: Books and Padayatty!"

Chapter 1

1. O'Rourke, "Nancy Drew's Father."
2. Watson, "Tom Swift, Nancy Drew, and Pals."
3. *Ibid.*
4. Greenwald, *Secret of the Hardy Boys*, 51.
5. Lange, *Edward Stratemeyer*, 32–33.
6. Rehak, *Girl Sleuth*, 26.
7. *Ibid.*, 98.
8. Lange, *Edward Stratemeyer*, 31–32.
9. "For It Was Indeed He."
10. Watson, "Tom Swift, Nancy Drew, and Pals."
11. O'Rourke, "Nancy Drew's Father."
12. "For It Was Indeed He."
13. O'Rourke, "Nancy Drew's Father."
14. *Ibid.*
15. McFarlane, *Ghost of the Hardy Boys*, 52.
16. *Ibid.*, 52–53.
17. D. Johnson, *Edward Stratemeyer*, 162.
18. *Ibid.*
19. Keeline, "Edward Stratemeyer: Author and Literary Agent, 1876–1906."
20. D. Johnson, *Edward Stratemeyer*, 2.
21. Keeline, "Edward Stratemeyer: Author and Literary Agent, 1876–1906."
22. *Ibid.*
23. *Ibid.*
24. O'Rourke, "Nancy Drew's Father."
25. D. Johnson, *Edward Stratemeyer*, 21.
26. *Ibid.*, 24.
27. *Ibid.*, 22.
28. Keeline, "Edward Stratemeyer: Author and Literary Agent, 1876–1906."
29. *Ibid.*
30. *Ibid.*
31. *Ibid.*
32. D. Johnson, *Edward Stratemeyer*, 161.
33. McFarlane, *Ghost of the Hardy Boys*, 53.
34. D. Johnson, *Edward Stratemeyer*, 162.

35. *Ibid.*, 168.
36. *Ibid.*, 169.
37. Keeline, "Edward Stratemeyer: Author and Literary Agent, 1876–1906."
38. D. Johnson, *Edward Stratemeyer*, 7.
39. O'Rourke, "Nancy Drew's Father."
40. Kismaric and Heiferman, *Mysterious Case of Nancy Drew & the Hardy Boys*, 123.
41. "For It Was Indeed He."
42. D. Johnson, *Edward Stratemeyer*, 42.
43. McFarlane, *Ghost of the Hardy Boys*, 198.
44. Greenwald, *Secret of the Hardy Boys*, 66.
45. Rehak, *Girl Sleuth*, 99.
46. "For It Was Indeed He."
47. Keeline, "Edward Stratemeyer: Author and Literary Agent, 1876–1906."
48. Qtd. in Feret, "Book Series and Character Development."
49. Greenwald, *Secret of the Hardy Boys*, 64.
50. Dizer, *Tom Swift and Company*, 13.
51. D. Johnson, *Edward Stratemeyer*, 11.
52. *Ibid.*, 51.
53. "For It Was Indeed He."
54. D. Johnson, *Edward Stratemeyer*, 52.
55. *Ibid.*, 53.
56. *Ibid.*, 13.
57. *Ibid.*, 16.
58. *Ibid.*
59. Quoted in Kismaric and Heiferman, *Mysterious Case of Nancy Drew & the Hardy Boys*, 120.
60. *Ibid.*
61. *Ibid.*, 123.
62. D. Johnson, *Edward Stratemeyer*, 16–17.
63. Greenwald, *Secret of the Hardy Boys*, 138.
64. D. Johnson, *Edward Stratemeyer*, 17.
65. Lum, "Just Who IS Carolyn Keene?"
66. *Ibid.*
67. *Ibid.*
68. *Ibid.*
69. Duffy, "Tom Swift and His Electronic Assembly Line."
70. *Ibid.*

Chapter 2

1. Greenwald, *Secret of the Hardy Boys*, 17.
2. *Ibid.*, 24–26.
3. *Ibid.*, 26.
4. *Ibid.*, 31.
5. McFarlane, *Ghost of the Hardy Boys*, 4–5.
6. *Ibid.*, 9.
7. *Ibid.*, 10–11.
8. *Ibid.*, 11.
9. *Ibid.*, 13.
10. *Ibid.*
11. *Ibid.*, 19.
12. *Ibid.*
13. *Ibid.*, 57.
14. *Ibid.*, 63.
15. *Ibid.*
16. Greenwald, *Secret of the Hardy Boys*, xiii.
17. McFarlane, *Ghost of the Hardy Boys*, 64.
18. *Ibid.*, 192–193.
19. *Ibid.*, 152.
20. *Ibid.*, 152–153.
21. *Ibid.*, 154.
22. *Ibid.*
23. *Ibid.*, 183.
24. *Ibid.*, 184.
25. *Ibid.*, 198–199.
26. *Ibid.*, 199.
27. Brian McFarlane, quoted in Weingarten, "The Hardy Boys."
28. *Ibid.*
29. McFarlane, *Ghost of the Hardy Boys*, 199.
30. *Ibid.*, 200.
31. *Ibid.*, 201.
32. *Ibid.*
33. *Ibid.*, 202.
34. *Ibid.*
35. Greenwald, *Secret of the Hardy Boys*, 200.
36. *Ibid.*
37. *Ibid.*, 230.
38. McFarlane, *Ghost of the Hardy Boys*, 203.
39. *Ibid.*, 205.
40. *Ibid.*
41. *Ibid.*
42. *Ibid.*, 210–211.

Chapter 3

1. Keeline, "Who Wrote the Hardy Boys?"

Chapter 4

1. Harriet Stratemeyer Adams, quoted in Rehak, *Girl Sleuth*, 199–200.
2. *Ibid.*, 200–201.
3. *Ibid.*, 202–203.

4. Greenwald, *Secret of the Hardy Boys*, 191.
5. *Ibid.*
6. *Ibid.*
7. Keeline, "Who Wrote the Hardy Boys?"

Chapter 5

1. "Television Receiving Set Production."
2. Rehak, *Girl Sleuth*, xx.
3. McFarlane, *Ghost of the Hardy Boys*, 209.
4. Bob Stall, quoted in McFarlane, *Ghost of the Hardy Boys*, 209–210.
5. McFarlane, *Ghost of the Hardy Boys*, 210.
6. *Ibid.*

Chapter 7

1. Greenwald, *Secret of the Hardy Boys*, 54.
2. Gabler, *Winchell*, 318.
3. Grant, *Passing of the Great Race*, 92.
4. Bayard Rustin, quoted in Slayton, *Empire Statesman*, 296.
5. LaGumina, *Wop!* 200.
6. Quoted in Veronesi, *Italian-Americans & Their Communities of Cleveland.*
7. "Luigi Galleani." *Wikipedia*. Wikipedia 2008. Answers. com 21 Feb. 2008. <http://www.answers.com/topic/luigi-galleani.>
8. Cramer, *Joe DiMaggio*, 100.
9. *Ibid.*, 102.
10. Kobler, *Capone*, 33.
11. *Ibid.*, 32.
12. *Chicago Daily News*, quoted in Kobler, *Capone*, 43.
13. *Ibid.*, 45.
14. Merriman, "Inn to the Past."

Chapter 9

1. McFarlane, *Ghost of the Hardy Boys*, 62.
2. *Ibid.*, 62–63.

Chapter 10

1. D. Johnson, *Edward Stratemeyer*, 41.
2. Caro, *Power Broker*, 323–324.

Chapter 11

1. Charles Fitzmorris, qtd in Kobler, *Capone*, 63.
2. Caro, *Power Broker*, 324–325.
3. Doyle, *Complete Sherlock Holmes*, 26–27.
4. *Ibid.* 36.
5. *Ibid.*, 1102.
6. McFarlane, *Ghost of the Hardy Boys*, 183.
7. *Ibid.*, 184.
8. Karnack, "Hardy Perennial."

Chapter 13

1. This information is fictitious. Edward Stratemeyer, quoted in Greenwald, *Secret of the Hardy Boys*, 55.
2. McFarlane, *Ghost of the Hardy Boys*, 79.
3. *Ibid.*, 65.
4. Billman, *Secret of the Stratemeyer Syndicate*, 63.
5. Prager, *Rascals at Large*, 103–104.
6. Billman, *Secret of the Stratemeyer Syndicate*, 92.
7. *Ibid.*, 91.
8. Crawford, *Lost Hardys*, 48.
9. *Ibid.*, 47.
10. "Take A Walking Tour of Haileybury."

Chapter 14

1. Cotter, *Wonderful World of Disney Television*, 3–4.
2. *Ibid.*, 185.
3. *Ibid.*, 184–185.
4. *Ibid.*, 190.
5. Finnan, "Hardy Boys on TV."
6. *Ibid.*
7. *Ibid.*
8. *Ibid.*
9. *Ibid.*
10. *Ibid.*
11. *Ibid.*
12. Durang, *Twenty-Seven Short Plays*, 158.
13. *Ibid.*, 160.
14. *Ibid.*, 161.
15. A. Johnson, "Anatomy of a Playwright."
16. Flynn DeMarco, quoted in A. Johnson, "Anatomy of a Playwright."
17. *Ibid.*
18. Madstage, quoted in "Secret of the Old Queen."

19. Bieschke, quoted in "Secret of the Old Queen."
20. Gordy, quoted in "Secret of the Old Queen."
21. Calerdine, quoted in "Secret of the Old Queen."
22. Maney, *Ghost in the Closet*, 62.
23. *Ibid.*, 116.
24. *Ibid.*, 227.
25. *Ibid.*

Chapter 15

1. Mathiews, "Blowing Out the Boy's Brains."
2. *Ibid.*, 652.
3. *Ibid.*
4. *Ibid.*
5. *Ibid.*
6. *Ibid.*, 653.
7. *Ibid.*
8. *Ibid.*
9. *Ibid.*, 654.
10. Ibid.
11. "For It Was Indeed He."
12. McFarlane, *Ghost of the Hardy Boys*, 27.
13. "Children's Book Week."
14. "For It Was Indeed He."
15. *Ibid.*
16. Trabasso, "Becoming a Reader."
17. *Ibid.*
18. Truby, "Fresh Look at Series Books."
19. Schroth, "Kick Your Foot Through That Screen," 11.
20. Winn, *Plug-In Drug*, 91.
21. *Ibid.*, 92.
22. *Ibid.*, 93.
23. Tunnell and Jacobs, "Series Fiction and Young Readers."
24. *Ibid.*
25. *Ibid.*
26. Sczerbinski, *Mystery in the Old Schoolhouse*, 40.
27. Truby, "Fresh Look at Series Books."
28. Sczerbinski, *Mystery in the Old Schoolhouse*, 46–47.
29. Laurie Pastore, quoted in Truby, "Fresh Look at Series Books."
30. Cart, "One Cheer for Series Fiction."
31. "Summer Reading Lists."
32. "Lower School Summer Reading Program 2005."
33. "Book List for Boys."
34. Krashen, "Free Voluntary Reading."
35. *Ibid.*
36. *Ibid.*
37. Bronski, "Sex and the Teenage Sleuth."
38. *Ibid.*
39. *Ibid.*
40. Inness, "Is Nancy Drew Queer?"
41. *Ibid.*
42. Stratemeyer, quoted in Rehak, *Girl Sleuth*, 97–98.
43. *Wilson Bulletin*, quoted in D. Johnson, *Edward Stratemeyer*, 163.
44. Sczerbinski, *Mystery in the Old Schoolhouse*, 13.
45. Hope White, quoted in D. Johnson, *Edward Stratemeyer*, 164.
46. Lillian Smith, quoted in Sczerbinksi, *Mystery in the Old Schoolhouse*, 20.
47. D. Johnson, *Edward Stratemeyer*, 166.
48. "MPL History — The Collection."
49. *Ibid.*
50. *Ibid.*
51. Greenwald, *Secret of the Hardy Boys*, 139.
52. Kismaric and Heiferman, *Mysterious Case of Nancy Drew & the Hardy Boys*, 120.
53. "Church Leader Demands 'Audit.'"
54. "Share What You're Reading."

Bibliography

"All Their Ways Are Helping Ways: Stories from the History of the Madison Public Library." http://www.madisonpubliclibrary.org/kann/collection.html (accessed May 12, 2007).
"Anti-Italianism." Answers.com, http://www.answers.com/topic/anti-italianism (accessed May 25, 2007).
Barnicle, Mike. "Made in Vietnam: Refugee/TV Law Analyst Living the American Dream." *New York Daily News,* December 11, 2000.
Benfer, Amy. "Who Was Carolyn Keene?" Salon.com, http://www.salon.com/mwt/feature/1999/10/08/keene_q_a (accessed May 12, 2007).
Billman, Carol. *The Secret of the Stratemeyer Syndicate.* New York: Ungar, 1986.
"A Book List for Boys." Parents' Choice Foundation, http:www. parents-choice.org/article.cfm?art_id=114&the_page=reading_list (accessed August 12, 2007).
Bronski, Michael. "Sex and the Teenage Sleuth." *Gay & Lesbian Review Worldwide,* September-October 2002, 9.5: 31+.
Burgess, Steve. "Perky Fellows in a Gay-Looking Speedwagon: The Hardy Boys Return." Salon.com, http://www.salon.com/mwt/feature/1999/10/07/hardy_boys/print.html (accessed March 11, 2007).
Caro, Robert A. *The Power Broker: Robert Moses and the Fall of New York.* New York: Vintage, 1974.
Cart, Michael. "One Cheer for Series Fiction." *Booklist,* October 15, 2000, 97.4: 430+.
"Children's Book Week: The History of Children's Book Week." Children's Book Council, http://www.cbcbooks.org/cbw/history.html (accessed May 12, 2007).
"Church Leader Demands 'Audit' of Collections for Sexual, Occult Content." American Libraries Online. American Library Association, http://www.ala.org/al_onlineTemplate.cfm?Section=march2004ab&Template=/ContentMA... (accessed May 12, 2007).
Cotter, Bill. *The Wonderful World of Disney Television: A Complete History.* New York: Hyperion, 1997.
Cramer, Richard Ben. *Joe DiMaggio: The Hero's Life.* New York: Simon & Schuster, 2000.
Crawford, Robert L. *The Lost Hardys: A Concordance.* Rheem Valley, CA: SynSine Press, 1997.
Dhindsa, Amar Dev. "Brown Man's Burden." http://www.chowk.com/show_article.cgi?aid=00000226&channel=civic%20center (accessed August 5, 2007).

Dirda, Michael. "Readerly Advice." *The Writer*, January 1998, 111.1: 7+.
Dizer, John T. *Tom Swift and Company: Boys' Books by Stratemeyer and Others*. Mattituck, NY: Amereon House, 1982.
Doyle, Arthur Conan. *The Complete Sherlock Holmes*. Garden City, NY: Doubleday & Company, 1930.
Duffy, Dennis. "Tom Swift and His Electronic Assembly Line." *Queen's Quarterly*, Summer 1997, 104.2: 260–74.
Durang, Christopher. *Twenty-Seven Short Plays*. Lyme, NH: Smith and Kraus, 1995.
Feret, Alice J. "Book Series and Character Development: An Unlikely but Powerful Duo in Book Choice for Read-Alouds." *Teacher Librarian*, February 2006, 33.3: 24+.
Finnan, Bob. "The Hardy Boys on TV." http://hardyboys.bobfinnan.com/hbtv.htm (accessed October 5, 2006).
"For It Was Indeed He." *Fortune*, April 1934: 86–89. http://seriesbookcentral.bobfinnan.com/indeedhe.html (accessed June 12, 2007).
Freireich, Paul. "Travel Advisory; Some New Touches at Shelburne Museum." *New York Times*, September 24, 2000.
"From Penny Loafers to Bellbottoms." *The Bayport Gazette*, http://bayportgazette.com/bg/16/three.html (accessed June 12, 2007).
Frye, Northrop. *The Educated Imagination*. Bloomington: Indiana University Press, 1968.
Gabler, Neil. *Winchell*. New York: Knopf, 1994.
Grant, Martin. *The Passing of the Great Race*. New York: Charles Scribner's, 1921.
Greenwald, Marilyn S. *The Secret of the Hardy Boys: Leslie McFarlane and the Stratemeyer Syndicate*. Athens: Ohio University Press, 2004.
Inness, Sherrie A. "Is Nancy Drew Queer? Popular Reading Strategies for the Lesbian Reader." *Women's Studies*, July 1997, 26.3–4: 343+.
"Italians." *The Encyclopedia of Chicago*. http://www.encyclopedia.chicagohistory.org/pages/658.html (accessed September 28, 2007).
Jenkins, Christine A. "The History of Youth Services Librarianship: A Review of the Research Literature." *Libraries & Culture*, 5.1. Winter 2000: 103+.
Johnson, Austin. "Anatomy of a Playwright: Hardy Boys Play Draws Crowds, Curtains." http://www.hardy-boys.com/gazette/archives/16/five.html (accessed May 12, 2007).
Johnson, Deidre. *Edward Stratemeyer and the Stratemeyer Syndicate*. Twayne's United States Authors Series. New York: Twayne Publishers, 1993.
Karnack, S. T. "Hardy Perennial." *National Review*. November 8, 2004, 56.12: 50.
Keeline, James D. "Edward Stratemeyer: Author and Literary Agent, 1876–1906." http://www.keeline.com/Stratemeyer.pdf.
_____. "Edward Stratemeyer Responds to Critics: Was There Really a Feud With the Boy Scouts of America?" Popular Culture Association National Conference, San Diego Marriott Hotel and Marina, San Diego. 24 Mar. 2005.
_____. "Stratemeyer Syndicate Pseudonyms: Bobbsey Twins, Tom Swift, Hardy Boys, Nancy Drew." http://www.trussel.com/books/strat.htm.
_____. "Who Wrote the Hardy Boys? Secrets from the Syndicate Files Revealed." http://www.keeline.com/Hardy_Boys.pdf.
Kirkpatrick, David D. "In Latest Hardy Boys Case, a Search for New Readers." *The New York Times*, July 29, 2001:1.
Kismaric, Carole, and Marvin Heiferman, *The Mysterious Case of Nancy Drew & the Hardy Boys*. New York: Fireside Books, 1998.
Kobler, John. *Capone*. Greenwich, CT: Fawcett, 1972.
Krashen, Stephen. "Free Voluntary Reading: New Research, Applications, and Controversies." Paper presented at the RELC Conference, Singapore, April 2004.
"Kyoto Sangyo University Extensive Reading Program Books in Order of Popularity." http://www.extensivereading.net/er/evalscr.html (accessed May 21, 2007).

LaGumina, Salvatore, ed. *Wop!* San Francisco: Straight Arrow Books, 1973.
Lange, Brenda. *Edward Stratemeyer: Creator of the Hardy Boys and Nancy Drew.* Philadelphia: Chelsea House, 2004.
Larso, Charles R. "Stratemeyer's Remarkable Writing Machine." *World and I,* April 1999, 14.4: 264.
"Lower School Summer Reading Program 2005." Loganville Christian Academy, Lawrenceville, Georgia.
"Luigi Galleani." Answers.com, http://www.anwers.com/topic/luigi-galleani.
Lum, Cynthia Adams. "Just Who IS Carolyn Keene?" About.com: Women's History, http://womenshistory.about.com/library/weekly/ucnancydrew2c.htm?p= (accessed July 7, 2007).
Maney, Mabel. *A Ghost in the Closet: A Hardly Boys Mystery.* San Francisco: Cleis Press, 1995.
Mathiews, Franklin K. "Blowing Out the Boy's Brains." *Outlook,* November 18, 1914: 652–654.
McFarlane, Leslie. *Ghost of the Hardy Boys: An Autobiography of Leslie McFarlane.* Toronto: Methuen/Two Continents, 1976.
Merriman, Woodene. "Inn to the Past: Downtown Cantonese Restaurant Points Back to City's Vanished Chinatown." *Post-Gazette,* http://www.post-gazette.com/lifestyle/2003 1209chinatown1209p1.asp (accessed May 12, 2007).
"MPL History — The Collection." Madison Public Library, http://www.madisonpubliclibrary.org/kann/collection.html (accessed October 12, 2006).
Murphy, Cullen. "Starting Over: The Same Old Stories." *Atlantic,* June 1991, 267.6: 18+.
O'Rourke, Meghan. "Nancy Drew's Father: The Fiction Factory of Edward Stratemeyer." *The New Yorker,* http://www.newyorker.com/printables/critics/041108crat_atlarge (accessed March 12, 2007).
Padayatty, Neil. "Catch 22: Books and Padayatty!" http://dlc22.blogspot.com/2005/08/books-and-padayatty.html (accessed May 12, 2007).
Prager, Arthur. *Rascals at Large or the Clue in the Old Nostalgia.* Garden City, NY: Doubleday & Company, 1971.
Praveen. "Ruminations of a Meandering Mind: The Bibliophile in Me." http://myarticulations.blogspot. com/2005_08_01_ archive.html (accessed August 15, 2007).
Ramnarayan, Gowri. "Children's Books, Part II." *Hinduism Today,* http//www.hinduismtoday.com/1995/5/1995-5-13.shtml (accessed March 21, 2007).
_____. "Great Children's Books... Alas, Still a Fairytale." *Hinduism Today,* http//www.hinduismtoday.com/1995/4/1995-4-04.shtml (accessed May 12, 2007).
Rehak, Melanie. *Girl Sleuth: Nancy Drew and the Women Who Created Her.* Orlando: Harcourt, 2005.
Roback, Diane. "A Year of Big Numbers." *Publishers Weekly,* March 19, 2001, 248.12: 43.
Schroth, Raymond A. "Kick Your Foot through That Screen." *National Catholic Reporter,* August 23 1996, 32.37: 11.
Sczerbinski, Jennifer Lyn. "The Mystery in the Old Schoolhouse: Why Children's Book Series Have Been Wrongly Excluded from the Classroom." Honors thesis, April 2004.
"The Secret of the Old Queen, a Hardy Boys Musical Adventure." *Kaliyuga Arts,* http://www.kaliyuga.com/QueenPg.htm (accessed May 12, 2007).
"Setting the Stage: About the Playwright." First Stage Children's Theatre, http://www.firststage.org (accessed May 12, 2007).
"Share What You're Reading: A Review by Andrew T., Grade 5, North Carolina." Scholastic.com, http://teacher.scholastic.com/activities/swyar/browseEntry.asp?id=22100&booktype=Mystery+%+Adve.... (accessed June 24, 2007).
Slayton, Robert A. *Empire Statesman: The Rise and Redemption of Al Smith.* New York: Free Press, 2001.

Springen, Karen. "Publishing: The 'Boys' Are Back. Nice Hair, Joe." *Newsweek*, May 30, 2005: 14.

"Summer Reading Lists." Old York Library, New York City. http://teacherweb.com/nj/Branchburg/OYlibrary/h1.stm (accessed May 21, 2007).

"Take a Walking Tour of Haileybury. The City of Temiskaming Shores." http://www.temiskamingshores.ca/htm/haileyburytour.html (accessed September 13, 2007).

"Television Receiving Set Production." *TV History*, http://www.tvhistory.tv/1947-53-USA-TV-MonthlyProduction.JPG (accessed April 8, 2007).

Thakur, Kakoli. "Harry Potter and the Indian Writers." *Day after India*, http://www.dayafterindia.com/july30/hp.html (accessed May 21, 2007).

Trabasso, Thomas. "Becoming a Reader: The Experience of Fiction from Childhood to Adulthood." *American Journal of Psychology*, Spring 1993, 106.1: 135+.

Truby, Dana. "A Fresh Look at Series Books: Ever-Popular, Series Books Can Open the Door to a Lifetime of Reading." *Instructor*, May-June 2003, 112.8: 21+.

Tunnell, Michael O., and James S. Jacobs. "Series Fiction and Young Readers." *Booklist*, September 15, 2005, 102.2: 64+.

"Unforgettable: Remembering Hardy Boys Author Leslie McFarlane." CBC Archives, http://archives_radio-canada.ca/400i.asp?ICCat=68&IDDos=292&IDCli=1543&IDLan=1&t... (accessed August 25, 2007).

Veronesi, Gene P. *Italian-Americans & Their Communities of Cleveland*. Cleveland Memory Project, http://www.clevelandmemory.org/italians/partii.html (accessed May 25, 2007).

Watson, Bruce. "Tom Swift, Nancy Drew, and Pals All Had the Same Dad." *Smithsonian*, October 1991, 22.7: 50+.

Weingarten, Gene. "The Hardy Boys: The Final Chapter." *Washington Post*, http://www.washingtonpost.com/wp_dyn/content/article/2005/12/05/AR2005120501092_pf.html (accessed April 19, 2007).

Winn, Marie. *The Plug-In Drug: Television, Computers, and Family Life*. New York: Penguin, 2002.

Wonk, Dalt. "Nancy Drew & the Hardy Boys in *The Wax Museum Mystery*." *Gambit*, http://www.bestofneworleans.com/dispatch/2005-08-02/thea_review.php (accessed May 12, 2007).

"Young Monster." *Time*, http://www.time.com/time/magazine/printout/0,8816,799619,00.html (accessed May 12, 2007).

Zumoff, J. A. "The Secret of the Hardy Boys: Leslie McFarlane and the Stratemeyer Syndicate." *Journal of Social History*, Winter 2005, 39.2: 589+.

Index

Numbers in **bold italics** represent pages with photographs or illustrations.

Adams, Harriet (Stratemeyer) **39**, **42**; assumes control of syndicate 38; birth and education 38; death 43; death of son in World War II 76–77; Grosset & Dunlap lawsuit 41–43; management of syndicate during Depression 40; requests for higher royalties 41; World War II treatment in Hardy Boys series 72–77
African Americans, depictions of 84, 114–120
alcohol 158–159
Alger, Horatio 27, 30
American Library Association's Winnetka survey 219
Applewood Books reproductions 18, 89–90
Arabs, depictions of 128
The Arctic Patrol Mystery 94, 143
Asians, depictions of 80, 85, 87, 107–114
Aunt Gertrude: characteristics 59–60, 149, 155–157; initial appearance 59; later role 89, 156–157, 199; McFarlane's creation of 59
Aunt Gertrude and the Boys (proposed radio show) 201

Bayport (fictional setting) 51; as both hometown and portal to excitement 190; Barmet Bay 190–191; geographical features 190–191; Haileybury, similarity to 190–191, **195**; location debate 193–198; rich eccentrics 131–132; Stratemeyer's initial description 190
Bayport, New York 196–197
Bayport Village, Ontario 199–200
Benson, Margaret (Wirt) 34, 44, 45, 76
Billman, Carol 11, 12, 14–17, 193
"Blowing out the Boy's Brains" 215–218
The Bobbsey Twins (series) 23, 32, 35, 41, 43
Boesing, Paul 212–213
The Bombay Boomerang 94, 199, 229

The Brett King Mysteries (series) 40
British editions 20
Bronski, Michael 225–226
Brooklyn Public Library 6
bumpkins 133–136
Button, John 66

capitalists 132–133
Cart, Michael 223
Children's Book Week **216**, 219, 224
class 130–137
The Clue in the Embers 106, 121, 125–127, 160, 170, 197, 199
The Clue of the Broken Blade 71
The Clue of the Hissing Serpent 93, 107, 158, 174
The Clue of the Screeching Owl 161
Cohen, Phil (chum) 8, 98, 100–101, 105, 106, 114, 180
Cope, Timothy 212–213, 214
Crabb Corners Boys 136
Crawford, Robert L. 193, 197
criminal type 171–174
The Crisscross Shadow 14, 80, 124–125, 142, 149, 156–157, 160, 163, 169, 172, 173, 199
cross dressing 111–112

Danger on Vampire Trail 95, 143–144
DeMarco, Flynn 211–212
dime novels 27–30
The Disappearing Floor 20, 69–71
Disney, Walt 84, 201–202
diversity 98–129
Duffy, Dennis 46
Durang, Christopher 210–211

ethnic humor 104–106, 109, 111–112, 124

federal authorities 170–171
"fifty-center" 32–35
A Figure in Hiding 61, 139, 167
The Firebird Rocket 93, 147–148, 196, 197
The Flickering Torch Mystery 61, 72, 74, 169, 171, 199
Footprints Under the Window 53, 73–74, 80, 85, 86, 107–113, 114, 117, 120, 121, 132, 199
"For It Was Indeed He" 26, 40, 219–220
foreign governments 171
foreign translations 20
Frye, Northrop 12
Fu Manchu 108

Gaines, Ervin 227
Garis, Howard R. 24
gay humor 145
gay satires 18, 212–214
The Ghost at Skeleton Rock 80, 127–128, 171, 186
A Ghost in the Closet 213–214
Ghost of the Hardy Boys 65
Gillis, Jackson 202, 204
Gilroy, Jerry (chum) 98, 180
The Great Airport Mystery 6, 11, 13–14, 53, 85, 92, 106, 138, 157, 158–159, 167, 173, 187
"The Great Purge" 40, 83–89, 205–206
Grosset & Dunlap 6, 33, 205; lawsuit 41–43

The Happy Hollisters (series) 40
Hardy, Fenton (father) 8, 51, 74, 75, 80, 91–92, 94, 95, 120–121, 128–129, 130, 133, 149, 150, 151–153, 158, 169
Hardy, Frank and Joe: ages 5–6; athletic skills 14; chores 165; confidence 17; connection with readers 17, 53; enforcers of security 166; freedom and independence 150; home 198–199; Irish ancestry 128–129; modesty and honesty 160–161; physical appearance 7, 12, **15**, **16**; relationships with girls 93–94, 138, 139–149; relationship with parents 151; respect for the law 174–175; school experiences 53, 54–55, 163–165; sex 138; social consciousness 77–78, 161; social responsibility 77, 96, 161; travels 10–11, 92–93; trust 157
Hardy, Laura (mother) 8, 148, 149, 153–156, 173
The Hardy Boys (series): action 177–178; African Americans, depictions of 84, 114–120; alcohol 158–159; appeal 7–8, 11–12, 150; Applewood Books reproductions 18, 89–90; Arabs, depictions of 128; Asians, depictions of 80, 85, 87, 107–114; British editions 20; bumpkins 133–136; canon 6; capitalists 132–133; class 130–137; Crabb Corners Boys 136; criminal type 171–174; cross dressing 111–112; debut 6; diversity 98–129; ethnic humor 104–106, 109, 111–112, 124; federal authorities 170–171; foreign governments 171; foreign

translations 20; format 8; gay humor 145; gay satires 18, 212–214; global impact 20–21; Hispanics, depictions of 120–122; humor and pranks 53–54, 58, 60, 95–96, 104–106, 134–135; identity theft 95; India, popularity in 21; influence 21–22; international intrigue 92–93; Ireland 128–129; Irish, depictions of 57–58, 109, 128–129; Italians, depictions of 86, 101–107; Jews, depictions of 98–101; law enforcement 104–106, 166–170; memorabilia 18; Native Americans, depictions of 80, 122–128; plot formula 9–10, 55; police and law enforcement 51–52, 57–58, 86, 104–106, 166–170; popularity 6, 11; "queer" use of 18–20, 214; race 103–129; racist stereotypes 84, 107–120; religion 157–158; respect for the law 174–175; revision of early titles 40, 85, 205–206; rich eccentrics 131–132; sales 6, 43; satiric parodies 18; suspension of disbelief 5–6; television productions 18, 21, 40–41, 84; terrorism 94–95, 96–97, 188; theatrical productions 18, 212–213; tobacco 158; trust 157; urban poor 77–78, 136–137; violence 177–178; "Weird Period" 66–71; wish fulfillment 12, 141, 147, 153, 156, 173; World War II, treatment of 72–77
The Hardy Boys and the Mystery of Where Babies Come From (play) 210–211
The Hardy Boys Casefiles (series) 6
The Hardy Boys in the Mystery of the Haunted House (play) 210
The Hardy Boys in the Secret of Skullbone Mountain (play) 210
The Hardy Boys Mysteries (series) 6
The Hardy Boys/Nancy Drew Mysteries (television program) 208–209
The Hardy Boys: Undercover Brothers (series) 6
Hardy home 92, 198–199
Hardy Men (film) 214
The Haunted Fort 193
The Hidden Harbor Mystery 84, 86, 115, 117, 139
Hispanics, depictions of 120–122
The Hooded Hawk Mystery 79, 80, 174
Hooper, Biff (chum) 8, 51, 55, 143, 145, 179–180
The House on the Cliff 85, 86, 87–88, 106, 107, 172, 178, 193, **194**, 205, 210
humor and pranks 53–54, 57–58, 60, 95–96, 104–106, 134–135
Hunting for Hidden Gold 17, 52, 57, 58, 66, 85, 86, 114, 164, 167, 181, 185

identity theft 95
Inness, Sherrie A. 225–226
international intrigue 92–93
Ireland 128–129
Irish, depictions of 57–58, 109, 128–129
Italians, depictions of 86, 101–107

Jews, depictions of 98–101
Johnson, Deidre 28, 32, 156
The Jungle Pyramid 92, 93, 147, 197

Karnack, S. T. 171–172
Klein, Joe 210
Krashen, Stephen 224

law enforcement 104–106, 166–170
Lum, Cynthia Adams 44–45

Madison Public Library 227
Maney, Mabel 213–214, 225
The Mark on the Door 99, 120–121, 122, 138–139, 171, 196
The Masked Monkey 92, 95, 107
Mathiews, Franklin K. 215–219, 221, 223, 224, 225, 226, 228
McFarlane, Leslie *49, 53, 63*; authority figures, attitudes toward 51–52, 57–58, 169; autobiography 65; background 47–8; Canadian influences 56–57; career with Stratemeyer Syndicate 34, 64; female characters 138; film and television career 62–64; freelance writing 48; hiatus from series 61; hiring by Stratemeyer 48; law enforcement, depictions of 57–58, 104–106, 166–170; newspaper reporter 47–48; revised editions, attitudes toward 65, 88–89; style in Hardy Boys novels 52–53; view of Stratemeyer's methods 27, 64; writing of Hardy Boys novels 51
Melcher, Frederic G. 219
The Melted Coins 76, 113, 191, 228
memorabilia 18
Mexico 121
The Mickey Mouse Club 41, 84, 201–206, 208, 209, 221
The Missing Chums 59, 141–142, 154, 155, 179, 182, 183, 185, 196
Moore, Anne Carroll 219
Morton, Chet (chum) 8, 9, 51, 55, 66–67, 69, 79, 81, 85, 91, 95–96, 98, 104, 108, 111, 116–117, 124–125, 130, 134–135, 142, 143–145, 161, 164, 167, 179–180, 187, 192, 199
Morton, Iola 18, 51, 79, 93, 112, 136, 139, 140–142
Mumford, E. W. 219
Murphy, Richard 206
The Mysterious Caravan 93, 101, 118–119, 128, 135–136, 145, 160, 164
The Mystery at Devil's Paw 80–82, 127, 149
The Mystery of Cabin Island 131, 141
The Mystery of Ghost Farm (*Mickey Mouse Club* series) 204–205
The Mystery of the Applegate Treasure (*Mickey Mouse Club* series) 202–204
The Mystery of the Aztec Warrior 121–122, 157, 161, 174
The Mystery of the Chinese Junk 93, 113–114, 141, 158, 160, 198, 199

The Mystery of the Chinese Junk (television production) 206, **207**
The Mystery of the Desert Giant 199
The Mystery of the Flying Express 71, 72, *73,* 139–140, 172, 199
The Mystery of the Spiral Bridge 158, 162, 197
The Mystery of the Whale Tattoo 164

Nancy Drew (series) 6, 21, 23, 35, 37, 40, 43, 44–45, 61, 201, 215, 219, 220, 221, 222, 223, 225–226, 227
Nancy Drew & the Hardy Boys: The Wax Museum Mystery (play) 211–212
Native Americans, depictions of 80, 122–128
New Line Television 209
New York Public Library 227
Nodelman and Reimer 35

O'Rourke, Meghan 26

Pastore, Laurie 223
Perez, Norah 78
The Phantom Freighter 62, 78–79, 140
police and law enforcement 166–170
Prager, Arthur 9–10, 192
Prito, Tony (chum) 8, 81–82, 98, 101, 104–107, 114, 125–126, 130, 158, 180
Prohibition 103, 159

"queer doin's" 18–20

race 103–129
racist stereotypes 84, 107–120,
Read, Richard 211–212
Rehak, Melanie 76
relationship with parents 151
relationships with girls 93–94, 138, 139–149
religion 157–158
respect for the law 174–175
revision of early titles 40
rich eccentrics 131–132
Robinson, Perry (chum) 9, 98, 130, 136–137
Rohmer, Sax 108
The Rover Boys (series) 11, 23, 31

satires 18, 210–214
Schroth, Raymond A. 221–222
Schwab, Bernard 227
Sczerbinski, Jennifer Lyn 223, 226
The Secret Agent on Flight 101 11, 92, *93,* 158, 223
The Secret of Pirates Hill 80, 157, 170
The Secret of Skull Mountain 79, 123, 142, 188
The Secret of the Caves 55, 71, 85, 122, 141, 158
The Secret of the Lost Tunnel 117, 123, 141, 197
The Secret of the Old Mill 88, 97, 101, 134, 153, 163, 173, 198
The Secret of the Old Queen—A Hardy Boys Musical (play) 212–213

The Secret of Wildcat Swamp 79, 148, 149, 154, 162, 173, 174, 186, 197
The Secret Panel 132, 199
The Secret Warning 61, 67, 117, 119, 173, 184
sex 138, 140, 142–148, 228–229
The Shattered Helmet 93, 144–145, 187
Shaw, Callie 18, 51, 79, 93, 112, 136, 137, 139, 140–142, 148
The Shore Road Mystery 53, 55, 74, 92, 172, 180, 183
The Short-Wave Mystery 77, 137, 171, 198
The Sign of the Crooked Arrow 79, 123, 135, 140, 172, 174
Simon & Schuster 6, 43
The Sinister Signpost 61, 74–76, 117, 162, 188
Smith, Lillian 226
social consciousness 77–78, 161
social responsibility 77–78, 96, 161
Squier, Edna (Stratemeyer) 38, 40, 67
Stall, Bob 64–65, 88–89
The Sting of the Scorpion 93, 96, 97, 119–120, 133, 197
Stratemeyer, Edward **25**; birth and childhood 27; creative methods 25–26; death 38; dime novelist 28; early career 27–28; family 24; "fifty-center" 32–35; formation of syndicate 32–33; income 24; influence 24; personal interests 24
The Stratemeyer Syndicate: author "brand names" 24, 27, 33; business operations 23–24, 25–27, 45; contract authors 27, 33–34; criticism of 217–221, 226; formation 32–33; formula for series books 35; girls series 34; Grosset & Dunlap lawsuit 43; marketing practices 35; popularity and influence of books 24, 27, 45–46; product line 35–37; revision of titles 40, 85; sale of syndicate to Simon & Schuster 43; sex, treatment of in series books 34; tot series 35
suspension of disbelief 5–6
Svenson, Andrew 40, 41, 85

The Ted Scott Flying Stories (series) 36–37
television productions 18, 21, 40–41, 84
terrorism 94–95, 96–97, 188
theatrical productions 20, 210–213
tobacco 158
The Tolliver Adventure Stories (series) 40
Tom Swift (series) 6, 11, 23, 24, 35, 37, 40, 219
The Tower Treasure 5–**7**, 8–9, 22, 33, 34, 52, 57, 58, 79, 85–86, 91, 95, 97, 104–106, 109, 110, 122, 131, 133, 135, 136–137, 141, 148, 151–152, 158–159, 167, 169, 178, 191, 196, 198, 200, 202, 203, 205, 215, 221, 229
Trabasso, Thomas 221
Trelease, Jim 221
Truby, Dana 223
Tunnell, Michael O. and James S. Jacobs 222–223
The Twisted Claw 67–69, 129, 186, 199

urban poor 77–78, 136–137

"Victor Horton's Idea" 28, **29**
The Viking Symbol Mystery 154, 198, 199
violence 177–178

The Wailing Siren Mystery 142, 148, 154, 160, 161, 169
Watson, Bruce 25–26
"The Weird Period" 66–71
What Happened at Midnight 6, 14, **15**, 60, 130, 136, 141, 157–158, 159, 184, 197
While the Clock Ticked 53, 122, 132, 185–186, 193
White, Hope 226
Winn, Marie 222
wish fulfillment 12, 141, 147, 153, 156, 173
The Witchmaster's Key 93, 128, 146, 228
World War II, treatment of 72–77

The Yellow Feather Mystery 141

www.ingramcontent.com/pod-product-compliance
Ingram Content Group UK Ltd.
Pitfield, Milton Keynes, MK11 3LW, UK
UKHW041935140426
5217IPUK00014B/491